SOFTWARE DEVELOPMENT RHYTHMS

SOFTWARE DEVELOPMENT RHYTHMS

Harmonizing Agile Practices for Synergy

Kim Man Lui and Keith C. C. Chan

The Hong Kong Polytechnic University, Hong Kong

WILEY-INTERSCIENCE

A JOHN WILEY & SONS, INC., PUBLICATION

Published by John Wiley & Sons, Inc., Hoboken, New Jersey
Published simultaneously in Canada

For general information on our other products and services or for technical support, please contact our Customer Care Department within the United States at 800-762-2974, outside the United States at 317-572-3993 or fax 317-572-4002.

Wiley also publishes its books in a variety of electronic formats. Some content that appears in print may not be available in electronic formats. For more information about Wiley products, visit our web site at www.wiley.com.

Library of Congress Cataloging-in-Publication Data:

Lui, Kim Man.
  Software development rhythms : using the flexibility of agile software practices in combination/By Kim Man Lui & Keith C.C. Chan.
      p. cm.
    Includes index.
    ISBN 978-0-470-07386-5 (cloth)
1. Computer software – Development. I. Chan, Keith C.C. II. Title.
QA76.76.D47L86 2007
005.1–dc22

                                                              2007019073

Printed in the United States of America

10 9 8 7 6 5 4 3 2 1

To my mother and my sister
— K.M.L

To my parents and sisters
and to Emily, Samantha, and Jeremy
— K.C.C.C.

CONTENTS

Part II: Rhythms

PREFACE

> This book helps us discover our own software methodologies in a way that respects the software development rhythms of both people and practices.

In the deep dark night, lying down on Kande beach on the shores of Lake Malawi, we looked up into the cloudless sky. Countless tiny stars were blinking at us. A little tired, or perhaps just mesmerized by those distant, mysterious lights, we closed our eyes and began to hear more, the peaceful slap of water on the little beach, and the small, almost concerted sounds of the dark night, throbbing in what seemed like a deep, rhythmic breathing. Nature is an incomprehensible concert of rhythms. Our Earth in its solar orbit spins through space composing the rhythm of day and night, endlessly recycling its four seasons. Following nature's rhythm, we wake to learn and sleep to remember, writing and rewriting our own programs in accordance with the very best universal software practice in a flawless symphony of rhythms. From heartbeats to footsteps, rhythms are a sustaining, momentum-creating vital force. In a world where complexity appears very much like chaos, we seek the confidence of being able to assign causes and identify correlations, but sometimes it is only the discovery of rhythms that allows us to see the order that sustains all.

Like any human endeavor, software development is complex and full of generalizations and correlations, but it is devoid of rules. To help us build software, we have disciplined software models and software project management methodologies. But the ferment of software development, with constantly changing teams and requirements and new tasks, means that there is no guarantee that any past successful method will succeed on the next software project. In fact, some project leaders who appear to adopt no method or methods that are scorned as "ad hoc" are able to get their software projects done on time. The secret of their success is the understanding of software development rhythms.

The knowledge of rhythms gives us a new perspective on some of the thorniest issues in software development. Methods that work for one team fail for another because even the most willing software teams can't achieve success with a new method until they come to understand its rhythms. Yet in the management of complex and multifaceted software development projects, where it is vital to harmonize and synergize both team and individual practices and processes, rhythms are a largely neglected theme.

Rhythms are not another methodology. There are many methodologies, and this book does not seek to introduce a new framework for building software or managing software projects. What is needed today is not more methodologies but greater wisdom in the application of the methodologies that we choose to use. The best way to do this is to understand and work in harmony with the rhythm of whichever methodology the team adopts. To do otherwise, to fail to understand and apply the rhythms of a method, is to make the method itself more burden than benefit, and to make the journey of a project long and difficult.

This book is not for beginners, In fact, we assume that you can already fish and have caught a few in your time. It is for people who want to refine or even rediscover some of the skills and techniques that can so easily be lost when we get into the habit of seeing things from just one perspective. Then, like someone who is fishing casting the line with a supple wrist and a steady rhythm, we hope to help you catch more fish than ever before, and to feel more satisfied as you do it.

Audience

We have tried our best to write a technical book in plain language. Those who are interested in software development and project management (software managers, programmers, researchers, etc.) should have no trouble with these materials as we explain and provide clear examples of any terms that might be outside those areas.

Along with Kent Back's *Extreme Programming Explained* (2nd edition), this book can serve as an advanced text on agile software development. It describes a number of project episodes and industrial cases suitable for use in case-based learning or for presentation to students as the basis of further work in group projects. This book is also a monograph as it presents many concepts that have not been adequately considered in books and scholarly papers on project management in general and software engineering in particular.

This book does address itself to a wide readership, but it is especially intended for *thoughtful readers in search of creative metaphors for project management and new insights into the complex field of software development.*

How to Read This Book

Generally, I would suggest that this book be read according to the chapter order. It is presented in two parts. Part I consists of three chapters. Chapter 1 introduces the idea of software development rhythms. Chapters 2 and 3 respectively discuss people and practices, clarifying some fundamental concepts in software development and asking some important questions such as "Why *shouldn't* we learn from experience?," "what are agile values?," "How can it be possible to weight different intangible software practices as heavy or light?," and "What can we learn from open source software development?"

Part II of this book is all about development rhythms. We are used to using the familiar terms "process" and "practices"—although not everybody is confident that they know the exact differences. We compose rhythms on the basis of software practices. To effectively demonstrate how software development rhythms are a powerful metaphor that we can use to analyze when best to use a software methodology, we take a number of more controversial software practices and consider their rhythms and compare them with some other more generally accepted software practices.

Once you have learned how an analysis of software rhythms can harmonize practices, you may like, as an intermediate step, to adopt the rhythms proposed in this book or modify them in any way. Feel free. Ultimately, however, it is important to realize that rhythms are not models and that in the end, we should all compose our own rhythms.

Special Acknowledgment

The book covers some topics and ideas that are outside the normal scope of software development. Fortunately, we were able to benefit from the kind advice and guidance of a number of renowned experts in these areas. Their precious time and professional advice were much appreciated. We cannot thank them enough. In alphabetical order, they are

Paul Davies, who critiqued our description of the physicist and pair programming

Don Forsyth, who provided his insights into pair programming from a group dynamics perspective

Michael McClellan, who reviewed the musical notation in this book

Richard Schonberger, who reviewed a number of sections connected with lean manufacturing and engineering projects

Frank Vigneron, who commented on the angel's gender

Joel Watson, who reviewed "Deal or no deal" and the game theory analogy

Philip Zimbado, who advised us about his prison experiment

Many highly experienced software professionals have done us the great honor of looking at one or two chapters of the book and providing valuable feedback. Many thanks to (in alphabetical order): Lawrence Bernstein, Grady Brooch, Magne Jørgensen, Pete McBreen, George Metes, Peter Middleton, Mark Paulk, Ioannis Stamelos, Royce Walker, and Sami Zahran.

Thanks to Martin Kyle for his useful advice on writing better using plain language. We appreciated John Nosek's insights on collaborative programming. We are delighted to have Angappa Gunasekaran's support. We thank Lai Shan Sit for her many funny cartoons illustrating our ideas. We would also like to thank our friends and colleagues, Jun Wang, Zheng Li, Polly Leung, Fei Dong, Ka Wing Wong, Whitney Lesch, and Rosalyn Farkas for their assistance.

Finally, we cannot thank two persons enough. We thank Kent Beck for inspiring our work on software development rhythms. Kent advised us on which topics to choose to focus on and he reviewed the whole manuscript for us. We also thank Paul Petralia, our editor, who told us from the very beginning that he liked the concept of the book and thought that it would motivate people to think about old things in *their* new ways. Without his encouragement there would not be this book. It is not coincidence that all of us believe that the idea of software development rhythms could be powerful metaphors and effective management tools. Rhythms are not methodologies, they are, rather, a meta-methodology – a methodology about developing new software methodologies!

KIM MAN LUI
KEITH C. C. CHAN

Hong Kong
January 2008

Part I: Essentials

1

NO PROGRAMMER DIES

The Bible shows the way to go to heaven, not the way the heavens go.

—GALILEO GALILEI

There is one question that is so frequently asked in software engineering that it may seem tedious to ask it yet again, but here it is, anyway: "What are the basic differences between software development projects and engineering projects (or manufacturing production), that is, say, between producing enterprise information system and building tunnels or manufacturing cars?"

The usual, dry, academic answer is that software is a conceptual, intangible, invisible artifact. This definition may be useful, but there is another attribute of software projects that distinguish them even more starkly from traditional engineering projects. The distinction, which is rarely mentioned, is that — while engineers may always be in danger — *software developers are never killed or injured while working on their projects.*

No matter how lousily or messily planned or implemented a software development project may be, nobody in a software team is ever seriously physically hurt at the office computer. There is a clear difference between developing Adobe and digging the Panama Canal, and this may be one reason why so many software development projects are hastily, carelessly, and sloppily managed.

> In 2005 the death toll from a tunnel project in western China broke a new record indicating project mismanagement and poor supervision of safety procedures. An investigation reveded that many fatal accidents

could have been avoided. This brought the issue of the rushed productivity for the project rather than workers' and engineers' safety, environmental concerns, and social needs under even closer scrutiny. The public severely blamed the chief engineer for the tunnel accidents.

—LOCAL NEWS IN CHINA, 2005

In real-world engineering projects, the prospects and costs of death are always looking over our shoulders, holding individuals personally responsible for the consequences of their decisions and actions. Thus, project managers must adhere to strict procedures and industrial standards: agreed-on plans, signed confirmations, written workflows, and timing. When an error occurs, a project management model enables us to track the work process, conduct a postmortem review, and identify errors; in addition, this may also involve financial issues of insurance and litigation.

Because life matters[1] and mistakes incur heavy costs, real-world engineering demands discipline, consistency, consideration, commitment to detail, and a strong sense of teamwork. The result is not just greater safety; it's also better products. You have to wonder whether software development can afford to continue in its current (often) irresponsible way. Are there any factors in society or the marketplace that will ever make it change? If so, what are they?

1.1 DEVELOPING SOFTWARE VERSUS BUILDING A TUNNEL

Many types of cancer are treated with radiotherapy, in which high-energy rays are used to damage malignant tumors. Given the danger of overdosage, the amount of radiation energy is supposed to be precise, and safely controlled by a computer system. The Therac-25 was developed for this purpose by the Atomic Energy of Canada Limited from a prototype in 1976 to a safety analysis in 1983 (Leveson 1993). Between 1985 and 1987, the Therac-25 overdosed a number of patients, killing five. Subsequent investigations blamed the software, but there's something strange in this. The programming code for the Therac-25 was built by only one person, who also did most of the testing. This is not even conceivable in a real-world engineering project, but in some software development the programmers are often responsible for their own testing. How did the software development process ever get itself into this mess?

---

[1]The ISO 9000, which have often been compared with CMM and CMMI, came from BS5750, which was adopted to control quality problems of bombs going off in munitions factories and bombs not blasting when they should have.

1.1.1 The Good Old Days?

In 2005, a Helios Airways Boeing 737 crashed in Greece, with the loss of all 121 on board. The suspected cause was a series of design defects in the 737 where the plane's pressurization warning alarm made the same sound as the improper takeoff and landing alert. Confusion over the reason for the warning may have contributed to the fatal crash. When things start to go wrong, it sometimes doesn't take much to spin them right out of control. Factors that may seem trivial in normal circumstances, may contribute to tragic outcomes when things aren't going according to plan .

Regardless of whether engineering product defects may be unavoidable, we are taught that rigorous development processes do remove as many as possible. A "rigorous" process normally means the separation between planning and execution. During construction, planned tasks should be designed to be strict to follow and easy to control. Ideally, constructive peer pressure should positively shape workplace behavior to ensure that a development process will be "as rigorous as possible."

Adopting that philosophy in engineering management, software development activities can normally be divided into two types of process—(1) *analysis and design as planning* and (2) *programming as execution*, with (2) following (1). This intuitive model, generally referred to as the "waterfall model" by Winston Royce (1970), is normally adopted when managing large software projects. These two processes are often chopped into smaller but still ordered processes. Dividing and conquering allows us to better allocate limited resources and control and track project progresses through a number of checkpoints and milestones. The analysis–design process is made up of such activities as software requirements gathering, system analysis and logical design, while the programming process is made up of coding, unit testing, system integration, and user acceptance testing, all of which are basically linked serially, one after the other. For the purpose of discussion, we consider here what is called a *four-stage waterfall model* as below:

Requirement→design→coding→testing (R→D→C→T)

The nature of the waterfall model makes it easy for a project plan to be executed the same way engineers manage their projects. Focusing on breaking down larger tasks into smaller tasks and putting them in the right order for execution better allows project resources to be allocated and conflicting problems to be resolved. With this idea of the separation between planning and execution behind a waterfall model, a project plan can be reviewed to optimize against time and resources. With this, we can then identify and weight various risk factors to draw up a contingency plan for a project.

Such a project management paradigm to develop software may sound intuitive, but one could easily discover that it does not encourage the exploration of interrelationships between people, programming tasks, and software practices. It can be difficult for some project managers to comprehend development synergies between these three elements, particularly in a situation where something can change unexpectedly during execution.

1.1.2 The More Things Change, the More They Stay the Same?

When project requirements are constantly changing, sometimes more rapidly than what we had imagined, and when developers know that what they are building is not what their customers need, they will start to realize that their software can be developed only by progressing in small steps so as to obtain constant feedback all the time. This is, however, easier said than done.

Our thinking is often limited by our past experience. For many software managers, their formative software experience is with the waterfall. Seeking to improve on it, we come up with an enhanced waterfall. As single-phase analysis for user requirements may rarely provide a full solution, more than one phase is often considered necessary, and for this, straightforwardly, we link two or smaller waterfall cycles together in a chain.

$$R \rightarrow D \rightarrow C \rightarrow T \quad \rightarrow \quad R \rightarrow D \rightarrow C \rightarrow T \quad \rightarrow \quad R \rightarrow D \rightarrow C \rightarrow T$$

There is really nothing new here. The same principles behind the waterfall model apply except that, in each cycle, one can plan according to the feedback obtained from what has previously been done. The current cycle will therefore be less stringent and more flexible than previous cycles.

The waterfall model, if strictly implemented as "one cycle" or some "bureaucratic procedures for turning back," may not be too popular in the commercial world. Many software teams take the concept of the waterfall model but implement their software projects more flexibly. Some teams adopt the enhanced waterfall model while still others may go even further to adopt an adaptive model so that the length and activities in each iteration can be dynamically adjusted. All these models can be considered as belonging to a waterfall family of models.

In some extreme cases in such a family, to deal with unexpected changes, some software managers would substantially revise their project plans on a weekly basis. Since they know that none of their team members could die or be injured, they are free to revise their plan to cope with any change when it occurs. Compared to software projects, in engineering projects this would be considered very unusual. It would be more normal to delay the project rather than risk changing what and how we have already planned and managed.

When project variables keep changing, a revision of a project plan is the way out of potential crisis. Many project managers do not care how often the project plans are revised as long as it is necessary. But, what really matters is our way of thinking being limited to the style of waterfall management, which always involves breaking down tasks into many sequential tasks, and resources, responsibilities, and any understanding of any bottleneck are planned along this line. Whenever there is any change, replanning is needed and it is hoped that the revised plans can reflect the situation as quickly as if such changes were already anticipated. This is undesirable as a software team does not manage change in this case; they are, instead, managed by change.

1.1.3 Behind Software Products

Let us look at the design and planning of manufacturing products and then come back to software products. If a product is supposedly made up of a number of components, subcomponents, and sub-subcomponents, and so on, then one can draw up a hierarchical architecture that consists of the complete product at the top with a hierarchy of subcomponents, which, in turn, are made up of sub-subcomponents, and so forth. This structure is called a *bill of materials* (BOM) and it is at the heart of operations in many assembly plants. It supports assembly task planning in manufacturing resource planning (MRP), as shown in Figure 1.1, where one plans when, what types, and what

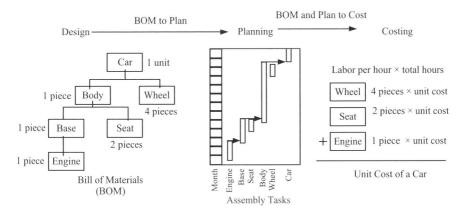

FIGURE 1.1 How bill of materials (BOM) can be used for planning and costing.

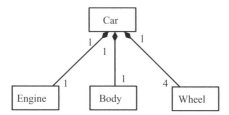

FIGURE 1.2 Class diagram for a car (simplified) that resembles bill of materials (BOM) but serves a different purpose.

quantities of materials or subcomponents are needed for production (Chapman 2006). The assembly task planning will allow costing to be determined (Figure 1.1). Subcomponent information can be used to do cost rollup calculation for customer quotations and for effective internal control over production costs.

Similar to engineering projects, software is often designed using a class diagram (see Figure 1.2), which resembles a bill of materials. Class diagrams help us understand attributes, methods, and class component relationships. Unfortunately, we could *rarely* use a class diagram to tell us how to do assembly task planning and costing. It would be good to have an integrated approach to tighten up or clarify what needs to be written and how a project should be planned. Only recently has it become possible to do this to some extent through the concept of a "user story" in eXtreme programming (XP), which can be used both for requirements management and project planning.

Compared to software tasks, other engineering tasks are often more tangible. Components built in a typical engineering project can be combined in the order suggested by a bill of materials (BOM) so that work progress can be objectively measured and quality can easily be monitored. This, when compared with software, is more tangible. For instance, as part of an engineering project, one can assemble an engine to the gearshaft and then form the base before installing the wheels and finally carrying out wheel tests. The sequence in which these tasks are performed could be designed in accordance with both physical constraints and economic efficiency, and this sequence somehow solidifies the idea of the separation of planning and execution into two stages.

In software projects, products cannot be assembled with this kind of job sequence as defined with class diagrams in the same way BOMs are, no matter how these products are designed. Programmers can work out login interfaces and main menu interfaces in an order that corresponds to how the users

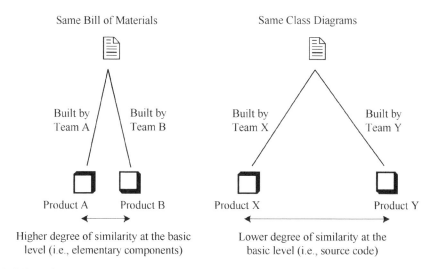

FIGURE 1.3 *Degree of difference* is a conceptual term measuring how two products can be built differently using the same design.

operate the system. But they can also do these later on.[2] There are virtually no restrictions on the ordering when we build with software components. Walker Royce (2005) of IBM suggests that software managers should manage software in the same way as managing a movie production rather than as a typical engineering production. To make a film, we have to effectively assess how all the elements of scenes of the film work together (actors, timing, lines, sets, props, lighting, sound, etc.) so that scenes of the film will be shot in a way that will minimize production costs and production time so that the film can be completed with the least amount of time and money.

In manufacturing, when two products, designed by two groups of engineers, eventually appear on the same BOM, we can almost speculate that these products should be built in similar ways. Furthermore, since products are built to follow the design as given by a BOM, if there are defects, either they are design problems or the products have not been made to plan.

Unfortunately, this same logic that is applicable to manufacturing does not apply to software development (refer to Figure 1.3). Unlike BOMs, class diagrams do not fully address code implementation. Given the same diagrams, implementation could be done in a variety of ways by different programmers. The programmer will not have to write the same software twice for a second installation, but may have to redo it for a second version,

---

[2]"It may make some kind of logical sense that you have to finish writing the login servlet before you start the logout servlet; but in reality you could write and test them in any order," said Robert Martin (2003).

and this can be done even without modifying the class diagrams! For instance, programmers may tune structured query language (SQL) algorithms for better performance when they know the characteristics of real data. Some software teams will adopt the practice of revisiting each other's code to detect defects and improve readability. Again, none of this necessarily implies redesigning the class diagrams.

In the case of software projects, not all that is well designed ends well! Worse yet, many software problems cannot be classified as problems even when the class diagrams or code are not written in compliance with the design. Bad code but good design is not that rare! In short, having qualified experienced system analysts do design using data models, unified modeling language (UML) diagrams, and so on, is not the only necessary condition for producing good software; we also need qualified experienced programmers to write code to build the system. Furthermore, with the right design and good-quality code, we need skilled testers to discover bugs in products. Managing these people effectively in a team, whether each member has just one role (e.g., system analyst, programmer, tester) or multiple roles requires a methodology for coordination, collaboration, and communication! Left to themselves, things may go wrong, and once they do, they will go from bad to worse. One cannot expect a bunch of the right technical people sitting together (without proper management or coordination) to produce software on time, within budget, and according to requirements if there is no development framework.

1.1.4 Deal or No Deal

Traditionally, software management emphasizes mainly relatively formal, rigorous, software development processes. Recently, agile development approaches have grown quite popular. There is now an agile or eXtreme version for formal methods, testing, database, tools, or project management. Although this new trend has attracted great attention in the software community, it has not taken over the waterfall model as the dominant approach. In fact, agile practices are often adopted within a waterfall framework. It appears that the waterfall model is either so intuitively better than the others or that software developers have been so used to it that they cannot think of any other ways better.

The popular TV game show *Deal or No Deal* displays a number of briefcases, each of which contains a different cash prize ranging from just one dollar to millions of dollars. A contestant who wins a game on the show is allowed to pick any of these briefcases as a prize. The contestant, however, is not allowed to open the briefcase until the end of the game. As the game progresses, a "Banker" offers the contestant a deal to buy the chosen briefcase. If the contestant rejects the deal, other cases can be chosen and opened while the banker continues to make offers to the contestant regarding the suitcase the contestant chose at the beginning. The contestant can either accept the banker's offer or take the cash prize inside the briefcase selected at the beginning of the game. It is interesting to note that many contestants who had chosen the right briefcase often accepted a lower-value offer from the bankers. They would have, say, accepted $250,000 dollars, rather than resisting temptations to hold onto the end to win millions. Even in the presence of favorable odds, it is interesting that many people are actually highly risk-averse (Post et al. 2006).

In a study involving 150 volunteers (Tversky and Kahenman 1981), who were asked to choose between a guaranteed $250 or a 75% chance to win $1000 dollars, the overwhelming majority (84%) of the participants took the $250 cash. Interestingly, when the choice was between winning or losing $750 dollars with a 75% chance, 87% preferred to try their luck. Mathematically, the odds were the same but not the subjects' perception of winning and losing.

Daring to take risk for a higher reward is an entrepreneurial attitude. For entrepreneurs to be successful, they need to be risk-takers. They need to understand the odds on success and failure, so that they can spot markets and seize opportunities before others do. If not, they need to have the gamblers' attitude. Compared to an entrepreneur or a gambler, how much risk is a software project manager willing to take when adopting a new development methodology? On the surface, this seems to be a matter of personal preference. However, it may be a bit more complicated than this. There is a chance that the members of a software team may not be so cooperative. They may try to stick to their usual way of thinking and work consciously or subconsciously toward it. If things do not seem to go as originally expected, these members may well place the blame on the manager. They may say that the manager should have been more prudent and should not have replaced the usual practice with something unproven. Is this prudence? Does fear overwhelm ambition? Or is it politics that has raised its ugly head?

Typically, user requirements continue to change and our competitors act and react much more quickly than we do. Even with all these arguments and hesitation, there is a chance that members of a software team will eventually be willing to adopt a new development methodology. But as software projects rarely go wrong at the beginning, it can take a significant investment of time and money before we realize that the old way isn't working.

Meeting deadlines is often a pressure to make us change our old way of working. Let us look at a real case here. In 1995, TechTrans, a Hong Kong software house with a technical staff of around 20 that specialized in the development of retail-chain points-of-sales (POS) systems written in C and Clipper, won a software outsourcing contract to redevelop an AS/400 application on a truly client/server platform. The system had to be written in PowerBuilder and Informix. At that time, no TechTrans programmer knew these tools. TechTrans could have used its existing Clipper database model for the Informix relational database. However, PowerBuilder is an event-driven programming tool under Windows 3.0, while Clipper is a programming language used to create business applications under the disk operating system (DOS). The project leader asked two developers to pair up to explore how to start their programming. The pair was expected to develop a set of code patterns that the other developers would try to follow. The project was managed using the waterfall model, and both the leader and the team firmly believed that this would be an effective, efficient, and less risky way forward.

1.2 DO-RE-MI DO-RE-MI

Experience keeps people growing professionally. The customers today are different from yesterday's customers, and so are members of a software team. For this, one can only expect software projects, and how they should be managed, to also keep changing. When projects cannot be effectively managed using the simple and familiar waterfall model, an iterative approach is used. This can revolutionize the way a software team develops software, but even though resistance to new ways of doing things can be expected, the resistance may be small as there is a familiar simplicity here.

"When you read, you begin with A–B–C" and "when you sing, you begin with do-re-mi."[3] A good place to begin iterative software development is with the waterfall model's requirements analysis (R) – design (D) – coding (C) – testing (T). The simplest way to perform iteration is to simply join two smaller waterfalls together as

$$R{\rightarrow}D{\rightarrow}C{\rightarrow}T{\rightarrow}R{\rightarrow}D{\rightarrow}C{\rightarrow}T$$

One benefit of iterative software development is that it can be adopted flexibly when coping with the inevitable changes that arise from customer feedback, communications, and working software. Because of changes and the issues discovered earlier, we have more realistic views to control projects to ensure that they are within scope, budget, and timeframe. Another benefit is that it breaks a protracted system analysis into more phases, and thereby actual

[3]From Rodgers and Hammerstein's *The Sound of Music* in 1965.

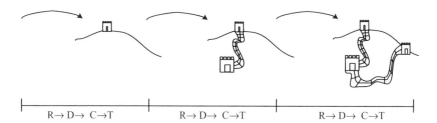

$R \rightarrow D \rightarrow C \rightarrow T$ $R \rightarrow D \rightarrow C \rightarrow T$ $R \rightarrow D \rightarrow C \rightarrow T$

FIGURE 1.4   Phase-by-phase development.

programming can start earlier. This is real progress for software delivery as design diagrams do not cover the details of how to code.

There are at least three ways to implement a simple iterative waterfall model. Most straightforwardly, a system is logically broken down into two or three modules, each of which could be consecutively released for production. It is also possible to implement one or two modules and withdraw the rest. The development approach is referenced as step-by-step or phase-by-phase. A metaphoric example of this approach is given in Figure 1.4.

The second way to implement iterative waterfall model is to review the system nature and functions and to define a kernel and its interface at the beginning (Figure 1.5). The goal of such an iterative cycle is to build new components that could be integrated with a kernel. Different software applications are assembled using the components, which are blackbox to the outside world, but are accessible via their defined interface. Components themselves can be written in several different programming languages as long as they are in full compliance with the interface specifications. This approach to implementing the iterative waterfall model is particularly useful when a number of different applications, each sharing the same reusable login components, are to be developed. Although this can appear to be ambitious, it is a very traditional computing approach. An example is for one to think of an operating system (OS) as a kernel and each application running on the OS, developed with the use of application programming interfaces (APIs), as components so that the computer running the application can serve as a dedicated point-of-sales (POS) or an application server.

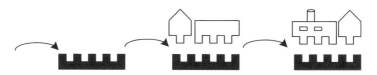

FIGURE 1.5   Component-based incremental development.

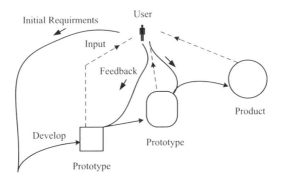

FIGURE 1.6 Evolutionary software development.

Brooks (1995) captures the spirit of evolutionary software development very well by saying "Grow, don't build software." This third way of implementing iterative software development is iterative, generative, and incremental (see Figure 1.6). With this approach, a small, immature prototype evolves through constant or regular customer reviews until the software has all the functionalities required. Customers are encouraged to reengineer their requirements so that the final product fits their business needs. With this approach, an early prototype may not even be software. It could be a paper prototype including a set of screen layouts showing the required functionality. However, the prototype must be sufficiently complete for customers to provide solid feedback.

All these different ways of implementing the iterative waterfall model can be adopted in the same project. They can be integrated to different extents into a hybrid iterative model. One way to do this is to have an outer loop taking a step-by-step approach so that each outer loop has several inner loops that can take, say, the evolutionary approach. Such a double-loop iterative model has been proposed and used with some successes as part of some agile methods such as the scrum (i.e., scrummage meeting, as in rugby) .

1.2.1 Iterative Models

As early as the 1950s, Deming popularized Shewhart's closed-loop model in statistical process control for business continual process improvement, to measure and identify sources of variations so that one can identify and manage the areas where improvement is needed. The feedback loop included in so many project management texts has been generally known as the "plan–do–check–act" (PDCA) cycle. The PDCA cycle is shown in Figure 1.7, which is self-explanatory. The PDCA cycle involves a solid grounding in identifying

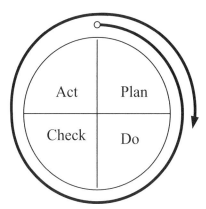

FIGURE 1.7 The PDCA cycle.

performance metrics and measuring them for analysis. The underlying principles have become the foundation of software project management.

Returning to a basic iteration like $R \rightarrow D \rightarrow C \rightarrow T \rightarrow R \rightarrow D \rightarrow C \rightarrow T$, we can see that the iteration does not tell us how to sustain actions! For this reason, a review session is normally needed after each cycle to determine whether we have done as planned so that we can realistically plan what the next cycle should be. In addition to this, we also need to reevaluate the different risk factors that may affect a project so as to ensure that we can better control budgets, resources, and schedules against the original project plan. Clearly, some supporting process areas should be considered to sustain the iteration of $R \rightarrow D \rightarrow C \rightarrow T \rightarrow R \rightarrow D \rightarrow C \rightarrow T$ so that each iteration delivers solid progress toward the final product until an application is released for production.

The PDCA and waterfall model activities, can be combined to establish a complete iterative model — the spiral model — as proposed by Barry Boehm (1988). This spiral model can be modified as shown in Figure 1.8. The sequences of $R \rightarrow D \rightarrow C \rightarrow T \rightarrow R \rightarrow D \rightarrow C \rightarrow T$ can therefore become, say, $R \rightarrow R \rightarrow D \rightarrow R \rightarrow D \rightarrow C \rightarrow T$ (see Figure 1.8). As expected, processes and practices are required to sustain such a model. It should be noted that this modified spiral model does not contradict the iterative waterfall model of $R \rightarrow D \rightarrow C \rightarrow T \rightarrow R \rightarrow D \rightarrow C \rightarrow T$ and software teams can choose to substitute it with the modified spiral model.

The spiral model was originally proposed to develop different prototypes at various stages of a project until the final product is completed. The use of such model is both generative and evolutionary. In practice, software teams may adopt a spiral model according to project requirements. The implementation of the iterative waterfall model can be flexible, and the three different approaches to implementing such a model can be integrated and hybridized.

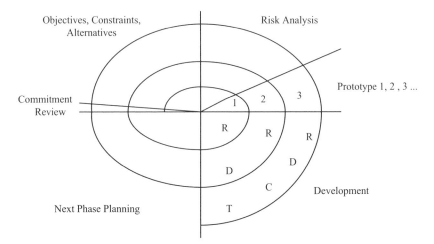

FIGURE 1.8 The spiral model (simplified version).

With these characteristics, the spiral model, which applies the ideas of the PDCA and a combination of these three implementation approaches, can be used rather flexibly with different software projects and thus has been generally accepted as much better than the waterfall model.

1.2.2 Code and Fix

Even though iterative software development approaches have their advantages, not all iterative approaches are desirable. The code-and-fix approach, for example, is repetitive. It involves writing code to clarify requirements for better design later. It is a time-buying strategy where the target is to release the software on schedule and to release patches afterward. It is common in software development that project pressure quashes discipline and that when software developers are under time constraints, they will naturally handle this pressure by jumping into coding immediately. Another situation in which developers would adopt a code-and-fix approach is when the application being developed is so popular that it attracts new, additional, originally unintended users who demand additional expansions in performance and functionalities.

Let us consider a real case as follows. In a retail chain of 45 outlets in a metropolitan area, operational staff might need to split their time between staying in office and visiting other stores. The human resources (HR) department therefore decides to have their information technology (IT) department write a system for them to allow staff to submit trip records electronically. Their goal was to replace manual forms with a database so that the HR department could quickly retrieve information relating to these business trips. The written requirements provided by HR were a brief sample copy of their current form!

The HR system, called *TripLog*, was written in under a fortnight in Microsoft Access using Delphi 6.0. Since the functionalities of TripLog were rather simple, so the HR staff were quick with their user acceptance testing. As expected, HR occasionally reported minor bugs, but these were quickly fixed.

After 2 months, the HR staff asked the IT team to distribute TripLog to user departments so that they could directly enter data into the system. After an additional 2-month period, the HR department decided to add vacation leave as a type of a "trip" in the TripLog so as to automate leave applications. Now that the number of users had unexpectedly increased, the system became extremely slow. Naturally, users start to request that the IT department to improve system performance and to have TripLog display leave balances.

The IT department decided to rewrite the system in MS SQL Server using Delphi 6.0. This took a month, but this was not the end of the story yet as TripLog continued to be the subject of modifications and eventually its user base included all staff of 150 back offices.

The development of TripLog was not disciplined, but the system was not complicated and the software team managed to do a good job. However, the software team actually redeveloped the system completely. The code-and-fix cycle in this case resembles the following sequence:

$$Code \rightarrow use \rightarrow fix(\rightarrow code) \rightarrow use \rightarrow fix(\rightarrow code) \rightarrow use \rightarrow fix \ldots$$

The activity shown in parentheses may occasionally be required.

The code-and-fix approach is different from the iterative model in that we could not tell when a development activity would occur and when one activity would switch to another. Although there was no sense of rhythm and events appeared to occur randomly, the pattern was iterative. This approach can be considered by some developers to be ad hoc.

1.2.3 Chaos

Timing and patterns are important in any kind of iterative model. There can be huge differences of days and even months in completion dates when the same iterative software activities are followed. In this section, we will see what an iterative model may look like when a cycle is as short as a day.

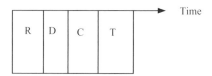

FIGURE 1.9 Waterfall topology.

Figure 1.9 shows a four-stage waterfall model over time. If we assume that there is a deadline to meet for each stage, the project can be tracked with four separate milestones. According to Parkinson's law, work expands to fill the time available for its completion. Therefore, it is rare for a software team to complete its tasks on time. Assuming the probability of delay in project schedule be $\frac{1}{2}$, for four stages, we can be very pessimistic about the chance of completing the project on time as $\frac{1}{2} \times \frac{1}{2} \times \frac{1}{2} \times \frac{1}{2} = \frac{1}{16}$. In other words, there is very little chance that a project is able to finish on time. Of course, many project managers would squeeze time from later stages to compensate for earlier delays, but this effectively shortens the time available for the tasks that are to be achieved in later stages. This may lead to sacrificing either quality, functionalities, or both.

To cope with this problem, we can implement an incentive scheme. When developers are able to complete jobs on time (see the "time box" in Figure 1.10), they receive a bonus pay. To implement this effectively, we need to assign different roles to different members of a software team at each stage. It is possible for us to assign different roles to the same developer. For instance, we can assign requirements engineers the role of software testing to test the final

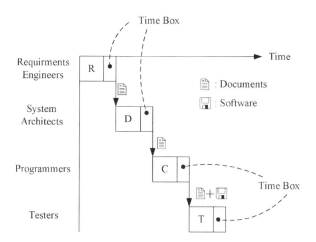

FIGURE 1.10 Waterfall in action.

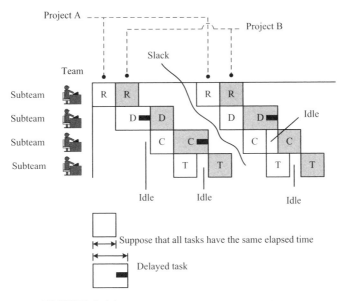

FIGURE 1.11 Delayed tasks and idle developers.

product and the role of coder to system analysts to enable them to write programs for verification.[4]

In addition to an incentive scheme and the assignment of different roles, another question arises as to how people in a team communicate and whether such communication is effective. For example, there is a need for well-written documents to be used as a communication tool between two sequential stages. Figure 1.10 illustrates the waterfall in action.

A software team may be involved in several projects at the same time with team members organized as divisions. Figure 1.11 illustrates how two projects can be run by the same team in parallel. Basically, each subteam either handles just one project at a time or the members deal with one project's tasks at a time. However, when documents passed down from a previous

---

[4]The idea of how quality control checkpoint can be integrated into each phase throughout the development as implemented in the V model. As in our simple example, the look resembles a "V" as shown here:

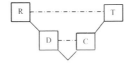

stage are difficult to understand, incorrect, or incomplete, the responsible subteam has to follow up. Thus, some subteam members will find themselves handling the tasks of two projects at the same time. Although this is quite typical in the real world, this kind of task switching adds no value at all to software development (Poppendieck and Poppendieck 2003). Human concentration is easy to break and hard to get back. Switching tasks between two projects eats up time (say, 10–15 minutes) as people reenter the flow of thought for a new task. Frequent interruptions are time-wasting.

Figure 1.11 illustrates another issue that is perhaps even more disturbing than task switching. Most staged models require the completion of one stage before it is possible to enter the next. This makes it difficult to plan two projects to avoid any slack-time between them! Compounding this is the fact that delaying some activities in one project will *tremendously* affect another project. Figure 1.11 illustrates how "delayed time" and "idle time" intertwine even though there is no real idle developer as the project plan can be revised as often as necessary.

To tackle these problems with the simultaneous management of multiple projects, we are brought to the arena of concurrent engineering. We do not wait for the completion of one task before the other starts (see Figure 1.12), and we allow different development processes to run in parallel. To allow a process to evolve more flexibly, we should not be confined only to documents. Instead, we hold more face-to-face meetings to facilitate proper communications. To manage single projects, we can also adopt concurrent software engineering (Figure 1.13).

Concurrent software engineering can be adopted by applying a model for managing single as well as multiple projects (Figure 1.13). The greatest benefit of such a model, called the *Sashimi model* (Raccoon 1995), is that it shortens the iteration cycle.

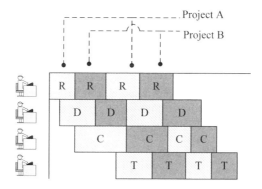

FIGURE 1.12 Concurrent engineering.

Involovemnt

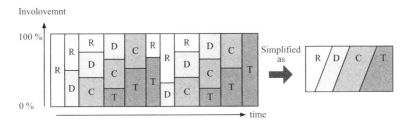

FIGURE 1.13 Sashimi model.

One way to expedite tasks is to shorten iteration cycles. Iteration cycles can be shortened by allowing many things to happen simultaneously. For example, the chaos model (Figure 1.14) looks at a team's activities as a whole, fractally. The model uses a short, small problem-solving loop, but unlike the case with code-and-fix, the chaos model can be very rhythmic as far as we anticipate when things work, when things can be used (i.e., how one loop turns to another), how to sustain the rhythm, and so on.

1.2.4 Methodology that Matters

The following statement was made by a finance director in charge of accounting, administration, personnel, IT, and purchasing departments: "My daughter, 15, was already building her home page at school! I just don't understand what our IT team is busy with."

Customers can be users within an organization, or they can be the external client of a software house. They may not see our service the way we do. Building and managing customer relationships are as important as developing quality software. Projects with teaming relations with customers could be twice productive (Bernstein and Yuhas 2005). When it comes to what

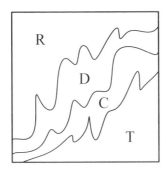

FIGURE 1.14 Chaos model developed by Raccoon (2006).

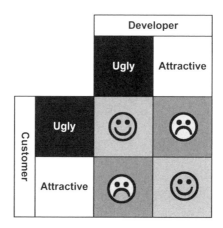

FIGURE 1.15 Customer–developer relationship.

customer-relations management (CRM) is, Ed Thompson of the Gartner Group presents the following matrix (see Figure 1.15). CRM, according to him, is all about how customers see the development team and how the development team sees them. When customers and developers regard each other as mutually ugly or mutually attractive, nothing can or needs to be done (shown as "☺" in Figure 1.15). But when the mutual perception is ugly–attractive, there is room to improve the customer–developer relationship.

From a developer's perspective, ugly customers are reluctant to participate in the development process [i.e., requirements management process and user acceptance testing (UAT)]. Such customers think that what and how software is built is not their concern. Of course, software that is not targeted to specific business processes or domain knowledge demands less user participation. Other than these kinds of customers, there are also customers who are not concerned with the details of software functionalities. For example, some people use Microsoft Word every day but have no interest in knowing anything more than what they already know even though there are better ways of doing things. Customers with that kind of attitude are not helpful. In fact, such attitudes can be harmful to a software team. From the customer's perspective, besides return on investment, satisfaction with the product or service, schedules and scheduling, speed of response, ongoing service support, and product quality are major concerns. Much of this is directly related to how a software team builds software, namely, software development methodologies.

Generally, customers do not like jargon or complicated flowchart diagrams. For this reason, the ideas of metaphoric communications or writing short descriptive requirements (see user story in Chapter 3) have been proposed. In addition, since many users, not trained as programmers, have problems with too many if–then-type requirements, keep them fewer than five.

From time to time, a software team has to give customers progress reports. Some software team will send their customers an enormous, perplexing updated project plan but customers like a product demo (demonstration model) or prototype. Instead of a report, it is therefore easier and more effective if an update of the latest progress status is reported by releasing a demonstration of working software. Owing to their organizational culture and operational processes, some customers accept only big-bang implementation, but it is still a good idea to release working software for a demo, or for early training.

In the commercial world, customer requirements are often dynamic. There is often much need for effective exceptional handling ability in an organization. Customers appreciate quick response from developers. How fast a software team can change a software to meet new business requirements depends on a number of factors. If one is to ignore technical issues and look only at development procedures, one may conclude that the implementation of bureaucratic document control and awkward team structure may make us change our work more slowly than we should.

Modifications can be made with these concerns in place and, after modification, it is necessary to retest the software. Moreover, after modification, retesting what software has worked is necessary. Testing and retesting are two basic concepts in software testing. Generally speaking, the purpose of testing is to detect faults in executed code that causes a failure, while retesting is done to confirm that the changes do not introduce error to other parts of the code (this is also known as *regression testing*). Retesting is often boring and tedious. Automating all or some part of the testing could be an answer to some of the problems mentioned here. Coding and testing need to be better integrated here for a more complete solution. Developers need to be able to write automated testing cases while coding.

When some developers leave a team, others will have to take over, and developers who take over will have to spend some time to understand and make changes to a piece of code. To do so, they may have to refer to technical documents or to read the code directly. This takes time as documents may not be written in such a way as to make them easy for other developers to follow. Ideally, developers should rotate jobs among themselves so that each piece of code can be maintained by more than one person. This, however, may not always be feasible.

All these development problems can arise at the same time, making it difficult to respond quickly to changing requirements. Changing our software development practices overnight will not lead to successes. We have to take small steps first. The iterative model discussed so far may meet this requirement as it allows us to manage processes, schedules, budgets, and risks. However, it is not complete. There is still something missing. We need to harmonize *practices*, *people*, and *software*, and this leads us to so-called software development rhythms, inspired by Kent Beck who says, in his XP book (Beck and Andres 2005), that rhythms operate at all different scales. A principle such as do–check can be applied to the process of doing before the process of checking or practice for doing before practice for checking. They are still do–check!

1.3 SOFTWARE DEVELOPMENT RHYTHMS

If you drop a frog into a pan of hot water, the frog will leap straight out. But if you put the frog into a pan of cold water and slowly heat it, the frog will sit there until it is cooked, unaware of the gradual changes in temperature. Well, maybe frogs are that dumb and maybe not, but there is an interesting point here. No one likes sudden, unexpected changes and, ironically enough, that includes techies such as software developers.

Suppose that a consultant is hired to coach a software team in a development methodology that has a number of new software practices. He asks the team to start with two or three practices and to gradually exercise others. Alternatively, he suggests that the team take a maturity approach in which the team advances toward software practices suggested by the methodology. For instance, an onsite customer requires at least one customer representative to be available onsite all the time. We begin with the representatives visiting the developers frequently enough to sustain personal contacts, then being available not less than 2 hours per day and eventually being an onsite customer (Nawrocki et al. 2003). Both approaches are widely used. The secret of making this successful lies in whether we have successfully complemented either way with the right rhythms of a development methodology while it is introduced!

For instance, Beck, in his book on eXtreme programming, suggests a "standup meeting" to start a day and software integration before calling it a day. Participation of all team members in these meetings is necessary. Developers have to be punctual; otherwise, time is lost in waiting. Not all people in every software team can get it done as easily as we thought. In some extreme cases, people who are not used to the time rhythm dislike the idea of morning meetings. A better way is to organize an informal morning coffee meeting for the whole team and to have a day-end gathering to orally confirm who could not join the coffee meeting the following day. We can see the

25

rhythm as morning gathering–work–day-end gathering. Once the team gets used to that rhythm, we may easy change to "standup meeting–work–code integration before go home."

Often a development framework can have many such rhythms playing simultaneously. In this case a software team should better get used to a thematic rhythm that actually drives the success of the framework. For example, in the iterative waterfall, the thematic rhythm can be design–programming–design–programming.[5] This thematic rhythm must be sustained; otherwise, the paradigm could be more harmful than helpful.

To sustain any rhythm, such as A–B–A–B, requires both strategy and execution. Determining what practices between A and B are selected and how they can be harmoniously combined to establish effective development strategies is the same as exploring when software practices work and when they can be used. Adopting the right strategy is only half of the story; we need execution, and we especially need to be able to sustain a rhythm. This issue will be revisited in Section 1.3.2.

1.3.1 Stave Chart by Example[6]

"Most people live within a wall of rationality that is defined by the real and the apparent limits of the world they inhabit" (Anderson 1993). Software professionals, by occupation, have been trained for so many years that they are mentally fixed to think in certain patterns. For instance, they often carry a preference of conditional logic when seeing diagrams looking like flowcharts. This is sort of reflection, and hence we are often being limited by what we see (Figure 1.16).

Development rhythm can be expressed in flowcharts as illustrated in Figure 1.16. However, the use of flowcharts may cause us to lose the ability to sustain, harmonize, and, most importantly, synergize. For simplicity and readability, we use stave charts to represent software development rhythms. We believe that the stave chart gives us a stronger sense of exploring deep harmony by putting two or more software practices in harmony. (For instance, in the sequence A–B–A–B depicted in the four different scenario in Figure 1.16, when practices A and B are harmonized to produce synergies,

[5]For those who have known eXtreme programming (XP), another example is that the thematic rhythm of XP is test–code–refactor; see Chapter 9.

[6] The authors would like to thank Dr. Michael E. McClellan from the Department of Music at The Chinese University of Hong Kong for technical comments on the "stave chart by example."

FIGURE 1.16 Different visual representations of the same thing affects our thinking.

the stave chart is a good choice.) The main purpose, however, is to help us think of software practices in rhythms.

Let us look at a simple rhythm of software practices such as A–B–A–B–A–B. The rhythm starting with A is denoted as 𝄞 ♩. Then we have 𝄞 A B A B A B .

FIGURE 1.17 ∩ Explained by code–fix.

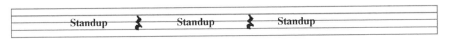

FIGURE 1.18 ⸓ Explained by standup meetings.

Since it is repeatedly moving between A and B, we use the symbol ‖: :‖ to show repetition. As with many rhythms, we are often concerned about which practice should come at the end. The rhythm will be ⸮ A ‖: B A :‖ B . Where we don't care about the order of starting and ending, a practice can be expressed as ‖: A B :‖ .[7]

Now let us look at another example of code–use–fix–(code)–use–fix–(code)–use–fix. Here "(code)" has an unplanned duration. It can even be skipped. The notation ∩ is placed over it to mean unplanned or uncertain practices. The rhythm tells less about when that practice happens and how long it may last. Figure 1.17 illustrates the rhythm of code–fix using a stave chart.

In some cases, we would emphasize pause and interruption. Sometimes, doing and holding onto something for a bit longer will unavoidably incur a stop or interruption. For example, when trying to have a standup meeting for an hour, team members will naturally ask for a regular break after 15 minutes. The symbol ⸓ indicates an interruption.

If we do not place ⸓ in Figure 1.18, then we would just write one "standup" instead of three. In this case, we deemphasize any interruption during a standup meeting.

The pause or interruption of an unknown duration can be really problematic. It is not wise to have a long standup meeting in the morning to discuss every project and technical issue that arose yesterday until all issues are resolved. Long meetings fragment, as shown in Figure 1.19. People may ask for breaks to return calls and do not return to the meeting on time. In addition,

---

[7]This a minor point, but technically, if something is enclosed in repeat signs, it will be repeated only once and everything within it should be repeated. So, for this example, the result would be A–B–A–B, nothing more and nothing less. There should be an indication that the section enclosed in the repeat signs should be repeated more times or an indefinite number of times.

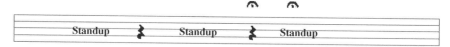

FIGURE 1.19 Long standup meetings.

urgent matters that should be handled soon may come up in the meeting and the meeting may have to be suspended.

Now we talk about the structure of a rhythm. Consider a rhythm such as A B A B A B . We can interpret this to mean that activity A is done to deliver something for activity B. Another meaning is that A and B are linked by time.

Another scenario is a bit more complicated. Some objectives of activities within A are to turn B. Normally, outputs of A are the input for B. But it is possible that A itself is much more important than its outputs and contributes much for B. The slur mark here A B indicates a special condition in which A itself triggers B.

Some rhythms have a faster tempo (e.g., hourly or daily basis). We use "Vivace" to represent that tempo as Vivace . The five lines on which practices or processes (e.g., A and B) appear are written such that, by comparing A with B, the higher it is on the stave chart, the more difficult it is or the more human dynamism is required for a team so that people will pay attention. However, in the real world, A B can be B A for some, but becomes A B for others.

The stave chart is self-explanatory. It is not a detailed workflow diagram. Basically, we have not invented any notation, although one of them has been slightly altered. The musical notation here parallels those between the compositional processes that Bach and Mozart used and the processes that programmers employ. We draw it on the whiteboard to coach software teams in development rhythms.

1.3.2 Game Theory

Companies from one country venturing into another are faced with a thicket of unfamiliar and easily misinterpreted regulations to which they must make their business operations conform.

Dave is a software leader who is going to take over a project to build an insurance application in a developing country. His software team has around 10 experienced colleagues, and they have successfully used the waterfall model to develop similar systems for almost a decade. What Dave needs to do is to lead the team and repeat the earlier success. However, unprecedented challenges are ahead of him.

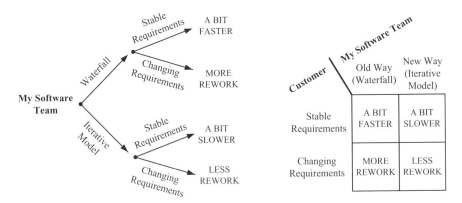

FIGURE 1.20 Software team playing their development game with customer.

The situation is more or less like exploring a game to determine the best strategy by understanding how the customer and the software team interact. When requirements are correctly formulated and relatively stable, Dave's team can do as well as usual. They feel confident. This way should therefore be considered as the faster or most expedient approach (see Figure 1.20). Unfortunately, the customers could ask for any change in their business requirements during the construction stage. More risks could result from the frequent change requests. In such a case, rework seems unavoidable.

Dave knows that the requirements could be unstable in that environment. A big waterfall model is not desirable. On the basis of his past experience, he works out a simple iterative model to build the system through evolution. There will be three or four releases, and review sessions will be held immediately afterward. During the review, the customers are allowed to raise any questions or comments for modification. Once satisfied with the progress, the customers have to pay the development fee. Rework can be minimized.

Although this sounds great, this could cause problems in Dave's software team, who may not be familiar with such an iterative approach. Adopting a new software paradigm is a team-level change! As the size of the development team is small and Dave has established a good relationship with the team, he can manage this situation. Nevertheless, the whole development process is definitely longer.

According to the maximum principle in game theory, players prefer to minimize the maximum possible loss. Thus, the project leader will plan for the iterative model because the loss is less.

This game theory analysis is satisfactory only if we can have data to understand the implications in detail. Moreover, change in software development is more than a yes/no issue. To fully analyze the game, the matrix shown in Figure 1.20 would have to be much more complicated. Still this type of tool is helpful for our strategic thinking about playing rhythms.

1.3.3 In–Out Diagram

When praised for brilliant, fantastic piano playing, Johana Sebastian Bach humbly said," There's really nothing remarkable about it. All you have to do is to hit the right key at the right time and the instrument plays itself." To play the piano well, we know how good a start is when attempting to tackle a piece of work that can have tremendous psychological impact on us. A good start motivates players to keep their focus and continue to strive for better results. A good beginning is work half-done. How a rhythm can be sustained is another key factor to be considered for a music player. One wrong key could break the melody immediately and could ruin all previous efforts!

Every rhythm can be represented as A–B–A–B regardless of what A and B are. They could be $R \rightarrow D \rightarrow C \rightarrow T \rightarrow R \rightarrow D \rightarrow C \rightarrow T$ or code $\rightarrow$ use $\rightarrow$ fix code $\rightarrow$ use $\rightarrow$ fix or anything at all. Each rhythm is uniquely different from the others. Some rhythms are easy to start but require a lot of effort to sustain, and external factors can also affect them negatively. Some rhythms, however, once we are used to them, are easy to sustain.

Sustainability is a key issue in software development rhythms. So often, a development rhythm no longer delivers expected values to both the team and the software but continues to be used. We use the in–out diagram shown in Figure 1.21 to represent rhythms as easy or difficult to start and to sustain. The in–out diagram provides a tool for strategic thinking. It is crucial to software development rhythms and is used throughout this book.

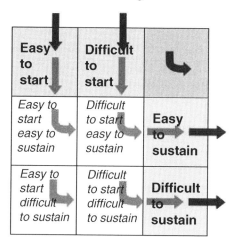

FIGURE 1.21 In–out diagram.

Easy-to-start	Difficult-to-start	↳
Interative Waterfall		**Easy-to-sustain**
Traditional Waterfall		**Difficult-to-sustain**

FIGURE 1.22 Dave's decision.

Both the conventional and the iterative waterfall models are easy to start with but difficult to sustain. Any changes can require substantial rework on software and its documentation and can also break the rhythm, at least temporarily. Changing requirements are less vulnerable to the iterative waterfall than to the conventional waterfall. Thus Dave's decision can be depicted in the in–out diagram in Figure 1.22.

In this book, we discuss the in–out development rhythm diagram on the basis of our experience. When putting this concept into action, it should be noted that all teams are different and all participants should reevaluate the diagram for their own team.

1.3.4 Master–Coach Diagram

The in–out diagram alone does not tell us what will happen to a software team when developers change with old hands leaving and new blood coming in. For better planning, there is a need to know that a worker has gone and taken his or her project knowledge and development experience.

Knowledge itself is an evergreen topic in philosophy. Ontologically, knowledge can be explicit and/or tacit. Explicit knowledge can be simply recorded in text, symbols, and/or diagrams. It can be articulated. Tacit knowledge is individual's actions, experience, values, enjoyment, rapport, or passion, or the emotions that they embrace. It is human knowledge. A software team putting rhythms into action has to work with tacit knowledge.

It takes time to learn and master new rhythms of practices in a unique development environment. Even a single practice such as two people collaborating in programming appears so simple, yet both people require hours or days to learn how to communicate well with each other. One dimension to

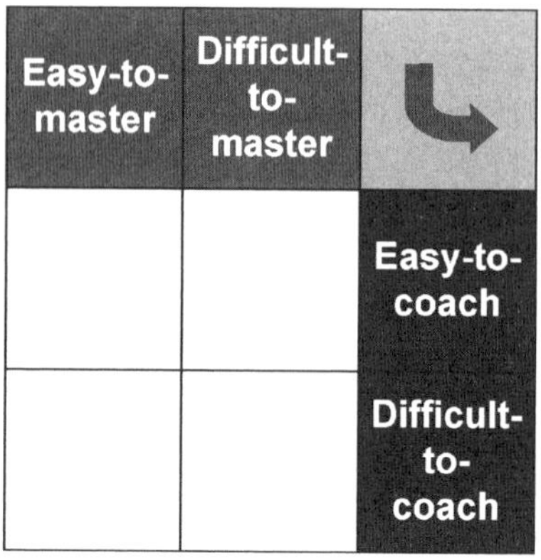

FIGURE 1.23 Master–coach diagram.

consider when adopting development rhythms is whether they are easy or difficult to master.

Newly hired developers may join a team during the development stage. Newcomers may find some rhythms easier to learn through on-the-job training alongside those who have already had experience with them or through previous project documents or even by absorbing the development atmosphere and culture. Newcomers start as apprentices to master craftsmen. However a skill is acquired, the ease or difficulty of acquiring a rhythm adds another dimension. Bringing team learning and newly hired programmer training together, we have the master–coach diagram shown in Figure 1.23. In formal terms, the diagram reflects knowledge transfers between those who have mastered the rhythm and those who have not.

1.3.5 No Mathematics

We do not need to perceive things through the use of mathematics. For instance, we can turn a burner to high and heat up a water-filled pot. The pot warms up and large bubbles rise to the surface. Eventually the pot boils dry. We have learned the principles of this phenomenon from our own experience. We do not need equations.

There is no mathematics in rhythms. Depending on how software practices are played as a rhythm, their synergy cannot be clear through understanding each of them individually. An example is shown in Figure 1.24. *Pair programming*, which is done by a team of two programmers who always collaborate on the same program together, is easy to start but difficult to sustain because the team has only two programmers, there is no partner exchange with

Easy-to-start	Difficult-to-start	↳
		Easy-to-sustain
Pair Programming		Difficult-to-sustain

+

Easy-to-start	Difficult-to-start	↳
Solo Programming		Easy-to-sustain
		Difficult-to-sustain

=

Easy-to-start	Difficult-to-start	↳
?	?	Easy-to-sustain
?	?	Difficult-to-sustain

FIGURE 1.24 Rhythms have no mathematics.

other pairs. If they work on the same task for long, it may not be easy for them to always maintain their concentration. *Solo programming* is easy to start and easy to sustain. It is hard to conceive of the in–out diagram of two rhythms as one just by understanding these two individual rhythms. We have to look into how a rhythm is established.

1.3.6 Where to Explore Rhythms

Iterations, patterns, and rhythms are interrelated. *Rhythm* refers to harmonized processes and practices in the sense that each element should be used at appropriate times so as to deliver synergistic values to people and software. Software development rhythms are also relevant when it comes to the use of different development strategies and how and when they should be executed. Both the in–out and master–coach diagrams can guide such analysis.

It is possible for one to identify many rhythms in good software development. Some are easy to start but difficult to sustain, while others are difficult to start but easy to sustain. In this book, we are interested only in those that are both easy to start and easy to sustain. There is no single one rhythm that applies to all kinds of software development. Identifying rhythms is a matter of observation and experience, and it may even involve many trials and errors. We have to try different rhythms out in our teams in practical situations. Agile practices are generally amenable to this kind of approach, and for this reason, rhythms of agile practices one of the main themes in this book.

Good software rhythms are required to ensure that a software team is productive and the software projects are completed successfully. For this, we need to know how to meet our new software teams, and how to recruit new software developers for our team. A software team has its own norms, and it is difficult for one to talk about a general template that can be adopted to achieve the same results with a different team. For this reason, instead of discussing some standard practices, we present some case studies. We will discuss software teams in developing countries to emphasize the importance of cultural elements in exploring the right rhythms. To make software team productive, a team must be aware that not all the knowledge gained from their software project experience may be helpful or useful. We return to this issue in Chapter 2.

It is tremendously challenging to tell a software team that they need to change their usual practice and adopt something better. As there are so many ways to build a piece of software, it is possible for some people to prefer one method and others to prefer a completely different method. To address such conflict in typical modern-day software development in Chapter 3 we discuss open-source software development that is almost diametrically opposite to the methods used to develop software in the commercial world. Almost every programmer believes that there is something to be learned from open-source software development, and in Chapter 3 we describe some of our experience with using agile software development processes.

Chapters 2 and 3 establish some basics and cover a very broad spectrum of topics in contemporary software engineering, touching on the essentials of programmers, social culture, project experience, team communications, software processes, and practices. The second part of the book makes use of proven techniques and applications in engineering management, sociology, industrial psychology, and group dynamics.

We explain software development rhythms in varying depths throughout the other chapters in Part II and discuss several software development rhythms. Many software rhythms are closely related to eXtreme programming (XP), and this is not just a coincidence. While many software teams have successfully adopted those XP practices, some teams are crying out loud to get out of it. I have often heard complaints such as "Kim and Keith, we already tried the agile practices before, but they did not work here!" We think that they get the software development rhythms wrong or they only get their old development rhythms right. Trust me! To succeed with any software paradigms, the mindsets and ways of working have to catch one critical element right: software development rhythms.

We hope that this book will help you become more aware of the rhythms of software development and see how they can contribute to the quality of both processes and products in your own firsthand experience of writing software.

REFERENCES

Anderson JV. Mind mapping: A tool for creative thinking. *Business Horizon* 1993; **36** (1):41–46.

Beck K and Andres C. *Extreme Programming Explained*. 2nd ed. Boston: Addison-Wesley; 2005.

Bernstein L and Yuhas CM. *Trustworthy Systems through Quantitative Software Engineering*. Hoboken, NJ: Wiley; 2005.

Boehm B. A spiral model of software development and enhancement. *IEEE Computer* 1988; **21** (5):61–72.

Brooks FP. *The Mythical Man-Month: Essays on Software Engineering*. Reading, MA: Addison-Wesley; 1995.

Chapman SN. *The Fundamentals of Production Planning and Control*. Upper Saddle River, NJ: Pearson/Prentice-Hall; 2006.

Leveson N. An investigation of the Therac-25 accidents. *IEEE Computer* 1993; **26** (7): 18–41.

Martin RC. *UML for Java Programmers*. Upper Saddle River, NJ: Prentice-Hall; 2003.

Nawrocki J, Walter B, and Wojciechowski A. Toward maturity model for extreme programming. *Proceedings of 27th Euromicro Conference*, 2001, p. 233–239.

Poppendieck M and Poppendieck T. *Lean Software Development: An Agile Toolkit*. Boston: Addison-Wesley; 2003.

Post TJ, Baltussen G, and Van den Assem M. Deal or no deal? Decision making under risk in a large-payoff game show. *EFA 2006 Zurich Meetings* 2006; available at SSRN: http://ssrn.com/abstract=636508 .

Raccoon LBS. The chaos model and the chaos life cycle. *ACM Software Engineering Notes* 1995; **20** (1):55–66.

Royce W. Successful software management style: Steering and balance. *IEEE Software* 2005; **22** (5):40–47.

Royce W. Managing the development of large software systems. *Proceedings of IEEE WESCON*, Aug (1970) p.1–9.

Tversky A and Kahenman D. The framing of decisions and the psychology of choice. *Science* 1981; **221** (4481):453–458.

2

UNDERSTANDING PROGRAMMERS

I believe because it is absurd.[1]
—FATHER TERTULLIAN

As the saying goes, "If you think you won't succeed, you probably won't," pretty much the same applies when we consider to what degree we often internalize other people's opinions about ourselves and to what extent they can condition the sorts of outcomes we get in our lives.

In a famous 1968 study, "Pygmalion in the classroom", two psychologists, Robert Rosenthal and Lenora Jacobson, informed elementary school teachers that certain students in their classes were, on the basis of the result of an intelligence test, highly intelligent (Rosenthal and Jacobson 1968). In fact, the students in question were simply a randomly selected group. Teaching continued, and at the end of the study students were tested again. The students for whom the teachers' expectations had been raised were found to have made strongly significant improvements in their test performances. This phenomenon is the self-fulfilling prophecy.

It's a paradox of humanity that we are individuals but our ideas about our individuality are heavily formed by those around us, especially by those with status.

[1]The original saying is in Latin as "Credo quia absurdum est," which means that if something (e.g., the son of God has died) is too absurd to have been invented, then it must be true (Rohmann 1999)

Software Development Rhythms: Harmonizing Agile Practices for Synergy
By Kim Man Lui and Keith C. C. Chan
Copyright © 2008 John Wiley & Sons, Inc.

37

So the self-fulfilling prophecy works in two directions. Teachers' expectations of students become students' beliefs about themselves. But students' beliefs in the teacher matters, too. When you go out to coach or lead a new software team, it is important to establish the team's belief in the leader so that the leader can help the team members believe in themselves. Letting the team know about your past successes will help your team now. Let them be proud of working with you.

Software development relies on people, and people rely on each other, in all sorts of ways. The success or failure of a software project can simply be a matter of self-belief and belief in the team. So think positively. Besides this, we also need to understand that each software team is unique and has its own strengths.

A Fortune 500 company calls you and invites you to advise its software teams. You are positive, confident, and optimistic. You arrive at the meeting with great training materials, some pretty good jokes about software development, and a passion to share what you know. But wait a moment! Are you sure you're ready? After all, what do you know about these people and what they want and need? How is your experience and knowledge relevant to them? You may be coming in to give them a complete overhaul, but they may just want a small improvement. They may like what they are already doing and just want to have someone confirm that they are more effective than anything new.

Team culture and personality traits can be another big issue. One physician may kill a patient with risky surgery procedures while another lets a patient die because she is too conservative to take risks. Yet both are trying to do their best for their patients.

Some of your team's current software practices may not be appropriate, but which practices should be dropped or changed, and what should replace them? To know what is worth learning, we have to know what is generalizable and what is specific to a particular project. A method that has been successfully used to implement one special project may have little or no value beyond that project.

If it is people who execute software methodologies, the execution cannot be too mechanical. Different teams implement the same model differently. So software methodologies should be more human-centered rather than process-centered. The thing to remember is that software methods are carried out by people and that people will always impose values on even the most obvious cause-and-effect practices.

Before we take a look at how and when software practices can be rhythmically combined, we must first briefly visit the realm of the psychology of programming. In particular, we need to consider how new software teams should be approached and made to understand working patterns, how to develop development rhythms by themselves, and also how new members should be recruited into the team. We also need to consider how cultural factors can affect software development and how software teams can make sure that they learn from their own experience.

2.1   PERSONALITY AND INTELLIGENCE

People are more sensitive to the issues of intelligence than personality. For example, how would you feel if your team leader said that you weren't up to the job intellectually? In contrast, how would you feel if she said you were stubborn? It is probably worse to be told that you are not smart enough. We are generally pretty tolerant of our human failings, or we are willing to concede that we have flaws or just have different personalities. But we don't like to think that we aren't as smart as our peers. You have to wonder whether we put too much emphasis on this slippery concept that we call "intelligence."

Early studies in psychology of programming on the relationship between psychology and computer programming did not directly deal with personality and intelligence. At that time, there was more interest in the evaluation of software tools in terms of performance. We looked at activities of programming design, code comprehension, and problem solving. Only then did we try standardized tests of intelligence to see whether they could be used to predict programming performance, and to screen job candidates. As expected, the correlation between intelligence assessments (e.g., figuring out the next number in a series) and programming capability was shown to be statistically significant. Yet, as Mayer and Stalnaker (1968) reported and as anyone in the workplace can tell you, there is actually no strong relationship between the test and the actual job performance of programmers. A piece of the puzzle appears to be missing. Is it personality?

Around 1997, we worked for a system analyst who was a dominating and directing person. He was very fact-oriented with no time for chitchat. As a programmer, this made him rather unapproachable and it also made it difficult for us to talk to him about, in one case, a database design of his that was not really up to standard. Knowing his ways, we decided to approach him in a very fact-based way. We did our research and collected plenty of references. Then we attempted to show him why his design may have had some problems. We knocked on his door. We were given 3 minutes before he requested us to get back to work. He did not want to hear about any problems.

Being wet behind the ears, we were a little taken aback by this. Shouldn't a person who expresses a belief in data be open to persuasion by the presentation of more facts? Actually, as we've since discovered more than once, the answer is "No." His interest in "facts" wasn't about "the truth." It was about his self-image of always being right. If facts were going to prove that he wasn't right, suddenly he wasn't so keen on them. That's personality in action.

Shell and Duncan (2000) say that subordinates who have personalities similar to those of their superiors will have a slightly higher incidence of job satisfaction if they are instructed by their superiors. Happy programmers work harder. They bring some sort of positive attitude into the workplace. As a consequence, problems seem easier to handle. It is, therefore, important that employees influence each other to create a pleasant, cooperative atmosphere. This is especially the case where there are a lot of individual, face-to-face interactions so that a small group of people can have a greater influence on others' behaviors. The more positive influence the members of a team have, the more skills and ideas they share, and the more we can get things done faster and better.

2.1.1 Virtuosi

A 1972 study showed that the fastest programmer could be as much as 28 times faster than the slowest programmer (Humphrey 1995). This may be of interest in certain contexts, but in terms of real-world programming products speed is just one element among many important ones. Programming includes design, algorithms, coding and, testing. Each of these requires different skills. As far as speed does matter, it is possible that a programmer is faster than his colleagues when writing program X but slower when writing program Y. We might say that a truly talented programmer can produce solutions to any programming problem more quickly than others can. But even this assumption does not take into account familiarity with the very diverse range of software products and development tools available today, the rise of interactive development environments that provide commands for checking and instant technical help, or the fact that the complexity of modern software demands teamwork.

Intuitively, however, one may still know that some programmers are just more skilled or proficient than others. What are we seeing in such people? Is it the domain knowledge they possess? One has to know enough about, say, logistic operations before one can write supply chain applications, know sales operations before writing customer relation management applications, manufacturing operations before writing a manufacturing resource planning (MRP) module, and so on. Often, it is a lack of domain-specific knowledge that makes programming hard. The more we understand business operations, the better we design and code for business operations.

Few people live such a hyperfull life or have such a varied career that they have not only the programming skills but also a knowledge of the world to the extent that they are expert in every facet of every project that they ever encounter. Life isn't that narrow, and most people aren't that smart. That is one reason why we need teams, to bring together people with diverse skills. But even then, the knowledge of each team member has to be available to other team members at various times, in different contexts, and in various accessible ways. This calls for managers to be able to create effective teams that focus on four core skill areas that are not addressed in text books on programming and never taught in courses on software design: (1) people collaboration, (2) task coordination, (3) effective communications, and (4) appreciation of cultural differences.

2.1.2 Meeting Your Team

Programmers live with and think with software activities, and the way they live with them and think about them affects the way we think and work. This matters because, surprisingly, among a group of programmers who you would expect to all have basically similar backgrounds, knowledge, and experience, there can be huge differences in the way they think about software activities. We shouldn't make the mistake of thinking that, when a software team adopts a particular programming paradigm, old or irrelevant or out-moded or even entirely contradictory programming practices and attitudes will just be immediately dropped or forgotten or left behind. No. People are creatures of habit and prejudice. The way they think about a software practice really matters and strongly affects the ways others around them think.

Programmers who have used the waterfall model for 10 years may have to struggle to adopt new programming practices (say, the agile practices as presented in Chapter 3). They do so not because such stuff is difficult but because their minds are just not ready for them yet. Every time we meet and try to help a software team, we have to understand their backgrounds and respect the way they develop software even though we might consider it stupid. How do we quickly know a new software team on the day we meet them? We ask them to draw circles—a little Rorschach inkblot–style exercise that almost anyone can do.

We give them paper and pencil and ask them to draw four circles, each of which represents their view of four basic programming concepts: (1) user requirements, (2) system design, (3) programming, and (4) testing. They may draw however many they want on the paper. Figure 2.1 shows some of these pictures drawn by developers. Next, we post the pictures where everyone can see them, and we see that within each category some drawings are similar

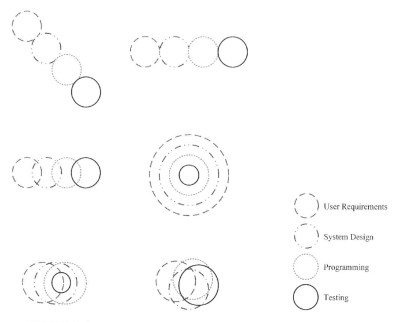

FIGURE 2.1   What does your team think of software development?

while others are very different. People usually find this part interesting, namely, how different people see the "same" thing differently.

Once the circles are drawn, we get into some interpretation. We ask people to briefly explain how what they have drawn reflects their working experience as programmers and how it represents the cultures of teams that they have been part of. One especially interesting phenomenon as these presentations proceed is that later presenters often start to draw on and modify their own drawings as they talk—in response to what they have seen and heard earlier; that is, the present peer input starts to modify how they are now seeing their own past experiences! This is the power of teams and this shows how teams can unleash powerful dynamics for better or for worse.

There is a lot of potential value and interest in this exercise, but it is important to be clear about what value you are trying to get out of it. It can produce information about individual attitudes to teams and their development rhythms. It can be an effective brainstorm for project management design. It can also be a good exercise in effective communication. (Get a team to interpret and explain someone else's drawing, then get an artist to explain it.) When you introduce your circle, it is a good, pretty much jargon-free way to get everyone on the same page about the approach being adopted in a particular project. And there are many other potential uses. This little exercise is a good starting point to show everyone that software practices matter, and that in fact they are at the heart of software design and quality.

2.1.3 Recruiting Programmers

We have met our new software team. Everything started beautifully. The team has done well! They developed programs according to what we coach them to do. Then, as always, the team needs to face a problem. The smartest guy in the team, who already learned everything from us, would now like to resign from his job. We need to find someone as good as this guy to replace him. The manager handed out a list of candidates with their resumes for the team's consideration. What the team needed to do then was to pick someone from among the list.

How do we know that someone is going to fit in with what we want to do in a smooth and productive way? This is well short of using a crystal ball. It is some kind of guessing game. Some software managers like to screen candidates using written tests, but it is very hard to write good questions to determine or assess a candidate's programming abilities or development experience. Some managers prefer, instead, to ask candidates to write a short program. This is a bit time-consuming, but it does at least test both their language skills and domain knowledge.

The programming aptitude test (PAT) is a common test for determining the ability of an individual to write programs, but it tells us nothing about specific personality traits relative to specific software practices or organizational cultures. Greathead and Devito Da Cunha (2004) discovered that student programmers who have a greater tendency to intuitive thinking approaches will do better at spotting semantic errors in Java programs (i.e., code review). Capretz (2003) surveyed 100 full-time software engineers and found that the majority preferred working with technical facts rather than with people. It may be just as interesting to ask people how they feel about working with software engineers. In most software organizations nowadays, the alone-with-my-screen model of software development is as passé as PacMan. Modern developers have to work closely together with colleagues and customers. Many organizations now expect their software teams to have some sort of diversity in terms of personality type.

There are many counts against personality tests. In some places, people are sensitive about such tests as they may appear to be a cover for racial, sexual, or other form of discrimination. There are also questions about how much trust we can put in them. Often enough, the personality test summaries that are spat out at the end of a questionnaire classify an individual in this group or that type, and they read pretty much like something from the daily newspaper's astrology page. Also you have to wonder how these limited categories account for variety. They never have anything to say about *specific* behaviors or *specific* circumstances. You read all the categories and wonder which vague generalization would include the behavior of an axe-murderer: "Prefers to set own goals?" "Requires little supervision?"

FIGURE 2.2 Asking specific interview questions will help you understand candidates' perceptions of and experience in software development.

Candidates don't like personality tests, either. They are suspicious of being categorized without a chance to defend themselves, of being classified under a general heading without a chance to show how they are special or unique. Most candidates would actually much prefer a job interview. They like open questions (e.g., such as that posed in Figure 2.2) that allow them to make claims and support them with examples, stories, and solid arguments. If they can talk about technical things and their team experience and can provide overviews and analyses, they are probably good candidates for any job that requires those things.

Ultimately, one part of hiring well must be to get the candidate to demonstrate the desired skills—whether they're technical skills (e.g., whether the candidate can program in a certain language) or transferable skills (e.g., whether the applicant communicates easily and clearly). So if you've got a job that requires people to sit through personality tests and get certain outcomes in certain columns, by all means, make a personality test a central part of the hiring process. But there are probably no such jobs.

2.2 OUTSOURCED PROGRAMMERS

Many software managers and coaches fly between North America and Asia to run software projects. Normally, these managers will tell you that it is difficult, but rewarding, to manage a team like this. Not the least of the rewards are the lessons we take home with us from other places. Learning from other places begins with respect, which is a keystone of such collaborative practices as pair programming (see Chapter 5).

As the Internet has globalized the demand for programming skills and data products, there are few geographic advantages any longer associated with any data manipulation activities. To the users, as long as it does the job, it makes no difference whether their code is written in Bangalore or Budapest.

Around the world, the distribution of skilled and less skilled programmers has no correlation to geography. It may correlate with other things, but certainly not with geography. So the "where" doesn't matter much any more. The focus now is almost exclusively on "how much" and "how good." This, in turn, explains the modern geography of programming as an answer to the "how much?" question, countries like China, Thailand, Malaysia, Russia, and Brazil and eastern European countries provide cheap programmers, making these places suitable for software outsourcing.

As for "how good," this raises the issue of "cultural capital"—the advantages and disadvantages inherited from history. One major type of cultural capital in the globalized world is of course, familiarity with the English language. Some countries like India have an advantage there. Those with a better facility in English will need less time to understand and pick up the latest technical tips. They don't need to rely on translations and won't fall victim to local translated Websites that may be putting out inaccurate information. This is a definite advantage when so many answers to problems are in fact frequently simply posted on the Internet for those who can read the source.

In the end, history and the markets may flatten out these distinctions, but for the moment they are a reality for every project manager to deal with. Managers should know the places that they are outsourcing to. You should remember that those places consist really of people and cultures with their own sets of local standards. Just because so much has gone global now and just because you sometimes don't meet face to face with the people who are working for you, you should not assume that teams or personalities are no longer relevant.

The right people are still necessary elements for good teamwork. With a little understanding of the local constraints on programmer behaviors in developing countries, you will be better prepared to get the best out the software teams you coach and lead everywhere.

2.2.1 Programmers in Their Environments

In Europe, manufacturing is moving to eastern Europe. In the United States it moves from northern to southern states, or across the border to Mexico. In Asia, it finds what it needs in formerly rural areas. Manufacturing has always done it—moving to places where land and labor are cheaper, and where governments are keen to provide or subsidize new, purpose-built infrastructure. In the same way that manufacturing plants spring up, so, too, can numerous small local software teams, either in-house or externally, to provide system solutions.

These software teams are defined by their local environments. They are composed mostly of local people and for various reasons; they may not be made up of the cream of the crop. Anyone who wants to build a software team in one of these regions, except perhaps for big corporate headquarters and top research universities, needs to realize that there can be big differences in standards and attitudes between those teams in some less-developed towns and the well-developed cities even though they may be in close proximity. These differences can continue to widen—very quickly—when a city, as is the case with China, becomes the focus of government attention.

The authors' experience managing software teams in China has revealed, briefly, four challenges that one needs to face when working in these areas with local teams:

- Your programmers will have very poor English. This means that they will not be able to make the most of new technical information available on English-language Websites.
- They won't know much about software methodologies. Currently, there are few books, written or translated into local languages, on this topic and even if there are, programmers are very unlikely to regard it as either practical or useful. Most translated books are about tools (e.g., Dreamweaver) and computer languages (e.g., Java).
- You will find that the people on your team are always on the move. Less developed areas might be remote from the well-developed cities in terms of practices and attitudes, but that doesn't mean that they are physically very far apart. In fact, less developed areas that are developing as active industrial areas are often within 250 kilometers of the more modern cities. This makes it easy for programmers to try their luck in the bigger cities and this makes it hard for team leaders to maintain stable teams.
- Most of the business is on the hardware side. Generally, 70% of business offers hardware support and only 30% provides software solutions. Therefore, they do not focus on software development as it is not their core business.

2.2.2 Programmers, Cultures, and Teams

The project manager recruited to lead a software team in developing countries must bridge between cultures. While language, management, and programming skills should not be neglected, cultural understanding of what software practices will and will not work is critical.

Local IT teams in developing regions will consist of a high proportion of inexperienced programmers. For them, your team and your project are just an entry in their resumes. They're heading for the city sooner or later, and hence, personnel turnover is usually extremely high. One must be prepared for frequent job handovers. Whether the software teams are in-house or external to a company, there is a balance of positives and negatives that you will have to deal with, some coming from the external environment (e.g., that slippery, hard-to-define thing called "culture") and some from how we handle those environmental factors (our corporate culture, e.g., how we communicate or how we use incentives). In the following lists, we summarize these factors.

The Negatives

- Managers usually have little formal training in software project management or software engineering.
- A high proportion of programmers are inexperienced.
- There is a high turnover of good programmers.
- Programmers either lack flexibility or are unwilling to display initiative. They rarely try new ways of solving old problems.
- Programmers prefer step-by-step guidance when learning and applying new skills.

The Positives

- The cost of programmers are low with monthly salaries ranging from US $62.50 to US $312.50.
- The software teams are small, around eight members or fewer.
- The programmers are willing to work very long hours (as much as 50–55 hours per week) without additional pay.
- The programmers are keen to learn any skills that they regard as "practical" or "useful" for their future jobs.

The Neutral

- Willing to accept comments about their mistakes. Unfortunately, they are prone to repeating the same kind of mistakes.

2.3 EXPERIENCED MANAGEMENT

We expand our knowledge of software by running software projects. We know how to say hello to our team and get along with different programmers. We know which approaches or development rhythms are suitable for some teams but not others because of team cultures or for other reasons. But have you ever wondered whether we could "mislearn" something because it is inherently difficult to learn from software projects?

The knowledge and experience that one gained through involving in various projects are treasures for an organization but so often only some of them are treated as valuable or worth collecting. Some managers are particularly keen to collect numerical project data for benchmarking and improvements as if the numbers have some undeniable, inherent truth. They can appear to be so narrow-minded as to ignore the fact that data must be interpreted according to how they are collected. This brings us to the importance of knowing how a project has been executed. How a team adopts software practices could be better understood by project events, meetings, and scenarios that are usually difficult to properly document. For example, it is unfair to judge how well two programmers are collaborating on a single assignment by the number of lines they have written. We have to understand software quality and the efforts involved in reworking and how they are related to job satisfaction.

Experience becomes exponentially more valuable to a company or team if it is recordable, teachable, and transferable—from person to person and from situation to situation. How can we add this value to experience? Given the right environments and incentives, it might help one to read and write about it, train it, model it, and mentor it. But all of this begins with recording it, making observations, and drawing the right conclusions—conclusions about our experience that are worth passing on.

With everything properly documented, it should be emphasized that learning from experience is not that easy. Some particular experiences may not provide lessons that are applicable to all software projects. One can confuse subsequence and consequence in software projects. For instance, just because one event (e.g., outdated design documents) often precedes another (*programming reworks*), we cannot conclude that the former is a cause of the latter. In other words, subsequence may not be the same as consequence.

2.3.1 Being Casual about Causal Relationships

Experience offers us a tangle of data and the relationships between cause and effect are not always easy to see from data. However, it is easy to just accept the first explanation for a phenomenon that comes mind. We really have to steel ourselves against this habit of blindly attributing causes to effects where, even if we know that there is a strong correlation between two events, we still may not know about the direction, the strength, or under what circumstances the causality takes place. For example, let's consider what might be the causal meaning of a strong correlation between outdated design documents and substantial programming reworks. There are four possible casual relationships.

1. *Outdated Design Documents → Substantial Programming Reworks*. Software developers have to completely rework their programs when they find out that they have followed outdated design documents to build software.

2. *Substantial Programming Reworks → Outdated Design Documents*. Software developers rework their programs to fix a number of bugs related

to system design but do not have time to update relevant design documents.

3. *Substantial Programming Rework* ⇆ *Outdated Design Documents.* Software developers have to rework their programs when they find out that the design document is outdated. At the same time, other developers detect design bugs and fix them but do not update the relevant documents soon enough.

4. *Changing Requirements* → *Substantial Programming Reworks and/or Outdated Design Documents.* A fourth factor, not tested for its correlation to the other elements and thus seldom on our radar, actually causes both substantial programming reworks and outdated design documents. There is no direct casual relationship between the rework and the documents.

Taiichi Ohno 1988, father of just-in-time manufacturing, suggests that anyone who is looking for a possible cause of a problem should ask "Why?" 5 times. For example

Why did we take much time to make a small modification in the software? *Because the same logic related to the modification was written differently and placed in more than one place.*

Why were pieces of the same logic put into so many different places in a program? *Because they were not grouped into a single submodule.*

Why weren't they grouped into a submodule? *Because the program was written by three developers and each wrote the same logic on their own.*

Why didn't the developers communicate at the beginning so that pieces of the same logic could be unified? *Because the developers thought we would communicate well through the design documents that they wrote at the beginning.*

Why didn't they follow the design documents? *Because they were written by the three developers and each part was read and understood only by the one who wrote it.*

Of course, Mr. Ohno didn't say you had to stop at five "why"'s (Ohno 1988).

2.3.2 Not Learning from Experience

It is often pointed out, but usually with a sneer, that people who believe that their temperaments are governed by the relative positions of stars tend to accept general personality descriptions as uniquely applicable to them and ignore the fact that such descriptions might equally be applied to many, many others, or even everyone (Forer 1949).

Of course, the trouble with this observation is that the same could be said of just about anyone who ever visited a psychologist. So, perhaps we shouldn't just pick on people who enjoy the simple-minded vanities of astrology. The fact is, most of us indulge in this kind of *intentional belief*— the behavior where we see what we expect to see and what we have learned to see. It is a very common and, in many circumstances, a very efficient behavior. But, of course, that doesn't make it a good software management practice.

The difficulty in learning from software projects comes with the fact that, because of the dynamic and multifactorial nature of many project-specific problems, the immediate or timely identification of the root causes of problems may be impossible. For example, changing requirements during implementation may lead to the ultimate abandonment of a software project, and this may arise from many causes, such as misunderstanding system limitations owing to ineffective user training, a lack of user involvement at the user requirement stage, or lengthy implementation requiring a review of potentially outdated business requirements. Given that the immediate identification of root causes is not always possible, it would be wise for problem solvers to take a Hippocratic approach to offer premature solutions to first ensure that they do no harm.

Premature bad solutions, however, are hardly worse than *delayed* bad ones. It may be, as Jørgensen and Sjøberg (2000) say, that much of the experience we obtained from IT projects could be in fact mislearned. Perhaps so. Then length of experience in IT certainly doesn't correlate with higher-quality professional judgments.

Even formal postmortem reviews may include much incomplete and/or incorrect information, and people are so tempted to jump to conclusions about causal relationships. Some common patterns or habits of thought can cloud the judgment:

Hypnotic Decision Making. The bases of our own decisionmaking are not always clear to us. In one study of buyer habits at a wine store, French and German music was played on alternate days. When German music was played, more German wines were sold than French and vice versa. However, in later interviews only 1 out of 44 customers mentioned the music as a factor in the purchase decision (North et al. 1999).

The Salience of Useless Unique Experience. We all enjoy unique experiences. They can make the best stories to tell other people. Unfortunately, they usually just contribute a lot to our prejudices and very little to the formation of useful generalizations.

Creating False Narratives. It is very common for us to take a fragmented selection of events from a project and re-form them in our memories as persuasive narratives. We reorganize events and unconsciously fill in gaps with plausible materials to make a nondisturbing, rational-seeming flow of events. Persuasive, but untrue. Don't rely on your memory. Remember that your memory thinks that its main job is to make you the hero of your own story. Just as the law has nothing to do with justice, your memory has nothing to do with the truth.

Believing Is Seeing. This is like intentional belief. We often formulate hypotheses or make generalizations, and then everything we see is made to fit into the theory (Preston and Epley 2005). We think that programmers like chatting online? We think that tall people are smarter than short people? We'll notice and take onboard as evidence any examples that confirm those beliefs. We'll just ignore any that don't.

So, how can we believe, and what can we believe? Part of the answer is to take on a range of diverse, evidence-based opinions and to record and reconsider what it is that we have learned. We have to consider alternative perspectives on the same event and challenge our own. We need to be aware of the biases and limitations inherent in our learning about a particular event.

Anyone can fall into the trap of project experience. Since so many software development rhythms can be worked out from project experience, we can very easily wrongly combine software practices. Rhythms that are easy to start and easy to sustain become important, as we should easily see values delivered to programmers and programming. Throughout this book, we will make use of a number of empirical findings in other areas that will broaden our perspectives in understanding when and how software development rhythms introduced here actually work.

2.3.3 Doing Things Right *Right Now*

"Works everywhere and always in the same way for everyone" would be a great promise for any software product. But there hasn't been a product yet developed that can really live up to that kind of promise. One may be full of confidence and may decide to adopt an "industrially proven" programming paradigm with lots of statistical support only to find that for some reason—or for many reasons—it just doesn't work for his or her organization.

At that point, the important question for a software program manager becomes "What now?" What do we do when the perfect plan turns out to have flaws? In many situations, the art of software management is the art of turning a sow's ear into a silk purse, of spinning gold out of straw. Software paradigms that work well for a project at the beginning may not be sustainable and may even end up as models for a mess!

Are there management techniques to prevent this? One technique is to be aware of the rhythms of software development. Because they are iterative, they allow us to check whether we are making progress, to check how real it is, and to see whether we are moving in the right direction. After each cycle, we can see what is more or less valuable and we become more confident that we are doing things right *right now.*

It is important not to assume that a paradigm or a part of paradigm is self-sustainable or to be overconfident because of previous success with a particular method or product (Figure 2.3). When things start to go wrong, we have to be able to change to other development rhythms. It is critical to

FIGURE 2.3 We may be misled by our past success.

have rhythms that are easy to start and easy to sustain and to use them as needed, and this is how we harmonize software practices for synergies.

REFERENCES

Capretz LF. Personality types in software engineering. *International Journal of Human-Computer Studies* 2003; **58** (2):207–214.

Forer BR. The fallacy of personal validation: A classroom demonstration of gullibility. *Journal of Abnormal Psychology* 1949; **44**:118–121.

Greathead D and Devito Da Cunha A. *Code Review and Personality: Is Performance Linked to MBTI Type*? Technical Report CS-TR: 837 of Computing Science, Newcastle University; 2004.

Humphrey WS. *A Discipline for Software Engineering*. Reading, MA: Addison-Wesley; 1995.

Jørgensen M and Sjøberg D. The importance of not learning from experience. *Proceedings of European Software Process Improvement*, 2000.

Mayer DB and Stalnaker AW. Selection and evaluation of computer personnel—the research history of SIG/CPR. *Proceedings of the 1968 ACM National Conference*, 23rd ACM National Conference, 1968, pp. 657–670.

North AC, Hargreaves DJ, and McKendrick J. The influence of in-store music on wine selections. *Journal of Applied Psychology* 1999; **84** (2):271–276.

Ohno T. *Toyota Production System: Beyond Large-Scale Production*. Cambridge, MA: Productivity Press; 1988.

Preston J and Epley N. Explanations versus applications: The explanatory power of valuable beliefs. *Psychological Science* 2005; **16** (10):826–832.

Rohmann C. *A World of Ideas: A Dictionary of Important Theories, Concepts, Beliefs, and Thinkers*. New York: Random House; 1999.

Rosenthal R and Jacobson L. *Pygmalion in the Classroom: Teacher Expectation and Pupils' Intellectual Development*. New York: Rinehart & Winston; 1968.

Shell MM and Duncan SD. The effects of personality similarity between supervisors and subordinates on job satisfaction, 2000. available at `http://clearinghouse.missouriwestern.edu`.

3

START WITH OPEN SOURCE

> If God had meant for us to be naked, we'd have been born that way.
>
> —Mark Twain

Software developed by organizations according to their customer requirements is hedged in by an intangible boundary. There are predetermined limits to its growth. Once it fills its niche, there it often stays. In part, this limiting boundary is defined not by customer requirements but by commercial considerations—especially issues of ownership.

The usual idea of growth is that it is driven by commercial needs. But commercial markets don't offer every good we want, and companies are in fact quite satisfied with offering fewer goods and choices if they can control a market and charge us higher prices. In other words, commercial markets aren't perfect. There are values that companies don't care about but people do.

Open-source software is a great example of this. It is exploding. It is taking on commercial giants. It is satisfying diverse needs that the commercial producers thought only they could satisfy. It's free. It's mysterious. Many have wondered exactly how open-source software development works.

We have talked about how to meet new teams and to recruit team members. It is time to ask a bunch of questions to explore your team's thoughts about what software development is and to share your understandings of the relationships between software practices, programmers, customers, and software. The success of open-source software development (OSSD) practices and artifacts is undeniable but is also something of an

Software Development Rhythms: Harmonizing Agile Practices for Synergy
By Kim Man Lui and Keith C. C. Chan
Copyright © 2008 John Wiley & Sons, Inc.

FIGURE 3.1 Redundancy and duplicated efforts in the workplace if coordinated as an anonymous open-source team.

anomaly when compared with many other software development processes. In our experience, it doesn't matter whether a software team is made up of waterfall model lovers, agile proponents, or ad hoc enthusiasts; they are always interested in OSSD.

What are the limits on the growth of open source? What drives an open-source software project? What sustains it? A paradigm that involves uneconomically large numbers of people asynchronously collaborating on tasks and tolerant of high levels of redundancy or duplication is not a very commercial way of managing a project (see Figure 3.1). How is this possible in the modern era, and what can we learn from it? Is it agile?

There are four important areas to consider with reference to open-source software:[1] (1) IT strategy, (2) OSS product management, (3) reusing open-source code, and (4) the OSS development model.

Companies re-form their business models and commercial strategies for open-source software. For example, some mobile phone manufacturing

---

[1] We might actually say five areas, including open-source licenses.

companies have already seen market opportunities and made their hardware with Linux preinstalled. Some have said that Linux has been the largest project in the annals of software development. Maybe so and maybe not, but certainly Windows Server 2003, which has been said to be the largest software development project in Microsoft's history,[2] was launched to handle the threat of Linux (Raymond 1998). Microsoft has continuously expressed concern about competition from open-source products. Nowadays, the open-source product is nothing more than software and it can be just one element of a total business solution for customers in the commercial world.

Using OSS products means making some changes in the way that we manage software projects as it creates a need to implement and integrate OSS products alongside other commercial packages. As for software implementation in the enterprise, Golden (2005) suggested a well-structured open-source maturity model. This model covers six key areas in which to assess and manage OSS products: software, support, documents, training, product integration, and professional services.

For further development, an organization may customize the open-source products. Reusing previous work of open-source software definitely accelerates development from the ground up. We will come back to this exciting topic in Chapter 4.

Finally, what lessons can we learn from so many open-source software projects? Is there any structured software model in these projects? Open-source software development has been well studied but it is still an area with many unknowns and uncertainties. There are some inherent barriers to understanding OSSD experimentally. It involves the collaboration of a large number of people from different cultures who may or may not be known to each other. They have diverse motivations, from killing time to personal interests to a role in a funded project. It is not easy to determine a suitable sample size or to manage cultural factors in a way that would satisfy the requirements of controlled experimentation. Yet this unconventional model would appear to have lessons to offer us in our commercial software development environments. Bringing the whole OSSD process into our commercial workplace is out of the question, but it may be feasible to adopt some open-source practices.

In this chapter we address the basics of software development. From the project management viewpoint, we explore commonality and differentiation between OSSD and agile software development.

---

[2] Microsoft's timeline from 1991, available at `http://www.thocp.net/companies/microsoft/microsoft_company_part2.htm`.

3.1 PROCESS AND PRACTICE

Processes and practices have been freely used in the software literature. Although we can usually tell the difference in context, some developers make the mistake of thinking that practices are just lightweight processes. To avoid confusion, we'll clarify the differences here.

Simply put, a software process is a collection of activities performed to achieve given goals. Therefore, a software process is a way of describing how work should be done (Sommerville et al. 1999). From the perspective of engineering management, the activities performed should apply disciplines for accomplishing the goals with a minimum of unplanned intervention.

Processes can be and often are automated with tools. This is important to recognize because processes with the same objectives and procedures could achieve very different results in terms of efficiency and effectiveness depending on whether the processes are executed using manual systems or automation. In practice, software processes are often semiautomated and use self-governing automation. It is not the same kind of automation that we see with machines in manufacturing environments, yet we continually seek to develop and adopt technologies to make our software processes more automated, such as the generation of code from user requirements.

Software processes should be recurrent and repetitive. This implies that we are concerned with how the same process can be performed better than previously. This brings up a topic called *software process improvement*. The resources taken up by the activities of a software process (e.g., cost and time) can be used to establish a baseline to continuously improve the process. Simplifying workflow among activities so that communication overheads are reduced and errors are discovered as early as possible may significantly improve the overall software process. Therefore, to optimize a software process, we have to deal with activities and ways of performing activities, which are collectively called *software practices*.

When we say "software practices," we mean two specific things. They can be ways to execute tasks (or activities) and/or activities (or norms/customs). The meanings can be best understood by example. In pair programming, two developers collaborating in front of a single machine is a way of programming. The tasks required to collaborate include design, programming, and testing. These are activities.

When a process is made up of one or two activities, it may be considered a practice. However, the reverse may not be true. A number of practices together may not be regarded as a process if there is no well-defined goal. Some practices are just more pragmatic and culture-oriented than they are goal-specific. For example, the practices *energized work* and *shared code*

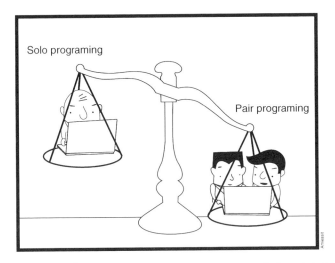

FIGURE 3.2 Are you sure pair programming is lightweight?

(Beck and Andres 2005) do not together explicitly indicate any objective. Along with other practices, energized work and shared code can be used to achieve certain things, or they alone are just organizational norms.

Depending on activities and their execution, software processes can be lightweight or heavyweight. And so it is with practices. The term *weight* is figurative (e.g., see Figure 3.2). It has no formal definition. Therefore, some may take the term *heavyweight* to mean ceremonial, nonadaptable, or bureaucratic. Yet this does not clearly explain why some agile practices are said to be lightweight. For example, a software practice called *pair programming* has two developers collaborating on design and programming tasks at the same time. We were once asked whether pair programming would be a lightweight practice. On one hand, pair programming allows people to work much closer so that there are fewer bureaucratic barriers to team communications. It is more adaptable when, for example, people call in sick. On the other hand, it can be nonadaptable when team members as the individuals previously enjoyed more flexible working hours.

The weightiness of software processes and practices is a matter of the values that arise from them and the degree to which activities directly benefit and contribute to core developers (i.e., people) and core software programming (i.e., products). So pair programming is lightweight. For example, a software process that requires writing all-embracing design documentation for commercial database applications may be considered heavyweight as it does not directly create value for the core development. Heavyweight processes have their place. In this case, detailed documents come in handy when we are going to outsource technical support and software maintenance abroad.

This simple definition does not consider customers because they normally are not interested in software development. But if developers make software right, this will result in delivering right-quality products at the right time and at the right price, and that is definitely a set of values that would benefit customers.

Lightweight and heavyweight are associated with people and products. Heavyweight processes and practices are less inclined to direct their effort and their values as directly toward people and products. Lightweight is the opposite.

3.1.1 The Four Ps of Projects

The Agile Manifesto (2001) declares that individuals and interactions are placed above processes and tools, working software above comprehensive documentation, customer collaboration above contract negotiation, and responding to change above following a plan. Agile software development is lightweight. The manifesto orients software development toward people and working software.

This movement appears to overthrow what programmers learned in traditional software project management in which programming tasks are commonly deemed either as an aggregate of tasks or as a set of components (subtasks). Adopting that kind of management model, software managers would be more interested in resources allocation or tools/methods to facilitate programming (or software development).

Although software project management provides guidance for team organization, its goal is to structure a group of members in order to optimize the resources and get high performance out of the team. Data collected from the processes and their results allows the monitoring and controlling of our activities. Facts are managed to dispel the myths and implications among people and activities. Little attention is given to the relationships between programmers and software in managing software projects as process procedures and control documents downplay the importance of such relationships.

To ensure that everyone in a team has the same understanding, we need to clearly address the mechanism of software processes. Often, the processes come along with a set of papers that guide and control what and how programmers perform programming tasks or develop software. The paper may go electronic, but its contents will be just the same: requirement specifications, entity–relationship diagrams, training manuals, and so on. Heavy documents in a small-sized project distract the team's focus from the working software product.

TABLE 3.1   The Four Ps (4Ps) in Software Projects

4Ps	Projects Managed by Waterfall	Projects Managed by Agile Software Development
Product	▲	★
Paper	★	▲
People	▲	★
Process	★	▲

Key: ★ indicates more focus than ▲.

Table 3.1 summarizes process, people, product, and paper from two different software project management perspectives. With fewer process management and control documents as in agile software development, it becomes more important to understand the links between programmers, programming tasks, and software. Programming—including requirements understanding, design, coding, testing, debugging, and integration—belongs to cognitive activities that demand both learning and understanding. A variety of skills required in software development are intermingled, such as problem-solving, planning, backtracking, quick thinking, and causal (cause–effect) reasoning. Even when individual programmers have all the necessary skills, they may not be up on new techniques. The response is to allow people to collaborate and share knowledge.

Jacobson et al. (1999) discussed the 4Ps of software development as process, people, project, and product. The new 4Ps for software project management (see Table 3.1) would try to help understand software methodologies in terms of the areas that differentiate the methods we use to manage software projects.

Now that the 4Ps can be used to identify how software projects can be managed, we can use them to try to understand open-source software projects (see Table 3.2). Obviously OSSD projects should motivate people to participate and products to share; otherwise, the project should not have been opened. Heavyweight documents are hard to keep up-to-date with frequent releases. Although some OSSD projects may have a set of full documents, the documents may have been developed before the project became open. To

TABLE 3.2   4Ps in Open-Source Projects

4Ps	Open-Source Software Projects
Product	Focused
Paper	Just-Enough
People	Focused
Process	Just-Enough

allow developers to make contributions at their own pace, the development process should be designed to be lightweight.

Open-source software development actually avoids the scenario depicted in Figure 3.3. The sharing procedures are simple so as to encourage people to try, join, and contribute.

FIGURE 3.3 An example of the need for OSSD.

3.1.2 Agile Values

In a general sense, any positive attribution to people and products in software development is the agile value. This, of course, is too broad. More specifically, as suggested in eXtreme programming, agile values can be communication, simplicity, feedback, courage and respect. But these are not a limit. They are just basic.

Some basic differences between open-source software development (OSSD) and agile software development (ASD) are listed below.

Communication

OSSD. For OSSD projects, developers are willing to share their own ideas and to get feedback from others. Communication is strongly built on rapid release and user comments.

ASD. Asking knowledge workers to work for extra 2 or 3 hours every day is not going to achieve any increase in productivity. To maximize their capabilities, we have to let them share their knowledge and experience so that problems can be dealt with better and faster. A lack of knowledge in a team could be just a symptom of a lack of communication.

Feedback

OSSD. For open source software development projects, opinions come from everywhere, critics, end users, and peer developers.

ASD. Software solutions by themselves can be artificially abstract on one hand and trick-specific on the other hand. When we are approaching a solution, we always need feedback. True value is delivered only at the moment that changes can actually be made in the software.

Simplicity

OSSD. For OSSD projects, to deliver frequent releases, developers always build software for today's needs.

ASD. You can write a complicated program or a simple one to fulfill the same requirements. Obviously, everyone will prefer a simple solution. Let us go a bit extreme. We need 3 weeks to complete a login function. There are two approaches: (1) we make the code done and runnable after 3 weeks, or, (2) the code is continuously done bit by bit and is partially executable every day. This is what we call simplicity: gracefully solving today's problem.

Courage

OSSD. For OSSD projects, this goes a bit further. The developers not only rewrite each other's working code and discard poor solutions but also share their own code in public, no matter good or bad it is.

ASD. Changing existing code for the better requires our belief, enthusiasm, and courage.

Respect

OSSD. For OSSD projects, developers are interested in and care about what others are doing and what has been achieved.

ASD. Respect for others and the respect of others are elements in motivating a team so that it enjoys challenges and achieving remarkable things.

Agile values are not accidentally established in the course of past successful project implementations. They also fulfill needs for a programming team that can *manage by self-satisfaction.*

Practices always deliver some values. But desirable values can be delivered only when the right practices are adopted by the right people at the right moment. Therefore, there may not be a simple mapping between values and practices. However, values may result not from just one or two software practices but from their synergies.

In fact, the same set of practices enacted by two teams may produce different effects: desirable or negative impacts. A team leader who has been understood to personally favor some agile practices demands that the team adopt them rigidly. In this case, the leader may ignore the fact that team members are not yet ready for the change. The team's culture can even result in hatred of the team leader and the new practices. For example, software teams that have allowed members to arrange their working hours within a broad timespan will feel constrained in pair programming where the whole team is supposed to work together and flexible working hours are gone. The team will be blind to agile values, and there could be a campaign against the leader by criticizing agile practices.

3.1.3 Zero-Point Collaboration

When a group of people collaborate on a new artifact from scratch, they will have to go through more steps. Software requirements are collected and then documented through conversations and meetings. Often, programmers will visit their clients' workplaces and talk to end users about their existing workflow. Then the team is asked to define a system architecture like a database model, class diagrams, or even a small prototype. To deal with a project like this, team members have to communicate with each other well and coordinate their subtasks. The proceedings of collaboration can be basically viewed as building something from nothing. This is called *zero-point collaboration*.

In some cases, team members are distributed in a number of locations or are varied in terms of their capabilities. In this case, the whole team will have tremendous difficulties in building something from nothing as software itself is abstract and the team members probably interpret the same things differently.

A few of the members, who probably share the same ideas, are able to develop something such as a data model so that others may easily follow the work. This kind of collaboration is the opposite of the zero-point as the whole team can become productive only when they are developing and adding to something. Once an artifact or a prototype has been built, other team members can see and ask questions that refer to that something.

3.2 OPEN-SOURCE SOFTWARE (OSS) DEVELOPMENT

Open source is a special development paradigm. Without budget constraints, customer pressure, and a schedule to meet, developers, users, and project competitors can speak equally. Projects are free to grow and even to produce child projects. The sky is the limit. Any part of the project canvas can be virtually extended so that other programmers can later add other things. If someone tries to add something malicious, there's a whole open community checking the work. This is the "Bazaar model" (Raymond 2001) for OSSD where no exclusive group controls the development; everyone who is interested in the development can take care of the project.

In contrast to the bazaar model, the "cathedral model" makes source code available, but the development is restricted to an exclusive group of programmers. Either way, it is the products themselves that have caught our eye. Many companies have adopted these products for commercial applications and governments around the world have officially supported the use of open-source software in civil administration, indicating that the open-source products have now come to be recognized in terms of not only software quality but also maintainability.

Between the cathedral and bazaar models there is a hybrid, the application kernel maintained by a group of programmers, like the cathedral model but where anyone can develop different open source plug-ins.

TABLE 3.3   4Ps in Some Open-Source Software Projects

4Ps	Features of Some Open-Source Software Projects
Product	Software cloning (or requirements cloning); software quality
People	Ugrammers
Paper	Same as for product and people, above
Process	Starting process, rapid releases

As there can be thousands of open-source software projects in or between the bazaar and cathedral models, it is not possible to generalize about open source. In this section we will therefore look at some features that may not be typical of every open-source project but that are helpful in contrasting it with the ways we develop the commercial development projects (often referred to as *closed-source software projects*).

Some of the features of open-source software projects are listed in Table 3.3.

3.2.1   Software Cloning*

Cloning in genetic engineering is the process of recreating an identical copy of DNA, the nucleic acid containing the genetic instructions for the biological development of an organism. Thus, cloning does not copy us (i.e., human body and mind) but our DNA. What is the DNA of enterprise software applications?

If we get the requirements for an existing system we can use them just like DNA to rebuild a similar system using other computer languages on other platforms. The two systems would have a very close functionality from a user perspective. The functionality of cloned applications should be of interest to us; otherwise, we would not clone them.

Why do we clone software? There are many reasons. In some cases, software applications that have been cloned should be either closed-source software or software built with many technical constraints so that further modifications are not that feasible. When such software applications interest programmers, it obviously must be the functionality such as application requirements and/or better performance, rather than the language used to write it. This provides us with a clue as to what motivates open-source developers to join a project and to spend time reading and writing code. Even though some programmers are not involved in the development because they are not familiar with the language used to build the software, they still enjoy providing their opinions and reporting bugs.

*The term cloning has been used in the open source community. For example, the early version of Miranda IM (Miranda Instant Messenger) regarded itself as a minimalist ICQ clone.

Example of Software Cloning

In 1991, Linus Torvalds, the initiator of the Linux project, needed a version of Unix for his PC. To improve its functionality, he made it known what he wanted to do and invited feedback from those who were interested in the product (Pavlicek 2000). Whether Linux has evolved beyond the Unix family, it was a cloned application of Unix.

3.2.2 Software Quality

The big question in open-source development is how software that has been developed through the collaboration of volunteer programmers could possibly deliver quality as good as we can get from a well-structured team using well-defined development processes. The cloned application may imitate the functionality of what we are going to develop, but getting complete requirements for software has nothing to do with code quality.

In terms of the number of developers, the Linux project has been recognized as probably the biggest project in the world. Ken Thompon, one of the principal creators of Unix, disappointed many open-source proponents by saying that he thought the quality of Linux varied drastically. Some of its source code was good, and some was not (Thompson 1999). This is just a sensible comment because after all, the software has been written by many different people.

Linux has often been assumed to be representative of all open-source projects, but it is in fact a uniquely large project, and writing operating systems is much more technical than doing other applications. We cannot generalize from Linux to other OSSD projects.

Stamelos et al. (2002), tried to quantify code quality in open-source development. One hundred applications written for Linux were studied using metrics such as cyclomatic complexity measuring the extent of linear independences (McCabe 1976) and vocabulary frequency measuring the sum of the number of the unique operands n_1 and operators n_2 (Halstead 1975). The results showed that the quality of code produced in these open-source projects was a little below the industrial benchmarking given by Telelogic's Logiscope. Interestingly, as the open-source project is running continuously, the open-source code in terms of software quality could be a little more maintainable in the next release than closed-source code (Stamelos et al. 2004).

Few commercial software vendors release source code or testing reports to their clients. Without that information, we actually know little about their software quality. So we can't criticize it, but that doesn't mean high quality code. In contrast, open source allows everyone to inspect the software quality at the code level. Obviously, we can't say on one hand that all open software is high-quality or on the other hand that bazaar-model-developed software is of a lower quality. To judge the quality of open-source software for use in commercial applications, we have to evaluate it project by project.

3.2.3 Starting Processes

Open-source software projects can have different starting processes. In some cases as just mentioned in software cloning, a single person (or a few known people) may begin by calling for public comments that arouse public interest. The project can be of purely personal interest. It can also be a funded project.

In other cases, the source code of commercial or academic working software products is released to the public and becomes a new open-source project. One example is Mozilla. Open-source projects initiated and supported by a number of organizations do not normally invite public developers to join the development, but what interested developers probably can do is to get involved in the customization and deployment of local language interfaces, for example, as in A-tutor.

Figure 3.4 provides an overview of how open-source projects like Linux and Mozilla are initiated. Personal interest in a software product—whether that interest is one person's or a group's—is the driving force in stimulating and steering an OSSD project. In many cases, the interest is in what the

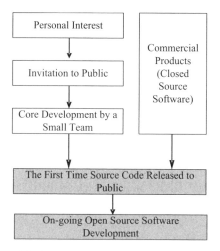

FIGURE 3.4 Open source software development.

product should be or look like rather than in how the product can lead to the development of an OSSD project.

Public invitations on the Internet to developers to participate may lead to the establishment of either a small core development team or the quick development of a prototype based on feedback. At this time, the team must be small, perhaps just one person. This is because when the product is at zero, it is both difficult and unproductive to create software on the basis of many comments and too many people and code changes. At this stage, the main goal is to release the product, despite its incomplete functionality. Interested developers can then focus on the product. Thus, an open-source project is product-driven. Without the first release, many developers can only contribute comments.

In other cases, closed-source projects that have probably been commercial products in the market are released to the public. This extends their user bases so that the companies can concentrate on providing professional services such as training and consultancy instead of selling software.

Software is purely artificial. It becomes less abstract only when we have experienced the use of software. In a word, zero-point collaboration, in which a group of people collaborate on a new artifact from the ground up, is difficult in a distributed environment.

Therefore, releasing source code is important in making others participate and hence to build the team. The success of requirements for open-source projects is that developers need to have something from the ground up that can be downloaded, installed, tested, and so forth, and it does not seem possible to build things from the ground up in the open-source style (Sandred 2001).

3.2.4 Open-Source Development Community

Once the first release is available to the public, the project team will rapidly grow. Some developers actively build more submodules while some others just play around and suggest potential features to enhance the software. Although this seems to have a structure of teaming, the OSSD team is just loosely coupled. The team has a higher degree of collaboration. Each individual can work on the product independently, accelerating its development in many areas such as debugging, performance tuning, refactoring, functionality enhancement, and testing on different platforms, such as Chinese Windows. But it is less coordinated.

As a consequence, people could be individually reinventing the wheel for the same problem until someone reports her or his findings. Once a solution (i.e., a program) is posted, the others would then look at the source for further improvement. In any case, effort can be duplicated, but others can build more on that program and later on release a more complete one.

Such low communication proximity makes the team work like a community, in which people feel the need to have a share in helping to build a software product and thereby having a sense of belonging to a group in the network where they live (having an identity, i.e., nickname; and social responsibilities, such as fixing their own program bugs once reported).

Surveyed from the open development community, open-source developers can be classified in terms of the extent of involvements and activities. For example, a project leader administers the overall project. Core developers manage concurrent version system (CVS) releases and coordinate others. On an either regular or irregular basis, codevelopers fix bugs, add features, submit patches, provide support, and exchange other information. Active users who probably install latest versions (rather than stable versions) submit their test reports and suggest potential enhancements. People outside of the above are free to examine the code and submit patches. When the cathedral model is adopted for the development, there could be a distinct difference between a developer raising an issue and some outsider raising the same issue (Xu and Madey 2004).

3.2.5 Ugrammers

No one likes to be responsible for more jargon, but we need a word to clarify the different and evolving roles of programmers and end users in the software world. Somewhere between a programmer and a user there is someone else, someone nameless. Armed with modern technologies and the knowledge of how to use them, these people are consumers who have become proactive. They are not easily satisfied with standardized products and are willing to let manufacturers know exactly what they want. Alvin Toffler, the author of *Future Shock*, coined a word "prosumer," which sounds like "proactive consumer," but he meant to combine producer and consumer. We may now at last be seeing the birth of this hybrid creature. Similarly, as the roles of the producer (i.e., programmers) and the consumer (i.e., end users) blur in OSSD, we are seeing the evolution of a new, hybrid creature, the "ugrammer."

Before, for lack of time and other reasons, developers could not customize or add features to closed-source applications for their individual needs. Open-source software projects give them the opportunity to participate in developing the application they are really interested in and a chance to have a wider impact. No longer just passive users but also active developers, they are two-in-one. They are *u*grammers. Consider the following definitions:

Programmers—those who build the software but they are not end users

Users (or customers)—those who will use the software (can be end users or the end-user supervisors)

Ugrammers—those who build and use the software

Traditionally, programmers have deliberately adopted a variety of user perspectives on the systems they build. But they are not necessarily real end users. The two-in-one role of the ugrammer contributes to the success of a software project. The ugrammers complement each other as their development knowledge and user experience provide insights into the product they build.

Two-in-one makes software development a new paradigm. For example, requirements management is a key area of software project failure. Some management methods advise sign-off requirements documents while some suggest tight collaboration between programmers and users. For programmers, experience of requirements management is often gained from domain knowledge that they previously gained from users. Ugrammers can use their own user experience to better evaluate requirements collected from others and can ask more insightful questions. This greatly enhances communications between ugrammers and end users.

3.2.6 Participant Roles

The intuitive way to understand any software project is to simply classify involved members into two roles, customers (or users) and developers, as a percentage. In this way, we can easily compare an open-source project with a commercial software project and understand some fundamental differences. How the percentage of project participants varies in the two roles tells us something about the projects. As illustrated in Figure 3.5, project participants in a commercial enterprise resources planning (ERP) project could be very separate. In this project, 25% of the participants take a pure developer role as programmers or system analysts. The rest play a pure end-user role, performing user acceptance testing, develop training manuals, and perform other tasks. In some commercial projects, some participants who adopt a 90% user role and a 10% developer role are often viewed as superusers. These participants can draw technical diagrams and even diagnose problems through systematic testing, which substantially helps the development.

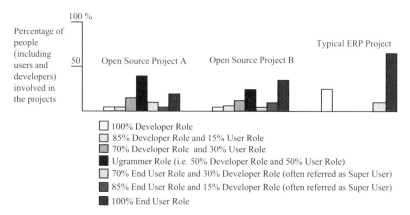

FIGURE 3.5 Software project participant roles.

In contrast to the abovementioned industrial project, the roles in many open-source development projects are any combination in any proportion of the programmer and user roles. In a case where the developers are the users (e.g., those who are involved in the development of Miranda-IM, Firefox, or Joone are the users), ugrammers can have a number of combinational distributions with active users as shown for projects A and B in Figure 3.5.

There is currently no evidence as to how these distribution curves (A or B in Figure 3.5) correlate to the success of a project; however, we believe that having ugrammers in a software project, particularly in a distributed environment, helps bridge the communication gap between the developers and the users.

3.2.7 Rapid Release

By breaking down system functionally, we may rapidly release a software product from time to time. However, this has to communicate well with customers; otherwise, it may not be always desirable. Let's look at a real industrial case.

We met an IT manager in 2004 who implemented a JSPWiki (open-source software) as a departmental knowledge base. A Website can be used to distribute information. It does not facilitate collaboration between people. But, when JSPWiki allowed people to log in and to easily edit available content, team members were able to follow documentation standards and then compile their working notes on practical experience and technical tricks directly on JSPWiki. This allowed departmental knowledge to be shared and reused (see Figure 3.6).

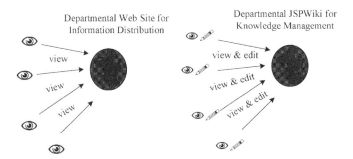

FIGURE 3.6   Unlike many other types of websites, JSPWiki allows individual logins and editing.

For example, someone may download a copy of JSPWiki to evaluate the functionality and plan for its implementation. The version was 2.1.134-alpha. The installation was done, and the server was up. Everything seemed alright until the team started browsing around the software and they realized that there was no interface for changing the default password!

From a customer perspective, the software was not that complete. This would not normally happen in many traditional commercial projects. Some software houses may release incomplete software packages to clients for training purposes yet claim that the products are prototypes. Otherwise, as some end users are "problem pickers," they will just view any incompleteness as defects. This may potentially damage the image of professionalism of the software house.

But what does "the expected completeness" really mean? It is all about the user's knowledge and experience. For example, any software requires authentication. Users will expect to be able to change their login profile somewhere on the software, just as other software does.[3] As so many users often do an apples-to-oranges comparison, it is better to put a release off until we get basic things done from a user perspective.

Open-source development projects somehow reverse the logic. Take our previous example. When the user authorization is done, the module and its source code will be quickly released. The work at this moment is complete from a ugrammer perspective. The ugrammer can modify related configuration files to change any password; unfortunately, this might not be regarded as "expected completeness" by general users. In short, open-source projects release their work products by the completeness of source code

---

[3] In agile software development, the developer and the customer truly participate in a software project. The customer can even prioritize a feature list for the developer. Thus, there is no expected completeness.

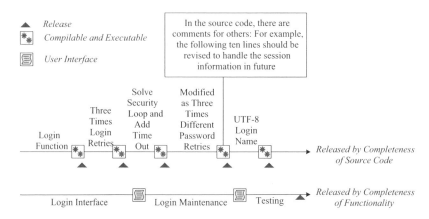

FIGURE 3.7   Rapid release demystified.

(i.e., compliable and executable) while commercial products are released by the completeness of functionality (see Figure 3.7).

Among other reasons, release by completeness of source code contributes greatly to rapidity of release, which, as mentioned, is critical for open-source workflow because other developers are able to further reuse the latest released source code so as to avoid doing duplicate work in parallel.

Figure 3.8 illustrates the relationship between rapid release and productivity. Four programmers who do not communicate with each other are all interested in spending their leisure time programming one submodule. They start by downloading the latest copy available to the public. Then we look at two situations: fewer releases and more releases. In the first case, the source code is released only when the whole submodule is done in terms of functionality. Development effort is duplicated until B eventually finishes and shares her work with others (see Figure 3.8, situation I). The other developers (i.e., A, C, and D) can obtain benefits afterward.

By comparison, in the second case, developer B shares the code earlier. Later on developer A can continue B's work in his spare time and release the completed version (see Figure 3.8, situation II). The elapsed time has been greatly shortened and, most importantly, it deals with the inefficiency that arises from the duplication of effort. The more source code is frequently shared, the more productive the open-source community can be.

3.2.8   Blackbox Programming

In the commercial environment, regardless of how software teams are managed, it is always recommended that the same set of software practices be

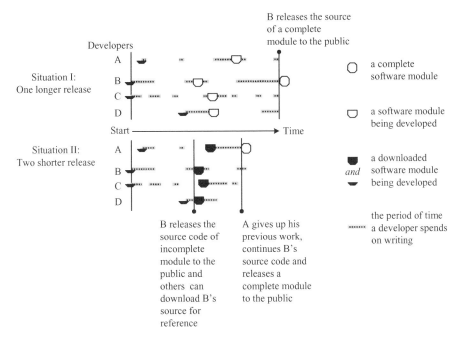

FIGURE 3.8   Rapid release and productivity explained.

adopted for a project, even though ways of programming by software teams may be adaptively evolving. As each developer probably works in a cubicle, all developers meet at regular meetings to share their individual experience so that some key software practices are consistently followed. More recently, agile practitioners have concluded that a cubicle-like environment is not good for team programming. An open and informative workspace environment allows programming ideas to be exchanged and practices adopted.

Open-source software development turns the abovementioned development experience upside-down. It is not hard to imagine that open-source developers just sit in their own offices or cubicles and work in their own ways. They may not coordinate in the same way as industrial team would. But this situation is not always the case. In some open-source projects, particularly in the cathedral model, some members within the core developer group know each other. They probably communicate better for collaboration (shown in Figure 3.9) and they can share their experiences of how to program with each other. In this case, the developers coordinate their on-hand tasks and even agree on their software practices.

Of the codevelopers, those who keep in contact with core developers and/or other codevelopers by email or through discussion forums may also be advised to follow largely the same software practices. In any case, there is

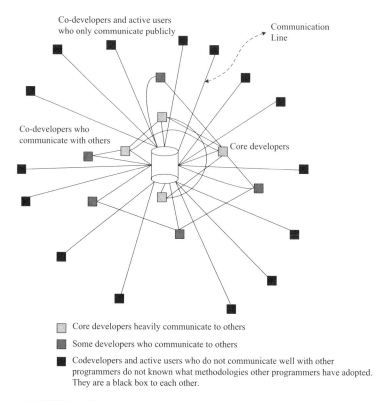

Co-developers and active users
who only communicate publicly

Communication
Line

Co-developers who
communicate with others

Core developers

Core developers heavily communicate to others

Some developers who communicate to others

Codevelopers and active users who do not communicate well with other
programmers do not known what methodologies other programmers have adopted.
They are a black box to each other.

FIGURE 3.9 Software project community and communications.

no broadly accepted way for these codevelopers to actually carry out their
own functions.

At the same time there may be many anonymous developers who only
communicate publicly through the project's Website, and it would be a most
unlikely accident if all of the members of this group were to agree to adopt any
single software programming practice.

In any case, writing source code under these conditions is a kind of
blackbox programming. Team members simply do not know how each
individual works. Some code in pairs, and some prefer to work out design
details first. A lack of knowledge about their programming practices also
means ignorance as to their code quality. Blackbox programming has no place
in team software development in the commercial environment.

3.2.9 OSS Practices

Many open-source practices may appear to be unique but in fact can be seen as
simply ways of covering all of the more familiar software project management

TABLE 3.4 OSS Practices

Areas	Practices
1 Software configuration management	Historical bug-fix records
	Well-established version control
	Different releases: stable, beta, and alpha
	CVS
2 People management	Prompt feedback
	Praise
	Anonymity, which eliminates bias regarding people and cultural differences
	Discussion forum
3 Project plan and project tracking	Rapid development release (nightly build)
	To-do list
4 Software quality assurances	Parallel debugging
	Public comments
	Code reading

areas (Table 3.4). The purpose of software configuration management is to record, control, and manage different versions of code produced by open-source developers. The purpose of people management in open-source development is to motivate, inspire, support, ensure communication between, and encourage team members.

There is no formal project plan for resources allocation, project schedule, and task priority. Instead, rapid release and the to-do list serve to minimize duplicated effort and to prioritize jobs. Software quality assurance is achieved by code inspection through code reading by a number of people on the Internet. Almost all of the open-source practices listed in Table 3.4 directly pave the way for people and products in the 4Ps.

3.3 OSS-LIKE DEVELOPMENT

The 4P analysis tells us that open-source development is similar to agile software development although their software practices may not be the same. Moreover, as mentioned previously, both deliver the same values, such as communication, feedback, simplicity, courage, and respect. They are interconnected. We are then interested in when and how software practices adopted in these apparently contradictory environments nonetheless tend to produce the same values. Answering this question will give use a better understanding of two major factors of a software development methodology: team size and team location.

The success or otherwise of past projects is an indicator of whether a software paradigm has been shown to work in one situation, say, a distributed environment. But the same paradigm will not necessarily succeed if used in another, say, a collocated environment. Perhaps some of its practices will still work and some will not. Those that do not work in one environment might be replaced with others that have worked in the same environment and that are compatible with the remaining practices.

3.3.1 Agile Practices

Unlike open-source development, which takes place across a distributed environment and implies the participation of large teams, many agile practices are most suitable for collocated teams. Let us look at agile practices that have been proved suitable for small, collocated teams. A typical example is eXtreme programming (Beck 2000; Beck and Andres 2005). Although it is not possible to manage small and large projects by using the same set of practices, it might be a good idea to try to manage software projects in such a way that the same values are delivered. For example, communication values can be delivered at a standup meeting in a collocated team and by instant messaging in a distributed team. Kent says that practices are situation-dependent but values do not have to change for every new situation. Agile values will guide project managers to try to manage a large project according to the same philosophy regardless of specific agile practices.

Now let us take a brief look at some agile practices. These practices are generally regarded as lightweight, but remember that the same practice could just as well be seen as heavyweight. It depends on whether its values are about people or products. Some of the practices are explained by their names, while the nature of others need some explanation. All of these practices can be adopted in a rhythmic way so as to achieve synergies, as will be discussed in Part II of this book.

> *Real Customer Involvement.* As far as developers are not ugrammers, both developers and customers must be in close communication to build software.
> *Informative Workspace.* This type of practice is opposed to blackbox programming. The workplace layout should encourage people to communicate.
> *Shared Code.* Source code is controlled by one or two team members. Source code should be owned by the development team to facilitate other agile practices.

Short Iterative Cycle. Short cycles provide a whole team with more rapid feedback, measurements of the last cycle for incremental planning, error discovery, and potential improvements for the next cycle.

User Story. Requirements are divided and written on a stack of cards so that programmers can estimate the work in each story for customers who prioritize the order of development.

Self-Organizing Team. Team members (equally or unequally) participate in decisionmaking as to how and what they could do best for people and software.

Standup Morning Meeting. Team members are less likely to waste time on trivia and will discuss recent and/or potential issues.

Refactoring. Existing code is reviewed and revised without changing its external behavior for better code readability and maintainability.

Pair Programming. Two people as one single unit collaborate on design and programming.

Incremental Design. This approach emphasizes that the simplest solution is always in place and that designs increment not by phase but by daily work.

Continuous Integration. To detect errors as early as possible, team members integrate their work frequently. Continuous integration puts the emphasis on working software in progress.

Test-First Programming. Simply put, before coding, it is advisable to write automated unit tests that could probably break a system.

3.3.2 Communication Proximity

Software practices in OSSD are for large, distributed teams as opposed to small, collocated teams. The dimensions that change from large to small will affect the way we manage our team. As mentioned, team location and team size are two important factors to affect the adoption of some software practices. But neither factor reflects values of communication, feedback, and so on. We therefore take as our two metrics communication proximity and team coupling (see Figure 3.10).

Communication proximity is a combination of factors that refer to the degree of distribution. They include human–human communications versus computer-mediated communication (e.g., face-to-face meeting or videoconferencing), synchronization versus asynchronization (instant messages and email), people identity versus anonymity (e.g., talking to people whom you know or to the public), and language.

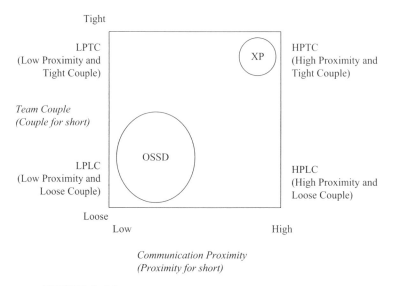

FIGURE 3.10 Communication proximity and team couple.

When communication proximity is high, people are located in the same place with a common language of communication. This implies that people know each other well enough to collaborate. In contrast, when communication proximity is low, people are physically distributed, and communicate anonymously and asynchronously.

Communication proximity strongly affects software practices that focus on people and place. Synchronous communications across time zones can hinder distributed pair programming. Even within the same time zone, distributed pair programming for two developers in Korea and Australia through videoconferencing still encounters the language problem and cultural effects. For non-English-speaking programmers, reading and writing are far easier than listening and speaking.

3.3.3 Loose and Tight Couples

The concept of loose and tight couples originates from that of weak and strong ties in sociology (Granovetter 1973). An example of a tight couple would be a well-defined reporting channel, while a loose couple might be a weak acquaintance such as a connection made willingly, anonymously, and voluntarily.

Team coupling has a tremendous impact on software practices that demand a lot of coordination. A loosely coupled team in distributed environment will find it much simpler to adopt reviews than will a pair programming team.

A loosely coupled team is not so much a team as a network or a community. Such a team is different from a global software team in which the members may not know others, but the team has a hierarchy and members have responsibilities. For example, the organizational structure will require a developer in London to reply to a colleague's request from Japan. This is not the case in open-source software development.

3.3.4 Collocated Software Development

The two dimensions that we have introduced are only metrics for relationships between a software team and a development environment. To learn more metrics, you may have a look at Cockburn's *Agile Software Development* (2002).

Open-source software development and eXtreme programming are alike in that they both highly value communication, feedback, simplicity, courage, and respect. Exploring how proven software practices in a distributed environment (e.g., OSSD) and a collocated environment (eXtreme programming) may correspond to each other would be of assistance in managing scaling issues in our existing favorite agile software model. We summarize key practices in OSSD and XP by process areas in Table 3.5.

Perhaps the most significant characteristic that makes OSSD successful is that open-source developers themselves are the end users. Since developers are playing both programmer and customer roles, they know exactly what they are writing. However, in many commercial software projects, programmers often require domain-specific knowledge to write the system, such as in

TABLE 3.5 Analysis of Practices in OSSD and XP by Process Areas

Process Area	OSSD	XP
Requirements engineering	Ugrammer involvement	Real customer involvement (on-site customers)
Requirements documents	Point listing	User stories
Project planning and project tracking	Rapid release (i.e., fast turnaround)	Short iteration cycle
Design	Evolution-like incremental design	Incremental design
Collaborative programming	Peer review	Pair programming
Software configuration	CVS	Continuous (daily) integration
Testing	Alpha release for those who would like to test	Automated test cases
Integration	Nightly build	Continuous integration

CRM and ERP. Practicing real customer involvement, the whole software team is composed of the roles of programmers and customers, while in OSSD each single developer can have these two roles.

In eXtreme programming, software project planning involves customers and programmers together developing estimates for the work to be performed, and defining the plan to perform the work. The rapid-release schedule itself can be a plan because the release time is shorter than the time we need to estimate and produce the software plan in a conventional approach.

Pair programming and shared code adopted for a collocated team and reviews in OSSD for a distributed environment are different practices but deliver the same values in communications and feedback. Therefore, when the dimension changes from collocation to distribution, we may prefer peer review. In the end, all software managers must understand that their past success may not be replicated when some metric changes. A good manager, however, has the imagination to see where the values of one approach can enhance the practices of another.

3.4 CONCLUSION

This and the previous chapter have covered the essentials of software development. We have seen that both open-source software development and agile software development address values and practices, but questions remain. What, in practical terms, does this mean that we should do? Should everyone dump their own values and practices and adopt these new ones, even if they are only half understood? And what if we can't get rid of our old values?

While not explicitly serving as guidelines as to what agile practices or processes should be used, software development rhythms do offer some answers to these questions. You do not need to be an agilist, and there is no lightweight or heavyweight in software development rhythms; rather, software development rhythms straightforwardly tell us three things:

1. Combine practices or processes rhythmically as your development rhythms. This step is very important. Although Part II will discuss in depth when and where individual agile practice works and when different software practices may be combined for synergies, you can always compose development rhythms with the software practices you understand most. However, it should be well understood which values are added to your software development when software

practices are rhythmically combined, although these values may not be the same as agile values. This means that they could make some positive contributions to process and paper, instead of to people and product.

2. Use the in–out diagram to understand the sustainability of your composed rhythms so that you can plan effort and resources to sustain the rhythms. The domain of easy to start and easy to sustain is much to be preferred. We have observed many agile practices combined into development rhythms to be domain-specific. As your development environment may unexpectedly change at any time, you may have to play another of your development rhythms in response.

3. Software teams have different learning curve and turnover rates, and this can tremendously impact your development rhythms so analyze the master–coach diagram for your project team.

In short, the practices of a software team are never pure. They are always combined either simultaneously or rhythmically. What is critical in software development is to understand when practices work better and when they should be used. Take eXtreme programming as an example. Although many teams successfully adopt eXtreme programming, others appear to encounter tremendous difficulties. Often, some team members are not yet ready to catch development rhythms for extreme programming. As a consequence, they fail to see the value of the whole.

REFERENCES

The Agile Manifesto, 2001. Available at http://www.agilealliance.org/home.

Beck K. *eXtreme Programming Explained: Embrace Change*. Boston: Addison-Wesley; 2000.

Beck K and Andres C. *Extreme Programming Explained*. 2nd ed. Boston: Addison-Wesley; 2005.

Cockburn A. *Agile Software Development*. Boston: Addison-Wesley; 2002.

Granovetter M. The strength of weak ties. *American Journal of Sociology* 1973; **78** (6): 1360–1380.

Golden B. *Succeeding with Open Source*. Boston: Addison-Wesley; 2005.

Halstead M. *Elements of Software Science*. North-Holland: Elsevier; 1975.

Jacobson I, Booch G, and Rumbaugh J. *The Unified Software Development Process*. Reading, MA: Addison-Wesley; 1999.

McCabe T. A complexity measure. *IEEE Transactions on Software Engineering* 1976; **2** (4):308–320.

Pavlicek RC. *Embracing Insanity: Open Source Software Development*. Indianapolis: Sams; 2000.

Raymond ES. Halloween Documents, 1998. Available at `http://www.opensource.org/halloween/`

Raymond ES. *The Cathedral and the Bazaar: Musings on Linux and Open Source by an Accidental Revolutionary*. Sebastopol, CA: O'Reilly; 2001.

Sandred J. *Managing Open Source Projects: A Wiley Tech Brief*. New York: Wiley; 2001.

Sommerville I, Sawyer P, and Viller S. Managing process inconsistency using viewpoints. *IEEE Transactions on Software Engineering* 1999; **25** (6):784–799.

Stamelos IS, Angelis L, Oikonomou A, and Bleris GL. Code quality analysis in open-source software development. *Information Systems Journal* 2002; **12** (1):43–60.

Stamelos IS, Angelis L, and Oikonomou A. Open source software development should strive for even greater code maintainability. *Communications of ACM* 2004; **47** (10): 83–87.

Thompson K. Unix and beyond: an interview with Ken Thompson. *IEEE Computer* 1999; **32** (5):58–64.

Toffler A. *Future Shock*. New York: Bantam Books; 1971.

Xu J and Madey G. Exploration of the open source software community. *Proceedings of NAACSOS Conference*, Pittsburgh, PA; 2004.

Part II: Rhythms

4

PLAGIARISM PROGRAMMING

Copy from one, it's plagiarism; copy from two, it's research.

—Wilson Mizner

A group of ants goes out to look for food. At first, they wander aimlessly, not knowing where to go. They spread out and crawl in all directions, in an apparently random fashion. But wherever each ant goes, it leaves a scent that it can follow back to the nest. At the same time, if one ant comes back with food, the other ants can follow this scent trail back to where this one ant found the food, abandoning their random search and instead all trooping back along the proven trail to where the food was found. In the ant world, an ant that can't follow the scent left by another will perish. Being a successful copycat is the intelligence of the ant.

Ants are playing a simple rhythm: seek–succeed–follow. Once food is found, others will follow that path without even calculating how far they are going. However, there is no reason to believe that the path is unique or is less dangerous. It is just one of many ways to the same place where the food is found (Figure 4.1). An ant alone has little intelligence, but the way ants cooperate with each other demonstrates community wisdom, a kind of shared-intelligence collaboration. It turns out that everybody brings food home.

Can we do the same thing, turning everyone into a programmer? More precisely, can programmers regardless of their skills be organized to follow a way to code successful small subprograms done by others, and to

Software Development Rhythms: Harmonizing Agile Practices for Synergy
By Kim Man Lui and Keith C. C. Chan
Copyright © 2008 John Wiley & Sons, Inc.

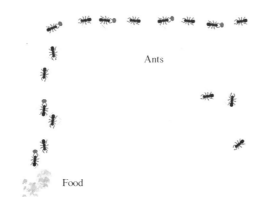

FIGURE 4.1 The trail is not always the shortest, but it guarantees some reward.

continuously repeat that way to code other subprograms, until a complete system is done? This sounds ambitious, but it is not impossible.

Perhaps you may think that I am suggesting "copy-and-paste" or "cut-and-paste" programming, which is nothing new. Understanding exactly where to copy from one program or procedure and to paste code into another is a common way to get a quick solution. But it can introduce problems. If we are not sure how the logic of the code actually works, along with the copy-and-paste code we may also get hidden bugs or incompatibilities with our existing code.

From experience we know that some programmers, the less experienced in particular, who do copy-and-paste programming are much less likely to properly test their program than when they write everything from scratch! Maybe they assume that whoever wrote the code was more experienced or responsible than themselves. Even when the copied code crashes, they feel they have a scapegoat and can forgive themselves for not doing a good job. After all, what has the world come to when you can't even be confident about the quality of what you copy?

Perhaps the biggest limitation of copy-and-paste programming is that it's practiced only by individuals. In an integrated team environment, copy-and-paste programming makes software configuration, standardization, code reading, debugging, quality, support, and maintenance difficult. Different developers may cut and paste different source code to get the same functionality for the same application. Clearly, it is not easy to scale copy-and-paste programming up to the team level, but it may be something worth doing. Here is our story.

When I was at school, my final-year programming assignment, an important task in terms of grades as there were no exams, was to write a program that simulated a flight path. The assignment was challenging, and only a few outstanding students could do it, so many students simply copied the better students' programs. However, they couldn't just cut and paste the code. They tried to understand the design and then to enhance simpler parts of the program, for example, by making user interfaces simpler, adding hotkey options, and providing better descriptive comments. In the end, some plagiarized assignments were better than the original because while they all provided the all-important simulation, the copied programs were more user-friendly. It is true that individual copied programs may have been substandard, but code like this, plagiarized with testing and modifications (or refactoring), can be economical.

We do not advocate an innovative method in programming; our endeavor is to seek disciplined mechanisms for easy coding. As you will see in Section 4.2 (which discusses making use of code written by others) and Section 4.3 (which provides a real case to readers), this may raise some controversial issues, so we should say now that we have no intention of challenging any system that rewards risk taking, or innovation. We all depend on that.

But at the same time we all have to admit that there is no such thing as total originality in any field or undertaking, and there is little point or advantage in programmers day after day reinventing the wheel when there are perfectly good models of wheels to be found all around us.

4.1 PLAGIARISM

Modern computing technologies continue to advance. So do programming languages. Yet basic instructions remain more or less unchanged while integrated development environments have evolved far beyond the old programming editor with reserved words highlighted. A typical example is BASIC (Beginners' All-Purpose Symbolic Instruction Code) developed in the 1970s. This BASIC evolved into the earlier version of Visual BASIC (VB) (1991), which uses template wizards and enables rapid application development, event-driven development, and other Features. VB continued evolving through the 1990s with a new version about every 1.4 years. When VB 6.0 came out in 1998, the VB programmers who had been busy with catching up on new features all these years had a long break till VB.net in 2002. VB.net, however, was a big change. Unlike writing small applications in BASIC in the past, we have to get very familiar with VB.net and its integrated development environment (IDE); otherwise, we will be very surprised at why the same application written in BASIC may take us much more time to develop in VB.net now.

Imagine that a talented hacker in 1980 saw the Christopher Reeve movie *Somewhere in Time* and fantasized about the same thing happening to him as happens to the movie's time-traveling hero. Right after watching the movie, he rushed to his lab and wrote a BASIC program displaying a large number count with a "takt" sound so that he could be self-hypnotized into a state that transcended time and space. As true love did not await him in the past, he had to bet on the future.

He traveled forward to our time. Before long, he was disappointed that he would never get used to our modern life—true love is anonymous and good sex is online! He wanted to go home. So he set about writing the same program again, but this time he had to do it in VB.net. He did not bother to read through the online language manual. Instead, he tried to get any demo source, then compiled and executed it. This working code established a baseline for the next stage. He studied how it worked, modified it, added his own code, and tested it. All these things were done in baby steps so that he could change back to his last success when there were unexpected errors. The program was quickly done. He returned home and joined Microsoft to develop Visual BASIC.

Plagiarism is an act that is considered unacceptable by many. However, under certain circumstances, for example, in software development in less-developed areas or with standard requirements, the conduct appears to be a productive way in which individuals with less knowledge can carry out programming. Now, the challenge is to scale up the paradigm for a small team.

4.1.1 Existing Code

In 1998 we were leading a small team in a brewery in southern China responsible for developing an ERP system for sales and distribution in the Chinese marketplace. We recruited two fresh graduates who came from the inland of China. At that time, many schools in the inland regions did not have enough computing facilities and equipment, and hence they were more focused on teaching by the textbook. As in the 1980s, students would design their programs on paper at home. Then they would type in their code and test it in the computer lab they booked. In this case, C was an ideal language to learn. As event-driven programming demands that a student spend much more time playing around with different events in front of a computer, it was not suitable to teach when the hardware resources were tight. However, windows programming had been around in the commercial areas there for few years. Such a gap between skills taught at school and skills needed in the marketplace was unbelievably big.

As expected, our newly hired staff knew little about Windows programming. In the first week, they played around with the development environment such as Windows 95 installation, Transmission Control Protocol/Internet Protocol (TCP/IP) networking software, Microsoft SQL server, and PowerBuilder installation.

In the second week, we gave them our PowerBuilder scripts with which to inquire about customer information written in PowerBuilder 3.0. They were asked to exactly follow the way we developed another two user interfaces for product and price inquiries. We told them where to change and to retrieve the right data they needed to revise the table names and field names. After 2 or 3 days, they completed it.

Plagiarism programming requires us to repeatedly test and then change a bit and then test again. This becomes tedious when we are unfamiliar with what we were trying to do, and little progress is made. To support and motivate the plagiarizing programmers, we needed to establish a people-caring environment for them.

4.1.2 Social Network Analysis

Although an organization chart may show how the leadership in a team is structured, surveys directly taken of employees about whom they talk to and collaborate with in their workplace illustrates another kind of relationship. The relationship of how information flows among a group of people can be easily visualized and quantified by social network analysis (SNA). A social network map consists of nodes that represent the people of a group and links that show flows between the people. The map show how knowledge may be shared, how decisionmaking happens, and who supports whom.

Social network mapping is straightforward. In our case, Kimman is shown in Figure 4.2 as a node with five direct links to other colleagues. As

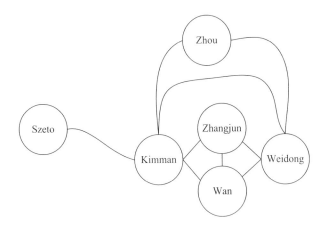

FIGURE 4.2 Social network mapping.

we can see, the newcomers, Zhangjun and Wan, may talk to Kimman, who deals with many people and activities. Szeto had only one connection but held a position of power. Zhangjun and Wan had the shortest paths to each other. They would inform each other of what was going on. As we see in Figure 4.2, if you plan to take over a software team, SNA will give you insights into how your team members talk to each other.

To quickly plagiarize another person's work, we need not only to have her program but to talk to her. An effective social network in the workplace facilitates communication and feedback. The network schematizes the team culture in which people collaborate. But how did the two plagiarizing programmers use our work to make theirs?

4.1.3   Being Plagiarized

Every program is written for some task. Although two programs written differently may achieve the same task, programs written in a similar logic probably achieve tasks of the same type. Thus, a set of similar programs and a set of similar tasks are our two domains of interest.

Suppose that a program is originally written to handle a particular task as in path 1 in Figure 4.3. Modifying part of the source, such as converting a FOR loop into a WHILE loop, would not change much. the program would behave the same (see path 2 in figure 4.3). this kind of modification is superficial.

Of course, we can change the logic for readability such as *abc* renamed as *monthsalary*, for maintainability such as removing duplications by function calls or for both such as trying to replace *nested-IFs* with *case*; this is refactoring, and it facilitates team communications through code.

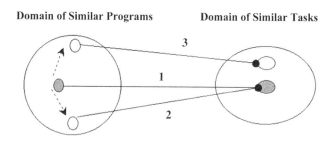

..... ➤ *Source Modifications:* **Code is revised to another version.**

———● *Achievement:* **Running a source performs a task.**

FIGURE 4.3   Illustration of plagiarism programming.

Often, we may just revise a small portion of code so that the program could be used to perform a similar yet different task or to solve a problem bigger than the one it was originally intended to solve (see path 3 in Figure 4.3). How to change the source or how to write source for change is the key to plagiarism programming.

A piece of source for updating a master table for a chart of accounts shows the same programming techniques as the one for updating a warehouse table. This is a sort of pattern. However, the code for a chart of accounts itself does not demonstrate how to plagiarize it for reuse. Thus, a plagiarized programmer highlights "the place where followers (i.e., plagiarizing programmers) should read in order to modify another part where followers should revise," or in order to be alert for some other issues. In addition, we may find highlighted code that remains unchanged when a table is updated so that followers need not do anything.

To do so, we use three different colors making sure that copiers know what parts to pay attention to and where changes are required. Blue is used to represent no change, green indicates the part requiring reading, and red is for modification. A piece of code is therefore like a series of colors of the form [B G R B G B R B ... B]. The coloring makes plagiarism easier for others.

Coloring in plagiarism programming serves indications. We selected our colors simply by intuition. The primary colors are red, yellow, blue, and green, which were first suggested by Leonardo da Vinci (Coad et al. 1999). However, text in yellow was not that easy to read. For some programmers, text in green was difficult. In this case, try pink instead.

The color series addresses how a program is to be reused and what coding techniques are required to process that data store. Plagiarizing programmers read the green part of the source and read/write the red part. What they need to do is change the red part of the program according to user requirements. They do not bother with any of the blue parts.

Let us look at how some fresh programmers may write code that deletes records from a table in SQL database programming. Without plagiarism, someone writes a simple SQL statement to get rid of a row such as "delete *tablename* where *col = condition*." However, the programmers do not notice that many other things should be written to support a recoverable database transaction.

Now, look at Figure 4.4, which shows another piece of code for deletion. The code does not actually delete a record, but it updates a flag that indicates logical deletion of that row. In addition, the code handles transaction rollback and a mechanism for error checking. We can revise a bit more to ensure that only one row is deleted each time. Plagiarizing programmers do not need to

```
begin transaction
...
// (i) allow to use "return," "break," etc. for only plagiarized code
//(ii) not allow to use "return," "break," etc. for nonplagiarized code
...
update tablename set status = 'D' where col='condition'
if@@rowcount<>1 //number of rows affected in this operation
        //if more than one row is affected, set
        //@@rowcount<=1.
                // If only 2 rows are affected, se
        //@@rowcount<>2
  and@@error<>0
begin
  raiseerror 50000 'error in update tablename setstatus'
  exec master..xp_logevent 50000
  rollback transaction
  return
end
...
// (i) allow to use "return," "break," etc. for only plagiarized code
// (ii) notallowtouse "return," "break," etc. for nonplagiarized code
...
commit transaction

Note:
Bold text represents blue (neither read nor write)
Italic represents green (read only and write occasionally)
Normal text with lighted gray highlights represents red
 (read and write)
```

FIGURE 4.4 When the piece of code displayed above is color-highlighted, the changes needed it will be visually obvious.

bother much about this. They should be concerned with only three pieces of semantic information:

1. Name of table where a row is to be deleted.
2. Condition under which a row is to be deleted.
3. Number of rows in which the operation affects—by default, only one row of deletion is allowed.

For example, when we want to delete an invoice INV00956, we replace tablename with INVOICE and col = 'condition' with INVOICE_NBR = INV1MAY01' (see Figure 4.4).

An old study has shown that most errors arise as the novice programmer tries to put the "pieces" of code together in a solution plan (Soloway 1967). Do not let programmers plagiarize code from a number of code samples. A practical question will have arisen as to how many code samples we need to highlight to be plagiarized.

Tables in any database application can be expressed in a tabular form and be manipulated by four types of operational commands. The operations include *c*reation, *r*ead, *u*pdate, and *d*eletion (CRUD). We can use (#, #, #, #) to show the number of different command types involving in a single database transaction. For example, (2,3,1,0) indicates that an SQL transaction has two INSERTs, three SELECTs, and one UPDATE.

Suppose that we develop an ERP application. The system can be functionally decomposed as a number of submodules such as open invoicing, purchase quotation, and the like. Each submodule could include four types of user interfaces: (1) data entry, where frontline users key in records; (2) data modification, where changes are made to the records; (3) data processing, where midlevel managers authorize business transactions to process; and (4) inquiries as to status and information (see Table 4.1).

A cross-product matrix can be constructed using submodules and user interfaces. From the data model, we may estimate CRUD. For example, CRUD for purchase quotation and data entry is (2,3,0,0), where we retrieve necessary information from three master tables—customer, product, and price—and insert new records into two tables: purchase quotation head and purchase quotation line.

For your first programming task, select those transactions that have average or higher numbers for CRUD. A transaction with higher numbers of CRUD has more instructional statements, which better serves as a pattern of a way of coding. Then color the code for plagiarism as discussed previously. Review the code colored by other colleagues. The original programmers need to roughly explain why this part of the code is red, green, and blue.

Undeniably, plagiarism is easy to adopt. The in–out diagram for plagiarism programming is shown in Figure 4.5. When plagiarizing, programmers can repeat-test and revise at the beginning, and progress here provides an incentive to carry on. Once they become familiar with the plagiarized code, they will naturally follow the same methods of programming. Therefore, it is easy to sustain.

TABLE 4.1   CRUD Analysis

User Interface	Purchase Quotation	Purchase Orders	Warehouse Stocktaking	Warehouse In–Out Data
Inquiry	(2,1,2,0)	(0,0,3,0)	—	—
Data entry	(2,3,0,0)	(0,0,1,0)	—	—
Data processing	(2,4,2,0)	(2,3,2,0)	—	—
Data modification	(0,4,2,0)	(0,4,2,0)	—	—

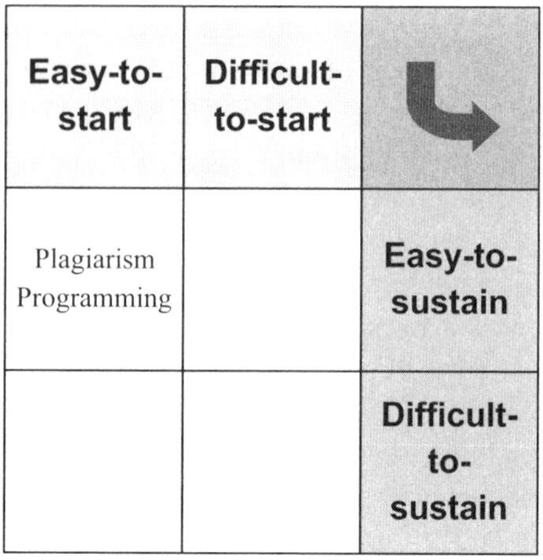

FIGURE 4.5 In–out diagram for plagiarism programming.

4.1.4 Turn Everyone into a Programmer

In mid-2000 we needed to recruit two more programmers to join our plagiarism programming team for a new project. As we were working in China's rural industrial sector, there were not many applicants, and those applicants we received had little experience in real software development. Given that it would take time to find experienced programmers, our bottom line was to find some programmers smart enough to plagiarize our existing code quickly even if they didn't know how to program.

We decided to use a job simulation test to select 5 or 6 programmers for an interview. We told the applicants beforehand that there would be a short, one-hour, written test. In the end, only 16 came for the written test.

Although the simulation test was intended to find candidates who would fit in with the team, this unexpectedly helped us understand in a quantitative way the efficiency of plagiarism programming.

Writing a Program. The job test was organized in two parts. For part 1, the applicants were asked to write an executable program on paper for computing n factorial ($n!$) in any computer language; the preferred ones were Transact-SQL and PowerBuilder Script, which were our development tools. Many found it difficult to complete a factorial program. This was no great surprise to us as we had already had a number of years managing inexperienced programmers in developing regions in China.

Some readers who do not understand the test environment may wonder why the applicants failed to finish such a simple program. In fact, many candidates may have technical skills such as Microsoft access, Web design, software installation, networking or hardware-related skills, but not programming. The candidates were graduates from inland areas who had traveled far away from home to the cities in southern China but did not succeed in finding an IT job there. Desperate, they would apply for any IT job even if they did not have the skills.

When they finished part 1 of the test they proceeded to part 2. We did not record the time as our objective was to find programmers for the company, but they returned their answers in around 15–20 minutes.

Plagiarizing a Program. In part 2 of the job test, we gave them three complete SQL programs, with the solution $f(n) = 3^n$. The programs were written in different ways: (1) IF–THEN, (2) WHILE loop, and (3) recursion. the applicants needed to revise each of them for the calculation of n factorial.

The candidates had to write down on paper those programs that should have been compliable: that is, with no syntactic errors. Roughly, they finished them in 30–45 minutes. The whole test lasted for around an hour.

Programs. Table 4.2. shows one candidate's result. He failed to write a program of n factorial. Part 2 contained three sample programs to be plagiarized. Although he had never done programming in Transact-SQL, the candidate was now able to modify two SQL programs correctly, in parts 2a and 2b in Table 4.2.

Part 2c used a recursive technique to solve $f(n) = 3^n$. As discussed, some programming skills were harder to follow than others, which would make plagiarizing challenging. Of three original programs of 3^n, IF–THEN, and DO loop were easier to perceive while recursion was not.

You Are Hired. For the interview, we selected the four applicants who did well in only part 1 and two of applicants who did well only in part 2. During the interview, we also asked how they liked the test the last time but did not tell them that we wanted to recruit two plagiarizing programmers for our in-house ERP development. The candidates gave us their view of plagiarism programming. The two whom we hired in the end showed great interest in plagiarism programming. We could not recall whether these programmers did well in part 1 or only in part 2.

Our experience here provides some reference for readers who are planning to recruit programmers for their companies. They may consider

**TABLE 4.2 Programming in Transact-SQL by a
Non-SQL-Knowledgeable Programmer**

Test Part	Source Code	Success

Part 1: no plagiarism	```
	A=1
	B=1
	C=1
	Input N
	For N to 1
	A+1=A
	A*B=C
	C=B
	End For
	Output C
	``
		×

Part 2a: plagiarizing an IF–THEN program	``` Create proc factorial (@y integer) as begin if @y = 0 return 1 if @y = 1 return 1 if @y = 2 return 2 if @y = 3 return 6 if @y = 4 return 24 if @y >= 5 print " out of the range!" end ```	✓

Part 2b: plagiarizing a DO-loop program	```
	create proc factorial
	(@y integer)
	as begin
	declare @result integer
	select @result = 1
	while (@y >=1)
	begin
	  select @result = @result * @y
	  select @y = @y - 1
	end
	return @result
	end
	``
		✓

Part 2c: plagiarizing a recursion program	```
	create proc factorial
	
	(@y integer) as begin
	declare @result integer
	declare @y_minus integer
	if @y = 0 return 1
	  select @y_minus = @y - 1
	  exec @result = fatr @y_minus
	if @y = 0 return 1
	``
		×

TABLE 4.2 (*Continued*)

```
              select @y_minus_1 = @y_minus - 1
              exec @result = fatr @y_minus_1
          if @y = 0 return 2
              select @y_minus_1 = @y_minus - 1
              exec @result = fatr @y_minus_1
          if @y = 0 return 6
              select @y_minus_1 = @y_minus - 1
              exec @result = fatr @y_minus_1
          if @y = 0 return 24
              select @y_minus_1 = @y_minus - 1
              exec @result = fatr @y_minus
          return (3 * @result)
          end
```

a job simulation test like this. Of course, if your development environment uses another methodology, you will have to work out your own job simulation test.

Insights. Some time later we reviewed the interview data and programs in a more systematic way. When part 1 is compared with part 2, is there any major difference between those who failed in part 1 but passed part 2?

There are four possible outcomes for their programs, as shown in Table 4.3. Figure 4.6 summarizes the outcomes of the job simulation test. Although three assignments in part 2 seemed to be the same, they were written in different algorithms. We compared part 1 with three results of part 2 in turn (i.e., 1 vs. 2a, 1 vs. 2b, 1 vs. 2c); the percentage of the number of successes soared 150%, 150%, and 75%. As shown in Figure 4.6, 4 out of 16 applicants (25%) succeeded in coding the problem in part 1; 10 out of 16 applicants (62.5%), in parts 2a and 2b; and 7 out of 16 applicants (43.7%), in part 2c. Clearly, plagiarism provides a certain degree of assistance in programming by inexperienced people.

Cognitively, "easy to do" and "easy to do by steps" (i.e., "easy to follow") are two different concepts. The first tends to be a subjective judgment of implementers. The second is more objective. For instance, coding a program of factorials by a recursion method is easier for people who are accustomed to doing it in this way. As for easy to follow, a DO loop could be more straightforwardly expressed in steps, as all people should already be familiar with this style. interestingly, in the factorial method, the best way in "easy to follow" is IF–THEN–ELSE.

Although the purpose of the test was to screen candidates, it was a bit stricter than the working environment of plagiarism programming as there were no verbal and informal communications providing feedback. Since it

TABLE 4.3 An Analysis of Four Outcomes

Outcome	Part 1	Part 2	Conclusion	Explanations
1	✓	✓	No conclusion!	Managed to complete both
2	✓	✕	Very unfavorable to plagiarism	Overthrew our belief about plagiarism as people are able to complete the assignment alone but fail to plagiarize it
3	✕	✕	Unfavorable to plagiarism	Demonstrated a fruitless attempt in part 2 even if the person is not knowledgeable about programming at all
4	✕	✓	Favorable to plagiarism	Turned everyone into a programmer

was a written test and we provided no spoken instructions, we also eliminated coloring.

4.1.5 Pattern Language

Christopher Alexander was an architect who developed the pattern theory in the 1960s that could be considered as an approach to arranging workspaces so that new employees would be able to learn by being in proximity to their mentors. This is called "master and apprentices." Patterns in architecture are

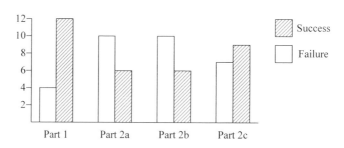

FIGURE 4.6 Job test results.

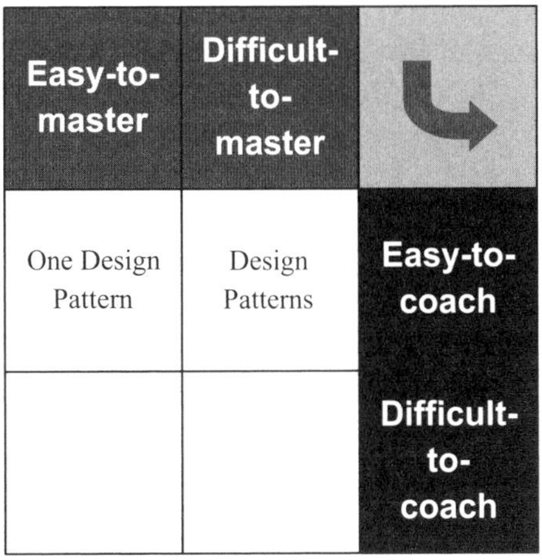

FIGURE 4.7 Master–coach diagram for design patterns.

perceptible; but patterns in logic are conceptual relationships among things and hence invisible. Shepard (2002) says that we remember pictures (with a success rate of 98.5%) so much better than words (90.0%) and sentences (88.2%) that were previously learned. Therefore, efforts required for human apprentices to learn visible patterns and learn design patterns are very different.

Anyway, inspired by patterns, the gang of four (Gamma, Helm, Johnson, and Vlissides) developed their classic work *Design Patterns*,[1] which are templates of descriptions of, conditions for, and examples of how to solve object design problems that can be used in many different situations. While this aspect of the pattern theory has proved useful for the problem under consideration, it should be realized that some patterns might be difficult to master and follow.

If mastering one or two design patterns sufficed to solve our programming problems, we would have no difficulty. Unfortunately, we have to master quite a number of patterns, and, most importantly, they are distinct from one another. Applying patterns to real problems requires experience. One good thing is that once our organization successfully adopts design patterns through a project, that application can serve as a solid example to help our team coach newcomers. Thus, design patterns are difficult to master but easy to coach (see Figure 4.7).

---

[1]If you have not yet read that book, we recommend that you read it. If you prefer Java code for explanation, Mark Grand's *Patterns in Java* is suggested.

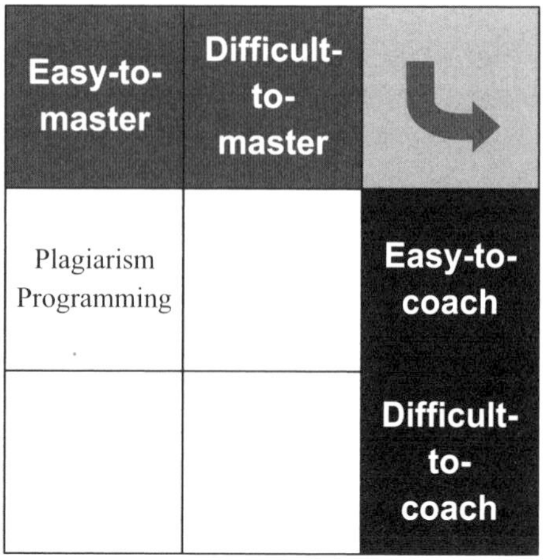

FIGURE 4.8 Master–coach diagram for plagiarism programming.

Plagiarism programming, as a tool that assists inexperienced (*if not weak*) developers in getting coding work done, can be an exploration of human cognition. We seek patterns for easy-to-follow code (i.e., knowledge of purpose) and patterns of ways to program (i.e., knowledge of structure) to help people complete their undertakings alone with little or no help from other team members, training courses, or references as these incur extra time. In this sense, plagiarism programming is code-oriented and design patterns are solution-oriented.

Sample code in plagiarism programming must be easy to follow. Figure 4.8 shows that the practice is easy to master, which does not mean that we can easily develop simple code to plagiarize any application. It simply says that once code is written to facilitate plagiarism (see Section 4.13), plagiarism becomes easy to master for others and they can coach newcomers on how to use that simple code for writing other programs.

In short, the purpose of plagiarism programming is not to think over generic application-independent solution built as a set of patterns (Gamma et al. 1995). For the purposes of plagiarism, design flexibility is not the same as easy-to-follow. We will clarify this point further in Section 4.1.6.

4.1.6 Software Team Capability

Nowadays, software development demands different kinds of skills. For example, writing client/server database applications necessitates the use of client development tools (e.g., VB, Delphi, PowerBuilder), SQL (PL-SQL, Transact-SQL, etc.), database administration and tuning (e.g., server manager, database denormalization), and network (e.g., remote access and proxy

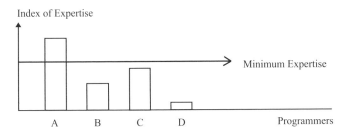

FIGURE 4.9 Minimum expertise for programming in which programmers B, C, and D could not work on their own.

server). If we are not technically strong enough to master technical difficulties, they will come back to haunt us.

Therefore, when coming across a technical problem, a team of more programmers stands a good chance of solving it. To do programming in a small software team, programmers have to be basically equipped with some minimum expertise [e.g., skills of inserting record(s) into a table, of database deadlock handling, of transaction rollback] that allows them to complete their jobs. For example, developers below that level could do nothing by themselves. Figure 4.9 depicts the idea. Programmers B, C, and D will have some trouble working on database programming. Unfortunately, programmers may not know how much they don't know. Software quality is therefore at risk. Our goal is to push down the line of minimum expertise to a lower position.

When I was around 5 or 6, I always carried some 10¢ coins to buy sweets. My parents did not allow me to spend more than 100¢ per day, so I had to know how much I had left if I spent 30¢ for a Coke and 40¢ for a burger. Unfortunately, at that age I had little math skills, so I solved the problem in a mechanical way. Here was what I did:

Step 1. I emptied my left pocket.
Step 2. I counted four coins and put them into my right pocket.
Step 3. I counted three coins and put them into my right pocket, repeating step 2.
Step 4. I counted the remaining coins.

Thinking about addition as the minimum expertise for paying money and buying things was transformed into simply counting coins and putting them aside. Addition is a higher skill than counting. So we did the same job using a lower-level skill.

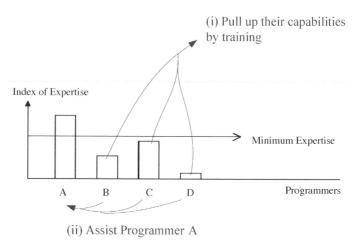

(i) Pull up their capabilities by training

Index of Expertise

Minimum Expertise

A B C D

Programmers

(ii) Assist Programmer A

FIGURE 4.10 Two solutions for what you would do.

Returning to Figure 4.9, what would you do if you were programmer A? Let us look at a number of solutions. You could intensively transfer your skills before programming takes place so that other programmers obtain the know-how, shown in (i) in Figure 4.10. This solution takes time, and its feasibility depends on the learning curves of your colleagues. In addition, personal turnover has not yet been factored in. The resignation of a well-trained staff member is detrimental to a small team.

You could take over difficult tasks yourself; other colleagues are just your assistants or are responsible for simpler jobs [see in (ii) in Figure 4.10]. This way is even less feasible. It ends up with a case in which programmer A has to do all system analysis and coding, while programmers B, C, and D may be involved in all testing.

The solutions suggested above are principally correct but not practically feasible. We have to adopt the right software practice, which can be pair programming discussed in Chapter 5 and its rhythm discussed in Chapter 6. Test-driven development discussed in Chapter 9 that tells us how we may progressively do programming right. Test-driven development is sort of microiterative; every small success establishes a baseline for programmers to go forward for more success, or go back to the baseline and start over again.

Plagiarism programming is also a solution; it pushes down the level of minimum expertise for more developers to do programming (see Figure 4.11). Although in software development there is no total solution (i.e., silver bullet), solutions are rarely absolutely incompatible. They could even become a great symphonic work if they are combined rhythmically.

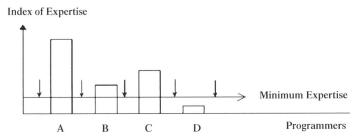

FIGURE 4.11 Push down minimum expertise so that programmers A, B, and C can work independently.

4.1.7 Rough-Cut Design

When the team adopts plagiarism programming alone, programmer A will work submodules for programmers B, C, and D to plagiarize. Since programmer A would never be able to complete every detail of the system design, there can be a case in which B and C write different code for the same feature in two submodules that they separately work on. For example, the value-added tax (VAT)[2] calculation repeatedly appears in a number of submodules. If the same things are not put together, we will have to modify a number of places every time there is a change in the sales tax. The better way is to use a procedure (or method) to handle all kinds of VAT in the system, that is, to achieve *high cohesion*, which in programming refers to how closely a number of operations in a routine are related (Shalloway and Trot Dec. 9, 2005; McConnell 2002)

The calculation of VAT needs to retrieve the selling price from a product code times the VAT ratio for the category of that product. Clearly, the VAT procedure includes the logic of getting the right selling prices.

However, a selling price of the same product can vary. One copy of a book is $10, but two are $15. A lunchbox is $10 but 10% off after 2:00 P.M. (14:00 hours). thus, the selling price as another function call should be decoupled from VAT so that when we have to change the business logic for the selling price, we do not have to bother about VAT.

Even so, skilled programmers may not be able to plagiarize programs and at the same time work on design problems with others; plagiarism programming is just a way of coding and does not handle any design issue.

To solve this problem, we have to do some sort of redesign after the code is done: refactoring (see Figure 4.12)! This does not mean that we wait to improve code in refactoring. In a situation in which many programmers are

---

[2]With VAT at 10%, a consumer should pay for the retail price times 10%.

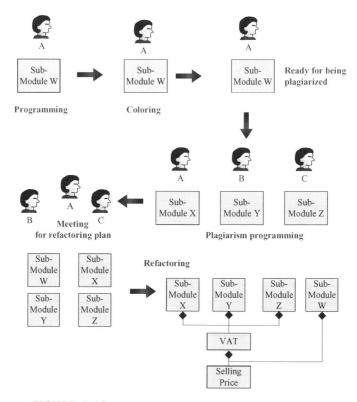

FIGURE 4.12 Plagiarism programming and refactoring.

inexperienced, programmers could do a rough-cut design (i.e., a rough plan), which provides a rough high-level view of the architecture. The purpose of rough-cut design is to share what we know so that we can avoid any mistakes through good communication. See rhythm displayed in Figure 4.13.

It is difficult to imagine how unwritten programs are similar to each other. Once the team has done the working software, it is easier to find similarities and combine the related logic. Thus, a design review (i.e., refactoring) is held during weekly meetings. The purpose is to identify improvements in the code

FIGURE 4.13 Refactoring to harmonize two previous practices.

that has been done. Programmers report on a list of functional points. When two or more functional points are alike, we may consider refactoring.

4.1.8 Training Is Not a Solution

The computer language continues to be developed; highly skilled programmers are in demand everywhere, needless to say in developing areas. Plagiarism programming provides managers there with a tool for running inexperienced teams. But why employ inexperienced programmers in the first place? In the cases we have outlined so far, there was no choice, but even if you do have experienced programmes available, using them may in many cases just be costly overkill. As one manager commented to me, "We aren't sending a man to the moon. We're building a trading database application for a brewery!" And then there's the issue of "experienced," which in certain circumstances can just mean "stuck in the past" as current programmers can be almost as inexperienced in the tricks and skills of tools of something like integrated development environment (IDE) as are many newcomers. Many programming errors are related to the programming knowledge being used (Ebrahimi 1994), and hence we often hear that the program worked before we updated the IDE.

Staff turnover and job handover are never-ending problems in software development. This is especially so when training takes a lot of time and expense. Your boss may at first appreciate your efforts in building up a competitive team even though the project moves slowly at the beginning. In the long run, the company may profit from your work, but when a well-trained member who has used your program as a finishing school hands in a letter of resignation to take a better opportunity somewhere else, your boss can't help judging you as a good technical coach, but a poor project manager, especially when newly hired programmers may repeat the old mistakes of the ex-colleagues whom you trained. So total training is not a total solution. The advantage of plagiarism programming is that it is just a simple software practice and senior management is happy to see new members producing acceptable work quickly and getting the project moving forward.

Finally, you may wonder why we call this "plagiarism programming." It has nothing to do with plagiarism! We will tell you why in the next section.

4.2 NOTHING FASTER THAN PLAGIARISM

When our software team is designing applications under time pressure, some of its members will naturally think about whether part of the code (i.e., the source or logic) has been developed elsewhere, how the other people have solved the same problem, where they may find similar source code, and finally whether we could reuse it. There is little chance that we are writing unprecedented logic.

Suppose that we are sure that what we are going to code for our application is part of a software source written by others. However, software is an integrated product. To extract the source code in the right place for reuse, we have to understand the structure of the software. The good news is that many programs available over the Internet are often as maintainable as if the program authors were actually writing for others, and that means that we just need to take a little time to figure the logic out. Once we learn where to change, we will be able to reuse the software. Reusing the software source that we successfully compile and execute is by all means faster than writing the same from scratch.

Once we identify where to extract, we need to test whether that piece of code is working as you expected. This is neither blackbox testing, where system behavior is determined by studying its inputs and outputs (Sommerville 1986), nor whitebox testing, where the system's behavior is analyzed by examining the code. We may go through only a part of the source. In addition, the source code may call other external libraries for which we do not have the source. Therefore, the testing is something in between black and white. If the extracted software does not work in the way we expect, we can go back and test the original program.

We may modify the existing code and build our application according to user requirements. Generally, the time that it takes us to repeatedly do test and revision and retest is much less than when we write everything from the ground up. As far as the program we plagiarize is executable and working, we stand a good chance of accelerating our own development. (See Figure 4.14.).

4.2.1 Immorality

Plagiarism can be defined as using or reproducing the work of someone else without acknowledging the source or obtaining permission. Mimicking the code of your colleagues introduced in Section 4.1 is not plagiarism. It is if we intend to get sample code from the outside. In fact, plagiarism has already hit the open-source world. Many software companies are using open-source software without honoring the relevant licenses (O'Brien 2005). Dishonest companies may even try to pass off open-source product to their clients as if it were developed by them.

Adopting plagiarism programming by taking advantage of open-source software to manage programmers in an in-house environment is a gray-area

FIGURE 4.14 Nothing faster than plagiarism.

issue. Staff actually get paid for the efforts of someone else, although there is no reselling for money.

Under the terms of the GNU general-public license (GPL),[3] plagiarism programming is acceptable. If we modify and distribute copies of the program or any portion of it, by the copyright holder under the terms of this GPL, whether gratis or for a fee, then we must give the recipients all the rights that we have. Other licenses may impose different limits on our rights to use software sources.

However, if we enhance GPL products for customers in a software-house environment, we must clearly understand that any derivative work incorporating any part of a GPL product is also licensed as the GNU GPL.

---

[3]Available at http://www.gnu.org/ .

Many open-source developers do not mind being modified for other purposes as long as the code stays free: "...I only have one requirement if you download either the source or binary, and that's what is free stays free. Make the world a better place if you want, but please don't take my code and try to make a quick buck off of it..."[4]

4.2.2 Unprecedented Code

Ed Thompson of Gartner Inc. (2004) says that around 80% of customer-relations management applications have been developed with a tailor-made approach. As customer behaviors and purchasing patterns differ in different industrial sectors, business processes of disseminating customer information and providing a deeper customer experience can hardly be automated in standard ERP applications or off-the-shelf software packages. Each customer-relations management (CRM) application has its unique features.

Two or more applications [say, CRM and supply chain management (SCM)] in the same family (e.g., database applications) can be designed in such a way that the reuse of core assets is planned, enabled, and enforced (Clements and Northrop 2001). Within the application, submodules can be common to other non-CRM systems. In short, there is no need to get CRM application source code in order to build your CRM by plagiarism.

Let us look at an example of how we can proceed with a CRM application development by reusing open source code. A manufacturing company wants to develop its CRM system. Part of the system will assist in simplifying customer requests. Customers can send their requests to a common email address, and the system, according to the domain names of received email addresses, automatically forwards them to their account representatives. In addition, the system needs to keep track if a request is handled within 2 working days; otherwise, an "alert" email will be sent to the account managers for their attention. The company aims to reply to their customers in 3 working days.

The system needs to retrieve emails from a Post Office Protocol Version 3 (POP3) server, extract the sender address of an email, record that header information and email body into a database, and send Simple Mail Transfer Protocol (SMTP) emails to corresponding account managers. Obviously, any program given for the four functions mentioned above will accelerate the progress.

Finding sample code may take time, but with luck we might get that code sample from computer books to start with. But there are some issues. The examples may be incomplete so that execution results in a compile error, some

---

[4]Available at http://mohairsofa.com/ .

libraries are missing, or they do not conform to the version of your compiler. In short, repeating the results may not be as straightforward as we might anticipate. Also, electronic sources may not be available; this problem is trivial if a piece of code is less than 100 lines. But a complete example may involve several hundred or 1000 lines. The best way seems to have advice from the authors or from those who have tried the same thing before.

Examples alone are presented only for reference. What is missing here is people who could share their experience and advise us where to look for the exact information.

4.2.3 People Network

We do not need to be experts to act like experts! Years ago, we were invited to give a presentation on software engineering at an international conference held in Paris. It was our first time there. A young Asian couple came and asked us for low-budget hotels. We probably looked like tourists. Clearly, the couple had a language problem, but so did we. I used my mobile phone to send text messages to friends of mine in Paris whom I had met in a chatroom (e.g., "I seek you" ICQ). They soon called me back . Even though not all of them were helpful, they could suggest one or two places to try. This story tells us two things: (1) "C'est toujours bien de parler un peu français à Paris"[5] and (2) building a people network is important for both information sharing and problem solving.

Open-source software development itself can be considered as a kind of people network. Many active open-source projects have their own discussion forums or newsgroups. Discussion forums may be using different communication channels: Network News Transfer Protocol (NNTP) messages, emailing lists, blogs, or chatrooms. Often, subscriptions are free. People there are willing to share or exchange their experience and program sources and libraries with those who are interested in them. The shared work could be originally written for open-source development or even private companies. We simply use the term "people network" to mean any form of open-source development and its related discussion groups.

In our CRM project, sample code for retrieving and sending emails could be obtained from the people network. The coding involves Socket programming and SMTP and POP3 protocols, which could be quite a task for a team of database programmers. We once interviewed a number of database programmers, and few were sure whether they could send email using Telnet. Database programmers are well versed in SQL programming and database tuning, but they may be inexperienced in network programming.

[5]"It is always good to speak a little French in Paris."

Our team can write an initial request for help to the people network. Of a number of replies, there are always one or two suggesting where we may be able to download the source code. If we get no reply, we rephrase our request. As those who reply are simply sharing with us what they did or got in the past, the sample program will normally work fine as long as we get the software configuration right enough. Now that the project team no longer needs to start everything from scratch, the team can focus on how to revise or integrate the software.

While it is possible to enjoy the past efforts of people in a network, they aren't part of the development team. To allow development resources to be used optimally, we have to manage and coordinate a way of assessing shared sources.

4.2.4 Rhythm for Plagiarism

System requirements and applications are always lengthy and specific to a domain. People not in the same industry may have problems digesting user requirements. Thus, we have to generalize a specific application to a nonspecific one so that there is a greater likelihood that members of our people network understand and thus provide informative and useful contributions. For example, rather than asking for help as to how to automatically forward to sales representatives in the CRM project, we should just request the source for an email client application. An action list is as follows:

1. Generalize particular user requirements into a common application that can still demonstrate the same techniques for solving our specific problem.
2. Send your problem to the people network.
3. Request any shared program that will employ that know-how in programming.
4. Obtain a shared program among replies. (If there is no reply or only negative comments, regeneralize your question in point 1.)
5. If you need to download the source, try to download stable versions.
6. Test and run the system. Request further help if any difficulties are encountered.
7. Software configuration management should keep the original source, using the latest source (with modifications in place) and the procedure to rerun it. and results and the modification made.

The sample code we are looking for can be embedded in either an open-source application or a complete open source library. In any case, finding the right copy of simple code is a critical step. Although this should logically come after our requirements have been studied, it is possible to start as early as possible in order to quickly gain technical feedback.

Whether the sample code is developed by the same software team or obtained from the people network is not an issue as long as we get the right code and repeat the results. Most importantly, the process should be completed more quickly than if we did it from scratch. Success will depend on the contributions of members of the people network, the complexity of the problem, and the capabilities of the software team.

After successfully testing the source, our team can proceed to revise the shared program according to the user requirements. As sources are not highlighted in color, the team will have to digest and figure out some semantics and syntax. Since it is not possible to read through every single line and it is not easy to fully understand the details of the program, relying on reading code is of little practical use. However, once the original program has to be successfully rerun, the team can always modify a small part of the program and retest it to gain more understanding. The team can always go several steps backward or, as a last resort, return to the original and start all over again if it is lost during modifications. Here are some more suggestions:

- The team may post more questions to the people network to solve technical problems in the source. Since people from the people network normally reply with short answers, they will not instruct us what and how to do anything in detail.
- Two developers work together to revise and to test. If the team has no idea where to revise, try to work in pairs, which will facilitate a heuristic search of an open-ended kind (Kaner et al.). Pair programming is discussed further in Chapter 5 and 6.
- The team can be split into two or three subteams to individually modify and test in parallel. All subteams will have communicated with one another; they share their findings and highlight modifications in color once any progress has been made. The process is as follows:

1. Revise the program by subteams.
2. Highlight any necessary modifications that should indicate any user requirements.
3. Communicate any findings with other subteams working on the same shared program by providing the revised program in color and results implemented.
4. Repeat above until the expected result is attained

FIGURE 4.15 Rhythm for plagiarism programming .

As we could not control the people network, by no means can we actually guarantee success, but we have learned that programmers, who cannot even plagiarize a solution for a problem of the same kind, cannot possibly devise that solution by themselves. Given this, plagiarism programming particularly facilitates software development in either of two cases: (1) the inexperienced team needs programming knowledge assistance or (2) the team does not have certain skills for completing part of an application.

In summary, a rhythm for plagiarism programming is shown in Figure 4.15. You may notice that "copy" is an abbreviated term. It means copying other people's success; that is, download the source, compile the program, then run and test it.

In eXtreme programming, we always stand on a baseline of the last success and make some progress forward. This can be done only with high-frequency iteration. The development team must successfully integrate the software and pass its unit tests before the team calls it a day. This makes a lot of sense. We cannot get integration and testing done by going home, throwing out today's code, and starting again from our last success. Today's code has become hard to maintain and should be trashed so that the team does not waste more effort in maintaining it. Besides, it may not be worthwhile to spend so much time fixing one day's code. So we don't fix it. We throw it away.

In plagiarism programming, if we modify the original program to the point that we lose track of the changes and can't see which changes are to blame for failures, we can always roll back to our last success checkpoint and restart again. This means applying a highly iterative rhythm (see Figure 4.15). Iteration frequency is an important concept in understanding the software development rhythm in any methodology that your team adopts.

4.2.5 Plagiarism at Work

Case 1: CRM A manufacturing company has three regional sales offices in Chinese cities: Huizhou (HZ), Shanghai (SH), and Beijing (BJ). Each office had its own IT support team, but the Huizhou team was the head team.

The company decided to go for its CRM project in 2001 after a long evaluation. The system had a number of modules, one of which was about customer communication solutions. The management believed that what customers really needed was "easy." To many customers, convenience is more

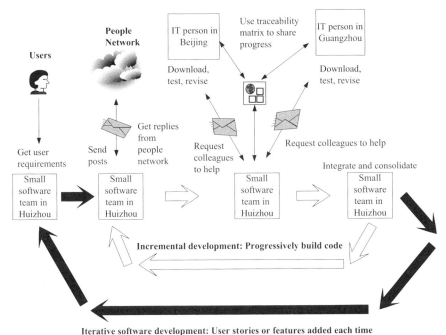

Iterative software development: User stories or features added each time

FIGURE 4.16   A case of virtual software development.

attractive than free. Therefore, the company wanted to establish a universal email address for all kinds of requests from sales orders to service complaints. Moreover, each request would be handled in three working days.

On the received email address, the system will record the header information and send an internal email to the responsible staff to follow up. In addition, the system counts the time. When no reply has been sent to the customer in 2 days, the system will send a reminder note. Section 4.2.2 has explained the application requirements.

Figure 4.16 illustrates the CRM project development cycle. At the beginning, the requirements would be related to the technical know-how of a general email program that sent and received messages. The Huizhou team at the head office therefore posted the requests to the people network (a Perl newsgroup) asking for any code samples for sending SMTP and receiving POP3 emails. The Huizhou team managed to get sample code. As the whole team was in a distributed environment, it was able to share these findings and coordinate its two remote subteams while the Huizhou team worked on other modules of the CRM. They first retested the program, which was always the first necessary step in plagiarism programming. The two centers worked independently and in parallel.

To avoid redundancy and share the progress of each team, they posted their results on the Intranet Website via VPN. Using a traceability matrix

TABLE 4.4   Traceability Matrix

Test Case	Huizhou	Beijing	Guangzhou
1. Rerun the original program	Yes (Nov. 11)	Yes (Nov. 15)	Yes (Nov. 16)
2. Change the POP3 server as our email server and Test	Yes (Nov. 17)	Yes (Nov. 19)	—
3. Retrieve the email header and print it out	—	Yes (Nov. 26)	Yes (Nov. 22)
4. Get the sender address and email body.	—	Yes (Dec. 27)	
Progress	1	4	3

(Kaner et al.) such as that shown in Table 4.4 enables each team to trace forward to each test case and backward from every success of other teams. The team should highlight its modifications with color coding for other teams to easily replicate and inspect. Once a team has managed to examine a particular test case, others can either learn how that test is done, or even skip that test and move on to other modifications.

The Huizhou team will examine all the resulting programs and may request further enhancements. Once the team can successfully integrate with other CRM submodules, the team may progressively utilize its remote teams for software development.

Case 2: Product Knowledge Training (A-Tutor) A retail chain selling Chinese herbal remedies had around 45 shops in Hong Kong in 2005. The company was planning to reach 50 outlets by the end of year. However, the high turnover rate of frontline staff caused setbacks to normal business operations in high seasons and limited their capacity to expand. Newly recruited staff seldom had knowledge of the functions of the different herbs that, according to Chinese medicine, can be used medicinally and for special diets. The staff in the chain had the job of not only selling the product but also providing advisory services and so required strong product knowledge.

The company produced a training video compact disk (VCD) on Chinese herbs and distributed the VCD to new staff; however, there were cases in which VCDs were not given to the staff promptly. In one case the number of VCDs needed to be burned by the IT department beforehand was incorrectly estimated by the training department, and when the company wanted to update some videoclips the company had to dispose of old VCDs and reproduce them.

The company launched an e-training project. One of the objectives was to allow colleagues to access videoclips online (see Figure 4.17). Two technical support staff who were responsible for networking and PC maintenance

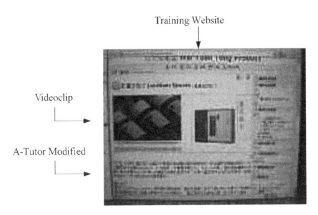

FIGURE 4.17 A company website to train new frontline staff in herbal product applications.

would be involved in the project. They downloaded and installed an open-source Web-based content management system, A-tutor (http://www.atutor.ca/).

To enhance the A-tutor for videodisplay, we had convert VCD file format into audiovideo interleave (AVI) format. Then, the support staff modified the PHP scripts and even though they were not programmers and knew nothing about PHP and MySQL, they managed to get the sample script onto the Internet and to modify A-tutor. The two staff members completed the project in 2 weeks.

4.3 BUSINESS AND RHYTHM FOR PLAGIARISM

The rhythm for plagiarism programming could sometimes help us do amazing things! It may also bring along more controversial issues on *copyleft*, in which original authors allow free distribution of their works. Here is our true story about business, copyleft, and rhythm for plagiarism.

In September 2005, we had a chance to meet the managing director of Swire Coca Cola. Coca Cola was franchised to a British company, the Swire group, to manufacture and distribute the product in southern and western China, Hong Kong, and Taiwan. The major competitor of Coca Cola was always Pepsi. In some regions Pepsi won while in others Coca Cola was ahead. Location is important in the soft-drink industry in that some locations have more extreme competitive consequences. When we order a beer in a restaurant, for example, our choice of drink excludes both Pepsi and Coca Cola. However, when we buy them in a supermarket, we may purchase all three.

In this short meeting, we had a chance to talk to them about our chatting robot, *Nammik*, and how Nammik may excel in a worldwide consulting firm,

ACNielsen, by its inexpensive, up-to-date market surveys. We were making a proposal about service, data, and ourselves, not about software and technology.

4.3.1 15-Minute Business Presentation

We were waiting in a small conference room. A man entered the room. His dress appeared unusual in a sizable British company. He was John from the United States, tall, in a casual shirt without a tie. We distributed our report to John. It was just one page long! We had around 15–20 minutes to sell what we had.

The company had already developed its own tailor-made ERP system many years ago, called the sales-and-distribution system (SDS). It was a powerful business operation database that supported and provided sales information in any dimensional breakdown. The manufacturing cost could be easily calculated from the sum of raw materials, logistic cost, expenses, and other factors. We all know that profits are sales minus costs and people running companies have to maximize profits by either increasing sales, decreasing costs, or both. Well, in reality, only small companies manage their business in this way. The strategy of a large company is monopoly, or at least market share, with big fish eating little fish. Therefore, Swire Coka Cola would always take efforts to expand their market segment and their share of each segment. The company purchased marketing data from ACNielsen to learn about its consumers and competitors. The date would assist the company to truly learn their business position and sales performance. John could understand his different regional sales and marketing teams by their key performance indicator (KPI), defined as follows:

$$\text{KPI(by region)} = \frac{\text{regional sales}}{\text{population aged 0–14 years}}$$

The KPI combined three types of information: data from SDS or ERP, demographic data, and marketing research. Thereby, it fairly reflected the business performance. As discussed, the sales amount, rebates, and volume [in hectoliters (hL)] by region could be retrieved from SDS. We may replace volume with sales, and hence we could have a number of KPIs measuring performance from different aspects.

As for demographic data, the National Bureau of Statistics of China published three populations of people at age of 0–14, 15–64, and over 65. However, selecting which one segment as target would necessitate marketing research data. Unlike demographic data, marketing research information can change unexpectedly. Section 4.3.2 discusses this topic in more detail. For now, we just need to know that marketing research helps us identify segments of our market and demographic data tell us the population of an age segment.

Box 4.1. shows our report. We presented data on a geographic map. In our proposal the KPI was indicated with colors for different sales performances.

BOX *4.1*

BUSINESS PROPOSAL

September 2, 2005

1. **Objective.** Different sources give new insights into business.

2. **Business System Proposed**. SDS merely supports the operational information. To understand market changes and to measure business performance, we propose a data warehouse that provides different views which complement each other. Such a system combines (1) basic data, (2) demographic data, and (3) market research.

Basic (ERP or SDS):	Sales, costs of sales (rebate), A/R (credit), volume,
+	and so on.
Demographic data :	Population information
+	
Market research:	Customer segment, competitor data analysis, and so on.

3. **Data Source (Real Data)**

	ERP		Demographic Data[a] (Age)				Market Research[b]
Regions	Sales	Volume	0–14	15 – 64	>65	Total	Lowest price of a can of (Pepsi/ Coca Cola)
Guangdong	—	—	20,593	50,799	6,283	77,676	2.0 RMB/2.0 RMB
Beijing	—	—	1,486	11,008	1,576	14,070	1.8 RMB/ 1.8 RMB

[a] Data from National Bureau of Statistics of China (NBSC) available at
   http://www.stats.gov.cn/tjsj/ndsj/yb2004-c/index.htm.
[b] Data from *Nammik* system developed by the authors.

4. **Information Fusion (Example).** In China, populations in different regions can vary significantly. Sales [or hectoliters (hL)] by region is not informative enough. Thus, "sales by region/population by region" can provide more information. Defining a benchmark, we may find key areas for improvement (see the diagram below).

SDS (Sales, Rebate, hL, etc.)	2003 demographic data (age 0–14)	KPI to help management learn more information

Different colors indicate sales performances.

5. Conclusion. Explore different ratios to discover any new business opportunity.

In each annual board meeting, John had to report on any change in the company's market and market share to evaluate their performance. Although our proposal indicated that we were advising a type of computer application, this was not the case. What we have not clearly addressed is how we could get "market information" by ourselves without expensive market measurement services from ACNielsen.

4.3.2 Marketing Research

Consumer marketing research is a form of applied sociology that uses sociological knowledge and statistics to help organizations understand consumer behaviors. Although there are many different kinds of marketing research, such as brand equity research, customer satisfaction studies, and consumer decision process research, the techniques used to obtain data are limited. Generally, the most commonly used method is the questionnaire.

In July 2005, we did some marketing research. We questioned more than 5000 Chinese people in a chatroom about their favorite drink and received around 500 complete replies. Figure 4.18 shows the result of our own marketing research.

As data provided by NBSC are presented in three groups (ages 0–14, 15–64, and >65), we may conclude that the population aged 0–14 years could be close to the right market segment of soft-drink consumers, and hence this age group was suggested for the KPI calculation in Section 4.3.1

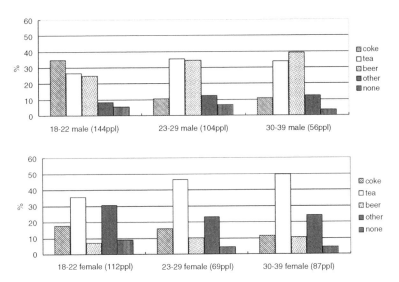

FIGURE 4.18 What is your favorite drink? ("None" means tapwater or particular preference) (real data by authors).

In a similar fashion, Figure 4.19 shows a contour map of China in which the population group at age 0–14 by province is indicated in the background and a small pie chart associated with each province shows Pepsi versus Coca Cola in percentage. Those who favor neither Coke nor Pepsi are shown as "neutral." The total number of intelligible responses from each province is shown below the pie charts.

Swire Coca Cola purchased data of this kind from ACNielsen annually. However, consumer behaviors can change significantly in a year. For example, Pepsi's commercial starring soccer star David Beckham had a tremendous impact on David's Fans (see Box 4.3 in Section 4.3.3). How do we get the latest marketing data, and how do they relate to software development?

4.3.3   Chatting Robot

Marketing data can be obtained from customers. Often we want to know not only who our existing customers are but also those who are not yet customers, and when they may become our customers. Since we have fewer current customers than noncustomers, getting to know the needs of noncustomers (i e., prospective customers) is a good start toward making them customers.

There are so many public chatrooms on the Internet. One of them is ICQ ("I seek you"). Although different chatrooms and instant messages have their

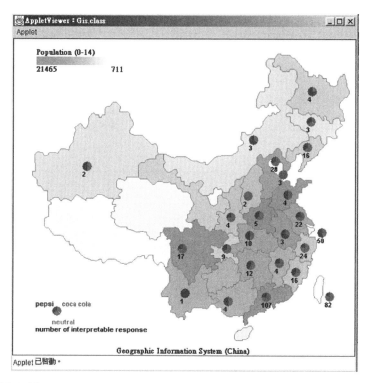

FIGURE 4.19 Coke versus Pepsi. (Taiwan population data not included). (Real data by authors).

own features, they were not very different in our case. ICQ can be a place to talk to people and to learn something from them, a bit like what we saw in the people network in Section 4.2.3.

When conducting a telephone survey or an interview survey, we have to design a good questionnaire. Therefore, a dialog-based questionnaire is designed and carefully examined. Then, our interviewers will log in to ICQ, search for people who are online and live in China, say "Hello" to them, and ask how they feel about Coca Cola and Pepsi. Our interviewer must be extremely patient as interviewees may be busy and may respond very slowly. They may be away or logged off. Our interviewers will have to talk to others. The process is unbelievably slow. The solution is to have more interviewers, which can become clumsy and costly. On one hand, we need to manage who has talked to whom, to avoid interviewing the same person twice. On the other hand, this kind of survey is expensive. The interviewees may log off anytime, leaving us an incomplete questionnaire that can rarely be used for statistical analysis. It would be better if we had a chatting robot to do the job.

BOX 4.2

THREE DIALOG SAMPLES (Aug. 2005)

Dialog 1

Nammik	I live in Hong Kong. Where do you live?
ICQ	I live in Yiwu City, Zhejiang.
ICQ	So you can type Chinese to me?
Nammik	Cannot read simplified chinese because i am using traditional Chinese Windows
ICQ	OK, no problem
ICQ	What is your job?
ICQ	Oh,has you been to another city of China? Except Hong Kong
Nammik	Can I ask you some questions about soft drink? i want to compare it with Hong Kong.
ICQ	I means which city did you go before except Hong Kong City?
ICQ	Ok
Nammik	How much is a can of pepsi there in rmb
ICQ	2.5–3 rmb/can.
Nammik	How much is a can of Coke?
ICQ	Nearly same.
Nammik	Which one do you like most? I mean Coke or Pepsi
ICQ	Both i don't like.
Nammik	That's cool.
ICQ	Which one do you prefer?
Nammik	I appreciate your help. Here is a joke for you. Tom: my wife is just forty. Kim: why don't you change her for two twenties?

Dialog 2

ICQ	oohhh—I like this city and I wanna work in this city
Nammik	That's great
ICQ	I'm in mainland [China].
ICQ	My English poor
Nammik	My English is not good either...dont worry...
ICQ	:-P
Nammik	Can I ask you some questions about soft drink? I want to compare it with Hong Kong
ICQ	My English poor I not know
Nammik	How much is a can of pepsi there in rmb
ICQ	Wat is mean?
Nammik	How much is a can of Coke?
ICQ	Oohh... 3
Nammik	Which one do you like most? I mean Coke or Pepsi

ICQ	Pepsi.
Nammik	Why Pepsi? Why not Coke?
ICQ	I think it has co2 more.
Nammik	I appreciate your help. Here is a joke for you. Tom: my wife is just forty. Kim: why don't you change her for two twenties?

Dialog 3

Nammik	I live in Hong Kong. Where do you live?
ICQ	Shenzhen
ICQ	Why you show you are 31 years old, and living in Singapore?
Nammik	That's great
ICQ	:-) why great ?
Nammik	Can I ask you some questions about soft drink? I want to compare it with Hong Kong
ICQ	Yes
Nammik	How much is a can of Pepsi there in rmb
ICQ	3.5
Nammik	How much is a can of Coke?
ICQ	The same
Nammik	Which one do you like most? I mean Coke or Pepsi?
ICQ	Coke
Nammik	Why Coke ? Why not Pepsi?
ICQ	Just like.
Nammik	I appreciate your help. Here is a joke for you. Tom: my wife is just forty. Kim: why don't you change her for two twenties.

Nammik is an ICQ chatting robot (see Box 4.2). We may write different dialog scripts (see Appendix). Nammik will talk according to that script. Differing from other chatting robots like ELIZA (1966), ALICE (by AI Foundation in 1995), and Dave (English teacher), which were developed to intelligently answer our questions rather than to conduct interviews, Nammik has been built to interview people.

Nammik does not have any sophisticated speech understanding engine. In of fact, we discovered that many people in the chatrooms do not speak English properly. For example, they say "what does it mean" as "wat is mean" (see Box 4.2). In Hong Kong and China, people may use their dialect "88" as "bye bye." Thus, according to the dialog script given, Nammik simply looks for keywords and related responses.

Although Nammik does not have text mining capabilities, we may easily extract responses after a related question. For example, to learn about "how people like Coca Cola and Pepsi," we can easily extract responses for that kind of question (see Box 4.3).

BOX *4.3*

WHY DO YOU LIKE COKE OR PEPSI?

Nammik	why pepsi? why not coke?
ICQ	i think pepsi is more sweet than coke i think children here prefer to pepsi
ICQ	see you next time!! i get off line
Nammik	why coke ? why not pepsi?
ICQ	i would like coke and pepsi
ICQ	i don't know
ICQ	but i would like coke
Nammik	why pepsi? why not coke?
ICQ	because of the advertisement, i like the football stars that are signed with Pepsi, like david beckham, and zidene
Nammik	why coke ? why not pepsi?
ICQ	i'd like coke because it's more classical brand for me, and coke's tasty i'd like a bit more
Nammik	why pepsi? why not coke?
ICQ	i like the logo of pepsi
Nammik	why coke ? why not pepsi?
ICQ	maybe I feel the pepsi is suit to the fashion people, and I m older:) actually, I don't refuse any brand

How challenging can it be to write Nammik? Well, many of programmers like us do not know much about ICQ protocol, network programming, and event-driven programming. Fortunately, basic knowledge of Windows API and "C" language skills is just enough. Nammik is simple and easy to write because many developers have already done the code for us to plagiarize. We just need to play the rhythm: copy–modify–test.

4.3.4 Old Song, New Singer

To build Nammik using plagiarism programming, we have to get a chatroom client application. There were a number of open-source ICQ clients. We used Miranda IM (http://www.Miranda-im.org) as our sample code. Miranda instant messaging (IM) written in C is built by a community of volunteers. It is an open-source project under the GNU GPL license. There is a chatting robot plug-in for Miranda IM, called ANNA (an implementation of an ALICE), but it is complex and does not meet our requirements.

Miranda IM architecture is simple and flexible. There are many powerful plug-ins (e.g., ICQ, Yahoo, email) that are dynamic-link library (DLL) files for the Miranda IM kernel (see Figure 4.20). To add functionality to Miranda IM,

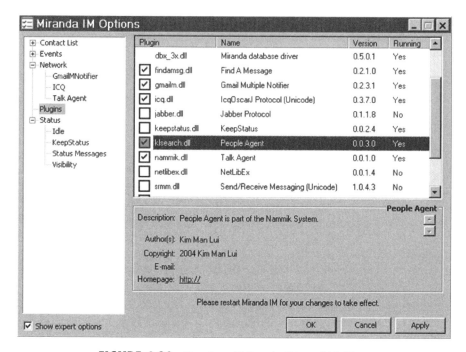

FIGURE 4.20   Plug-ins of Miranda IM are DLL files.

we have to develop our own plug-ins. We downloaded a small plug-in source, modified it a bit, and tested it so that we knew how that plug-in could interface with the Miranda IM kernel.

Nammik has been built in a rhythm of modify–test since we and our student programmers knew a little about ICQ protocol and network programming. Figure 4.21 shows the architecture of Nammik.

Send/Receive Messaging Plug-in   With this plug-in, we could type in and send our instant message in a dialog window. The plug-in was modified to display all posted and received messages. In addition, we could send the ICQ text through function calls (see Figure 4.22). Because we have to code–modify–test the plug-in, the plug-in is not regarded as a reusable component in this case.

People Agent from IcqOscarJ Protocol Plug-in   The original plug-in provides searching functionality of on-line ICQ users shown in Figure 4.23. Those online users are random. It is possible that some of them to whom you have just talked are also listed. Besides, we have to type in welcome messages one by one.

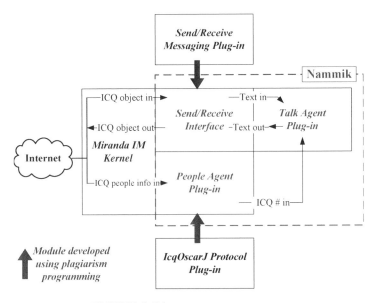

FIGURE 4.21 Nammik architecture.

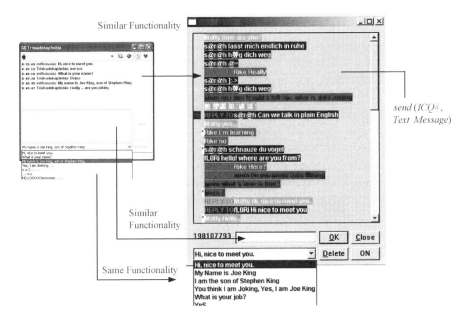

FIGURE 4.22 Send/receive messaging plug-in modified using plagiarism programming.

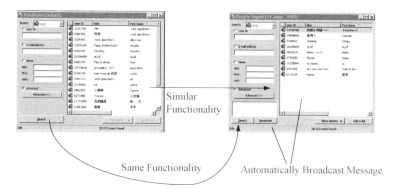

FIGURE 4.23 IcqOscarJ protocol plug-in modified.

We modified the plug-in so that it filters out people we met already and broadcast a "welcome" message to new people. When they respond, Nammik's talk agent will take over the dialog. In short, the function of people agent is to automate "find/add contacts" in the IcqOscarJ plug-in.

Talk Agent In essence, the talk agent is an interpreter of the dialog script. Figure 4.24 illustrates its function. When the execution pointer is on line 330, it sends a message through a say() function call to the ICQ user whom we are talking to, and the execution pointer changes to 340, the next line of 330. Then Nammik will wait for a response.

Although the talk agent is the core part of Nammik, its code is about string handling and matching, which is much simpler than both IcqOscarJ protocol or send/receive messaging plug-ins in terms of data structure and exceptional handling. We rely heavily on the rhythm for plagiarism to build Nammik. Nammik is an old song with a new singer because Miranda IM has almost every code we need.

How can we tell dancing from body shaking? It is rhythm. In the same fashion, rhythm makes the difference between copy-and-paste programming and plagiarism programming. Without rhythm, plagiarism programming just becomes cut-and-paste and software projects managed by plagiarism will sooner or later end up in a mess. Plagiarism programming has a strong sense of what activities should follow after we copy other people's work. The rhythm helps the team members communicate with each other.

Some readers may notice that we rarely mention software disciplines. The reason why is because software development rhythms implicitly demand that people be disciplined and that there be a team effort to sustain them.

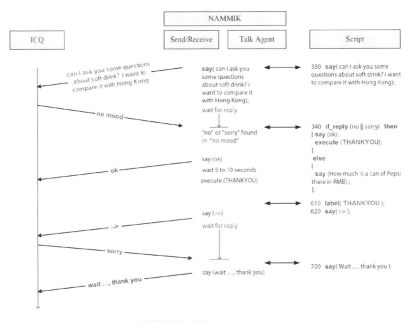

FIGURE 4.24   Talk agent.

REFERENCES

Clements P and Northrop L. *Software Product Lines: Practices and Patterns*. Boston: Addison-Wesley; 2001.

Coad P, Lefebvre E, and de Luca J. *Java Modeling in Color with UML: Enterprise Components and Process*. Upper Saddle River, NJ: Prentice-Hall PTR; 1999.

Ebrahimi A. Novice programmer errors: Language constructs and plan composition. *International Journal of Human-Computer Studies* 1994; **41**:457–480.

Gamma E, Helm R, Johnson R, and Vlissides J. *Design Patterns: Elements of Reusable Object-Oriented Software*. Reading, MA: Addison-Wesley; 1995.

Gartner Inc. *Customer Relationship Management Summit 2004*. Oct. 4–6, Scottsdale, AZ, The Westin Kierland Resort and Spa, Stamford, CT, 2004.

Grand M. *Patterns in Java: A Catalog of Reusable Design Patterns Illustrated with UML*, 2nd Ed. New York: Wiley; 2002.

Kaner C, Bach J, and Pettichord B. *Lessons Learned in Software Testing: A Context-Driven Approach*. New York: Wiley; 2002.

McConnell S. *Code Complete: A Practical Handbook of Software Construction*. Redmond, WA: Microsoft Press; 1993.

O'Brien KJ. In open source, an unexpected trap, *International Herald Tribune*, Dec. 9, 2005. Available at http://www.iht.com/bin/print_ipub.php?file=/ articles/2005/12/09/business/open.php .

Shalloway A and Trot J. *Design Patterns Explained: A New Perspective on Object-Oriented Design*. Boston: Addison-Wesley; 2002.

Shepard RN. Recognition memory for words, sentences and pictures. *Journal of Verbal Learning and Verbal Behavior* 1967; **5**:201–204.

Soloway E. Learning to program=learning to construct mechanisms and explanations. *Communications of The ACM* 1986; **29** (9):850–858.

Sommerville I. *Software Engineering*. 5th ed. Reading, MA: Addison-Wesley; 1995.

5

PAIR PROGRAMMING

> Three thousand years ago, scholars in pairs studied the Torah by taking up opposite positions on each issue. Three thousand years later, we write programs in pairs by taking up doing and watching roles on each piece of code.

"Spend less"[1] is a new rule for corporate executives in an article "IT doesn't matter." As we all know, it is getting more difficult to achieve a sales advantage through IT investment but easier to put a company at a cost disadvantage (Carr 2003). This brings us to another two protective rules: "Follow, don't lead" and "Focus on vulnerabilities, not opportunities." The idea is to get cost benefits by keeping ourselves less than state-of-the-art competitive.

This reminds us of a paper product manufacturing company we visited some years ago. The management employed many uncompetent staff that were unbelievably loyal to them. Perhaps for this reason the staff worked harder and made up for their deficiencies to the point that they were cost-efficient. The company could have cut its administrative staff by half and replaced them with more competent people who the company would have had to pay even more. It wouldn't have been economically worthwhile. The company that employed too many less-than-competent individuals turned out to be more productive and faster than a company that was "optimally"

---

[1] Spend less on information technology (IT).

Software Development Rhythms: Harmonizing Agile Practices for Synergy
By Kim Man Lui and Keith C. C. Chan
Copyright © 2008 John Wiley & Sons, Inc.

staffed. The idea seems as odd as pair programming, in which two people who are working on a single task that just one person could complete alone.

Let us clarify what we mean by pair programming. *Pair programming* is the hallmark of eXtreme programming (XP). It defines pair programming as two programmers sitting side by side to collaborate on a unitary job that includes the design, coding, and testing of a piece of software. One programmer acting as the driver controls the keyboard/mouse and actively implements the program, and the other programmer, serving as the observer, continuously watches the work with a view to identifying tactical defects and providing strategic planning. Therefore, it is not pair programming if they subtask the program so that one does one set of code and the other does another set of code.

It is likely that the observer may write part of the code faster or may get bored watching or tired of explaining her/his ideas to the partner. Thus, they rotate their roles. Done with the right timing, both are having fun and maximizing their contributions. When more than one pair participates in software development, partners of each pair need to be periodically exchanged. This may seem a bit complicated, but each programmer can get involved with every single line of code. This supports code standards in action and creates synergies within the pairs.

According to this definition, few non-XP programmers would have tried pair programming, although they may have collaborated with someone in front of the same screen while writing some code. But why can't both have keyboards, and work on the same file simultaneously, communicating orally to coordinate their efforts? The one-keyboard/program/driver element creates a bottleneck in the process. Should we just take collaborative cognition as the idea behind how and when pair programming works, it can be understood as the driver writes the code and her/his partner actively provides any kind of assistance in order to achieve higher-quality software.

To distinguish this from eXtreme programming by name, we might better call it *collaborative programming*. We easily generalize triple programming and side-by-side programming (see Chapter 6) as collaborative programming. Fortunately, it is not that necessary to rigorously differentiate their definitions, and we believe that many programmers have once worked in a way of pair programming, or more precisely, collaborative programming.

5.1 ART AND SCIENCE

A number of problems with pair programming have been widely discussed in the past. Developers who are new to pair programming will probably ask a number of basic questions that many others have raised or responded to. To start with, we are going to have a short review of some frequently asked questions (FAQs) such as whether a programmer prefers to work alone as in solo programming and not work aloud (vocally) as in pair programming and so on (Williams and Kessler 2003). Afterward, we can move forward on more mysterious issues: Why pair but not triple? Does pair programming actually speed up the completion of a software project?

These questions might be related more to art than to science. Because many practitioners may have their own perspectives on them, they are divided and vocal in pair programming. Different people understand pair programming as meaning different things, and this has made it somewhat controversial in some circles.

However, we will, by drawing on the existing understanding of collaborative work, offer some general recommendations for forming pair programming teams, but that these recommendations are guidelines that may, in some cases, be less than effective when put into practice.

In this section we are primarily presenting commonsense ideas about pairs of people working together. In Section 5.2 we will address each of these concerns and show how pair programming, combined with proper design of the program environment, can offset some its inherent limitations.

5.1.1 The Right Partner

> *FAQ*: Two heads are better than one! But pair programming works well only with the right pair as the partners complement each other's knowledge.

Our intuition tells us that with the right pairing two heads are better than one, and to some extent this is the case because paired programmers will always complement each other as long as two people think differently and have different focuses. For example, one observer may focus more on alternative programming design. We're generally unlikely to get two people who think so similarly that they may as well be just one person.

There are frequent cases in which today's business needs require unpredictable programming changes and programmers have to modify what they have done. The difficulties of such revision depends on how much they have already coded, how many changes are required, and how they are able to effectively modify existing code to respond to those changes. In such a coding game, programmers working in pairs complementing each other's ideas make better teams. It is not an issue about a right partner, but it demands close collaboration to meet the new challenge and get the job done.

Two brains may tackle projects more creatively and efficiently than one (Constantine 1995). Saying that two heads are better than one is too bold. People, methodologies, and tasks should be put in place so as to ensure in-depth understanding of when a software practice works and when practices are connected. "Work well" relies on what kind of task can be better solved by pair programming.

In group dynamics, studies of group composition suggest that groups with optimal diversity will work together more effectively than others. In practice we have to carefully balance the need for similarity against the need for complementarity and/or diversity. Diversity is good for creativity, but it can cause tensions within the group that may eventually undermine productivity. A group of programmers (including a pair) may end up fighting, chatting, or even worse, flirting. But these are problems with social professionalism. They can occur in any form of team programming, not just pair programming. In these situations, developers are simply not mature enough or sufficiently self-disciplined to respect their team members in the workplace.

5.1.2 Noisy Programming

FAQ: Many programming tasks can be so challenging that developers need to have a quiet place to think about them. Pair programming, however, is noisy.

A "quiet" place is not the same as a "silent" place. Quietness can be subjective. Programmers may feel like listening to music and would still consider it quiet if it helped them get the job done. You know! Playing Mozart to children for 10 minutes enhances their spatio-temporal reasoning, as shown in Figure 5.1.

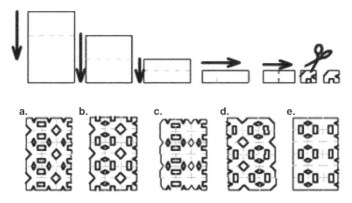

FIGURE 5.1 Spatio-temporal exercise.[2]

---

[2] The answer is (b) (Hansen 2001). http://coe.sdsu.edu/eet/Articles/ mozarteffect/start.htm.

Some programmers prefer working in a cubicle, where they can create private environments with decorations or photos. In reality, many of us work in an interrupting environment. After being interrupted by the mobile phone, a programmer might not be able to concentrate for at least 15 minutes (DeMacro and Lister 1987).

Some don't like to be watched. They need to be trusted. This can be due to personal traits or cultural influences. Some of our colleagues are nocturnal and enjoy writing code late at night. This is their ideal quietness. A need for quietness can be just a matter of personal preference. Some programmers prefer to work alone in what they regard as a quiet place, although they may, of course, be online with ICQ and irregularly hear the sound of an incoming message.

5.1.3 Just Training

> *FAQ*: Pair programming facilitates on-the-job training for newly hired programmers; however, paired programmers will be a waste of time once they receive enough training.

We can rephrase this as "Pair programming is not mutually beneficial to paired experienced programmers." When we pair two experienced programmers, we should ask what kind of problem they are going to solve. Are they going to solve a simple problem, or are they going to solve a very difficult problem?

A newly hired programmer might ask questions that an experienced programmer would regard as stupid, and, of course, such questioning may affect productivity, but this situation is not in general representative of team productivity.

Collaboration demands sharing and task focus. It is important to learn how to practice pair programming and how programmers play their roles. For example, it can be a mistake to regard pair programming as a training session in which the driver writes code and explains what she is doing in detail whereas the observer, as her secretary, takes notes of everything that is said. People share knowledge through the code. This is a bit different from training.

Finally, the most obvious FAQ, by which a manager is bewildered, can be the next one.

5.1.4 Pay to Watch

> *FAQ*: Why is a job that can be finished by just one person now still done by one person but with one watching?

Tasks that can be completed either alone or together always present theoretical and applied issues (Stasser and Dietz-Uhler 2001). When all members are independently capable of doing their work, pair programming will cut the team productivity in half. This seems counterproductive, but the people who have tried it now swear by it.

In programming, a task isn't necessarily done well or even completed. Often, owing to hidden bugs and requirements changes requested by users, rework is necessary and, in the worst case, this can happen when the original author has already moved on. Another programmer takes over the modifications. If the code is not written for easy comprehension, is hardcode development or spaghetti code, that programmer will have a hard time. How do we solve them all? Pair programming throws light on a bottom line for software quality problems.

The issue then becomes whether a company is happy to pay twice as much to get better result:

1. We must understand how much salary a programmer earns. This depends on the country or, within the same country, the region where the hire is working.
2. Suppose that an energetic but less experienced programmer costs $50. Then two will cost $100. From a quality perspective, the question now is whether, if working together they will produce something better than a more experienced programmer who costs $100.

So, why adopt pair programming? What is more, we might need to convince senior management about the adoption of pair programming. Our reply should be determined and sensible. The advantages of pair programming must be potential so that we are willing to tackle problems with adoption of pair programming and to present to our management. Otherwise, we shouldn't risk it.

Ultimately, anyone who is considering adopting pair programming will have to think about these issues because for all of its complexity, one thing about pair programming is clear—it is more than simple collaboration.

5.2 TWO WORLDS

Medieval philosophers tell us that if an object or a thing happens to be true or exists in some but not all possible worlds, it is contingent. To the contrary, it is necessary if it exists in all possible worlds; for example, in mathematics, 1 and 1 is 2. It is always held true in any possible world. That simple distinction between these *two* truths eventually helps some mathematician logically prove the existence of God (Gödel 1995). Apparently, that pair programming is beneficial to software development is a contingent truth.

Imagine that there are two worlds: a moneyless world and a money-led world. At first glance, this may seem a bit unrealistic, but it does not matter. We are merely interested in how pair programming may work in these two worlds. How these two worlds may come to exist is a job for economists.

5.2.1 Moneyless World

In the moneyless world, we will prefer a working style that has more support for staff learning. Knowledge is power. Pair working provides opportunities for learning from each other. In addition, we would like to minimize any risk due to staff resigning or becoming sick. Another advantage comes with quality. In computer programming, removing defects as early as possible by having an observer help is always ideal. All these can be achieved by pair programming without balancing staff costs in a moneyless world.

Learning. Pair learning or pair work is a type of cooperative learning that is often defined as a range of concepts and techniques for enhancing the value of learner–learner interaction (Tan et al. 1999). Cooperative learning has been associated with gains in achievement, such as for assignments, thinking skills, enjoyment, interethnic relations, and self-esteem. This sounds pretty good.

The idea can be further extended to develop problem-based learning in which learners work collaboratively in small groups to analyze (or solve) a case. With no clear-cut right or wrong answer, the objective is revealed to the learners toward the end of the case.

Pair programming creates an on-the-job learning environment. It is a combination of cooperative learning and case-based learning. The process of analyzing and critiquing software written by others is a way for learning about design and code. There is no clear-cut right or wrong in system design and writing code. Thus, each software application can be considered an individual case in which a team of paired programmers explores the best and fastest way to complete it.

There is a body of research looking at how groups learn versus how individuals learn. Groups are not as fast as individuals when it comes to acquiring new manual skills. The group, once it learns, may be collectively smarter than the individual, but it will take longer to reach that state. A group of two (i.e., pair) will often take less time than will a larger group to acquire the skills necessary for collaboration.

In short, pair programming brings the benefits of cooperative learning to a workplace.

Personnel Turnover. In a conventional software project, we practice either solo programming or pair programming. Each member has been given different responsibilities. Some of them are given very important ones, and some are given less important ones. There are two extreme cases: (1) members' jobs never overlap one another, so that the jobs are complementary, together forming a useful combination of skills; and (2) members' jobs overlap in a way that knowledge and skill in doing their jobs are shared. In the moneyless world, we would prefer case 2.

With pair programming, the risk from losing key programmers is reduced, because there are multiple people familiar with each part of the system. If a pair works together consistently, then there are two people familiar with this particular area of the program. If the pairs rotate, as is always suggested in pair programming, many people can be familiar with each part.

There is an amusing idea in project management. A project manager takes over a very tightly run project and has to try hard to maximize team efficiency. The manager has carefully assign tasks to team members so that no tasks overlap. The project has gone two-thirds just as planned. To celebrate this success, the project manager invites the team to dine out. When they are walking across a street to a Chinese restaurant; you see a truck steered by an obviously intoxicated guy who is picking up speed and going to hit them. You shout to warn them. Everyone leaps out of the way except one unfortunate team member who is hit and killed on the spot. Bad enough for the manager by itself, but even worse because this accident has killed not just a team member, but the entire project, because the truck number for the software project is just one.

A "truck number" is defined as the number of team members that would need to be hit by a truck to have an impact on a project. If it is one, losing any single member of a team will mean the loss of skills or techniques that are critical to the success of a project. A high truck number can protect us against personnel turnover.

Error Detection. Software inspections were introduced in the early 1980s. Although there are many consistent, positive findings to support software inspections, not many software teams have fully adopted the inspections. From an informal USENET survey, only 20% of 90 respondents practiced software inspections (Cockburn and Williams 2000).

There is little doubt that a second look from others at existing code provides a useful, fresh perspective on our work. In software inspections and peer reviews, inspectors can look at the program and identify (troubleshoot) the problem. They provide supporting data and may even consider solutions and fixes. Software inspections and peer reviews serve as a vital final check on software quality. However, they cannot detect errors that are not there yet or are about to appear. Sometimes, inspectors may discover a design defect that requires a number of fundamental changes in the program. In this case, we may have to consider an add-on patch approach to hiding the defect instead of substantial reworking.

In pair programming, your partner is a safeguard against potential design defects. The driver may actively ask for the observer's opinions. Explaining our code to the partner helps us learn more about design defects in our code. What is more, pair programming will not compromise on quality, and paired programmers are willing to make changes while developing the code. They will remind each other that better quality will save on maintenance.

Although pair programming can be considered as problem identification on a minute-by-minute basis, we also see pair programming as being about defect prevention whereas software inspections are concerned mainly with defect detection. In this way, pair programming is complementary to software inspections.

Pair Pressure. When two programmers are committed to their work and respect each other, in pairs they put a positive form of pressure on each other. The programmers admit to working harder and even more intelligently on programs (Williams and Kessler 2003). They do not want to disappoint their partner. In pair programming, any mistake made by either that causes rework later will burden the teammate.

5.2.2 Money-Led World

Notwithstanding the advantages of the moneyless world, there is one important element missing. It is programming productivity. While other advantages of pair programming are determined, its productivity remains a bit uncertain. Even though we ignore the money, it is still not obvious that pair programming is better than solo programming.

As expected, pair programming has been challenged on the basis of productivity as we need to pay two people for a single job. The question is not whether those advantages that exist in the moneyless world can outweigh concerns about money. We have to justify the productivity of pair programming against solo programming; otherwise, we should consider other ways of programming in the money-led world.

For example, software experts proposed (or rediscovered) alternatives to pair programming such as mutual programming, in which two programmers write their code but mutually inspect and test it (Keefer 2002), and two-person inspections, in which programmers are needed to pair up and inspect their design or code (Bisant and Lyle 1989).

In comparison of these two worlds, pair programming does have many advantages, particularly when we intend to ignore productivity. Unfortunately, we cannot pontificate about paying double for a job that can be done by one programmer.

5.2.3 Economics

Undoubtedly, talented programmers may write a piece of beautiful code that other programmers are just not able to or take much longer to write. These programmers are rare, and for this reason they are expensive. The ideal case is that an application is divided into a number of parts according to the degree of difficulty. The ideal case in terms of economics is expert programmers who are responsible for more difficult tasks and less experienced programmers for easier ones.

In this case, we may expect a quality threshold and we are satisfied with software as long as its quality is higher than that threshold. The implication of this is that for programming modules requiring less skill, we would employ graduate-level developers as long as their salary ratio multiplying total finished time satisfies the condition of minimum cost.

With regard to pair programming, we may ask "Why employ two programmers when the same job can be fairly done by one?" In terms of economics, this question can be answered with the question "Why employ experienced programmers when graduates can do the job?" Since matters of economics are central in pair programming, by "economical" we mean here that programs of an expected quality are produced at the lowest cost.

One pair programming study shows that pairs took longer person-hours than individuals on average but the percentage of pairs passing the test cases was 86% while individuals, 70% (Williams et al. 2000). If software quality were good enough for just 70% of test cases passed, pair programming would not be adopted because it would be uneconomic. The focus of programmer economics is on the production of quality programs at the lowest cost.

5.2.4 Mythical Quality–Time

The focus of programmer productivity is on the production of quality programs as fast as possible. Cost—in our definition of economics—is replaced with time because we consider a fixed salary ratio among all levels of programmer. This makes it clear which programming practice (in pairs or singles) produces better-quality programs most quickly per person. Unfortunately, the two independent constraints, time and quality, cannot be easily understood without a common relationship.

In pair programming, the mythical quality–time has baffled many people who struggle to understand why to pay two people to perform one person's programming. It has been known that pair programming will take around 15–42% person-hours on the same task yet produce a higher-quality program (Williams et al. 2000; Nosek 1998).

Time and quality are not easily exchangeable. Taking a conservative view of time and quality, we may assume that they are not exchangeable. Also, we can always take software quality as a justification for pair programming when quality means everything.

5.2.5 Elapsed Time Accelerated

Suppose we estimate that a program can be done in 10 person-days. The program can easily be broken down into two submodules that are shorter than 10 person-days. Assume that each submodule takes 5 person-days. As long as we have two programmers working in parallel, we can get the program done in 5 days.

We may not be satisfied with that schedule. We would like to continuously divide these two submodules into smaller ones for programming. Eventually, there will be two cases in Figure 5.2:

1. For some submodules, when developers estimate that each submodule is done in less than one day, this can be the optimum size of a

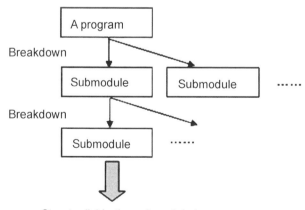

Stop to divide the submodule because:

- the submodule can be finished in a day (or half a day)
- not easy to break down something smaller

FIGURE 5.2   The smaller you divide, the more time you need to think how to divide.

programming task to work, and we will not further divide the submodule.

2. We simply cannot easily divide some submodules into anything smaller for two or more programmers working in parallel. Moreover, we get much more time overheads to think about how to divide when we keep breaking down a submodule further.

Suppose that we manage to break the program down into 10 atomic tasks and each requires one person-day, with enough workforce we stand a chance of getting it done in one day. We may still frown on our efforts because we have yet to deal with how to expedite work on atomic tasks. Can the whole program be completed in less than a day?

In a word, for atomic tasks, pair programming may be a way if we would like to complete them as soon as possible. Pair programming can shorten the total elapsed time. Even though in some case pair programming takes the same time to finish programming exercises as does solo programming (Nawrocki and Wojciechowski 2001), pair programming will not take a longer elapsed time.

In today's market, getting a quality product out as quickly as possible is a competitive advantage that might even mean survival. There is a problem in our analysis for speeding up a software project in reality because we have to consider economics in a money-led world. We will see how to accelerate software projects in the next section.

5.2.6 Critical Path Method

A telecommunication client comes to us and consults about its small mobile computing software project. They want to complete the project sooner than they planned as they have received unannounced information that the competitor may launch its product next month.

The project plan is shown in Figure 5.3 and Table 5.1, in which a project composed of six tasks whose precedence requirements have been planned and whose duration have been estimated.

	Task	1	2	3	4	5	6	7	8	9	10
A	Create database tables for data entry	▓									
B	Implement a login interface		▓								
C	Write interfaces for user enquiry			▓	▓						
D	Produce user reports			▓	▓						
E	Build interfaces for data entry		▓	▓	▓						
F	Perform an integration test							▓	▓	▓	

FIGURE 5.3 Project plan.

TABLE 5.1 Project Specification and Estimation

Task		Duration, weeks	Precedents
A.	Create database tables for data entry	1	—
B.	Implement a login interface	1	A
C.	Write interfaces for user enquiry	2	B
D.	Produce user reports	3	B
E.	Build interfaces for data entry	5	A
F.	Perform an integration test	4	C, E

Naively, we know that if we can cut the elapsed time of every task in half, the 10-week project will be done in 5 weeks. For this reason, we advise the client to do everything in pair programming! However, this does not sound professional to our client.

We quickly ask ourselves which tasks are very relevant to shortening the completion time of the project. In 1957, DuPont developed a technique called *critical path method* (CPM), observing that a task that can be done one day faster will make the project done one day faster. The reverse is also true; a one-day delay in that task will end in the project being delayed by one day.

The CPM involves two steps: (1) *forward pass*, to calculate the earliest date, and (2) *backward pass*, to obtain the latest date. When the earliest date is the same as the latest date, any change at that point will affect the completion time of the whole project.

Starting at week 0, the earliest date to finish task A is week 1. As tasks B and C cannot start until week 1, the earliest dates for task B and task C are weeks 2 and 6, respectively. In a similar fashion, we can calculate all the earliest dates as shown in Figure 5.4. We can see at the endnode that the earliest date to complete the project is week 10.

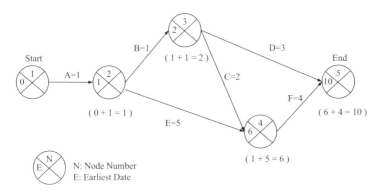

FIGURE 5.4 Forward pass.

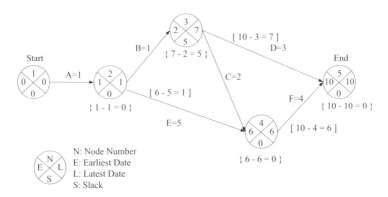

FIGURE 5.5 Backward pass.

The next step is to retime the network starting at the endnode as the latest date. The latest date for the project should be the same as the earliest date, which indicates that the project is done as early as possible. We start at week 10 at the endnode (i.e., node 5). The latest date to start tasks D and F are weeks 7 and 6 without affecting any outcome shown in nodes 3 and 4. In a similar fashion, we complete the diagram, and the results are shown in Figure 5.5.

If task B is finished at week 2 as planned, its subsequent tasks, C and D, can be started as late as at week 7 without any impact on project completion. We have 5 weeks with an empty slot in between, which is called "slack." Saving such time does not help us complete the project earlier. Slack at each node is the difference between the earliest date and the latest date.

To find the critical path, we simply look at the nodes whose slacks are zero. Now all we have to do is assign resources and put time-critical tasks in control. The correlation between CPM and pair programming becomes obvious to us. According to CPM, we advise our client that tasks A, E, and F *must* be done in pair programming, shown in Figure 5.6. If any of their elapsed times are shortened, the project will be completed earlier.

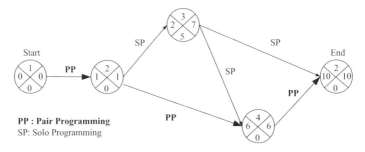

FIGURE 5.6 Tasks on critical path by pair programming.

In this section, we have combined traditional software project management (i.e., CPM) with agile practice (i.e., pair programming). If you are running a project like this, this may be a way to accelerate your project economically.

The critical path method has been questioned by agile project management. As software itself is artificial, most task precedents can be avoided (Robert 2003). For example, we must design before we can begin coding, but coding and design can be developed simultaneously.

5.2.7 Why Two, Not Three: The Antigroup Phenomenon

Many programmers who have been involved in open-source software development may easily believe that more eyeballs are better, a generalization that is often referred to as Linux's law. Have we ever doubted that there can be a case in which, given more eyeballs, the truth just goes a bit far off?

A well-known horse-trading problem by Maier may help to refute the popular myth: "Why pair programming, not triple programming." The horse-trading problem states that "A man bought a horse for $60 and sold it for $70. Then he bought it back for $80 and again sold it for $90." On average individuals normally work out a solution in 3 minutes. However, not all of them can correctly understand the problem and calculate how much the man actually earns.

In 2006 we asked computer science students to solve a horse-trading problem. There is a significant improvement in the average percentage of correctness from solos to pairs. However, from two to "three and four," the percentage of correctness drops. So does "five and six"! How can this happen? Why two? Why not more? The results shown in Figure 5.7 are consistent with sociologists' findings.

When team members provide their answers in turn, which is often the case in small team discussions, rather than by anonymous voting, an

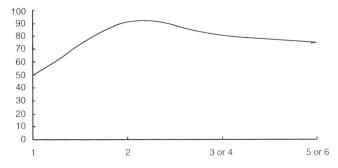

FIGURE 5.7 Three heads are better than one but worse than two.

FIGURE 5.8 Triple programming and antigroup.

individual's decision will be influenced by the degree to which the individual identifies with or sees her/himself as being similar to others. In particular, this happens when the majority starts out with the same answer. The minority will feel less confident of their opinions. Thus, if the majority is holding an incorrect answer, there is a greater likelihood of team errors occurring (Figure 5.8).

In the case of two, there is no majority or minority. And two reaches an optimum in which we always perceive a 50–50 chance on either side. As a consequence, we will give a second thought to a problem. In pair programming, when considerable disagreement arises between two people, the pair may put the problem aside and work on something else. Often, the solution can be around the corner but the pair is simply unable to see it the first time.

5.2.8 Software Requirements Are Puzzles

Understanding software requirements in many cases can be compared to solving puzzles. Puzzles are intentionally designed for the players to work out tricks. Moreover, puzzles sometimes give you a feeling of being almost solved. Many of the tricks are about our perceptions and cultures as well. For example, we will not guess that a gregarious person who talks about many interesting things at a cocktail party is a programmer. We picture programmers as people of few words, or even as introverted.

```
Trans_profit = - 60 + 70
business = business +
Trans_profit
Trans_profit = + 70 - 80
business = business +
Trans_profit
Trans_profit = -80 + 90
business = business +
Trans_profit
Print business
```

FIGURE 5.9   Pseudocode of horse-trading (see also Figure 5.10).

Compare the following two paragraphs. How much are they alike?

1. A man and his son are in a serious car accident. The father is killed, and the son is rushed to the hospital emergency room. On arrival, the attending physician looks at the child and gasps, "This child is my son!" Who is the physician (Gladwell 2005)[3]
2. On the back of an ATM card it says that if your ATM login fails 3 times, the system will not allow further logins. But you just failed once; the system has already blocked any further attempts. How could this happen?[4]

We understand system requirements from a number of users at different levels: from operators to managers. The requirements we collected can often be inconsistent, misleading, incomplete, and ill-defined. If we are lucky, we may notice the problems in the requirements and then ask the users for clarification. However, there can be a case in which we just misunderstand the requirements!

Let us come back to our horse-trading problem. When someone asks us to write a system by giving the requirements as the horse-trading problem, we may finish the problem with a piece of code (see Figure 5.9) and not realize that we have been wrong even at the beginning of writing. Not all programmers can correctly grasp the user requirements as if they thought that they fully understood and surely solved this small horse-trading problem without any need to have a second look. Therefore, users often say to us, "This is not exactly what I want." As discussed in Section 5.2.7, pair programming helps us understand requirements better.

---

[3] *Answer*: The physician is his mother.

[4] *Answer*: The system does not reset a retry counter to zero when you successfully log in the system every time.

```
paid = 60
sold = 70
paid = paid + 80
sold = sold + 90
business = sold - paid
Print business
```

FIGURE 5.10 Pseudocode for horse–pig-trading (compare to Figure 5.9).

Interestingly, once we have really solved a puzzle it is no longer a puzzle. We can reframe the exercise as follows. A man bought a horse for $60 and sold it for $70. Then he bought *a pig* for $80 and sold it for $90. Believe it or not, everyone now can do it right (see Figure 5.10).

5.3 PROGRAMMING TASK DEMANDS

More users today are computer-system-literate and demand a system that has more functions and is easy to use. The system should be flexible to change and could be delivered sooner. On the contrary, programming tasks involve a greater variety of skill sets than before. Unsurprisingly, programmers who do well at one programming task might not be equally good at other programming tasks. In addition, it makes sense that what one person could do in the past may now actually require the combined efforts of two or three people, and hence it is expected that programmers have to closely collaborate to meet such demands.

Software teams that go with agility will work in a different way by writing less technical documents and sharing their thoughts more. However, to optimize the team performance in the context of the task type, we need to properly identify programming task demands.

Other factors such as team motivation and personality traits also affect programming productivity. But, regardless of these factors, we often misunderstand that the productivity effect of teams is the sum of the efforts of members.

Imagine that there would be a team of two programmers who could try their best to contribute project efforts of 2 and 4 units. Let us look at whether their total contribution as a pair can be 6!

5.3.1 2 and 4 Is 6

Tasks or activities that are aggregated can be divisible into a number of subtasks required of members working in the same way. They are classified as

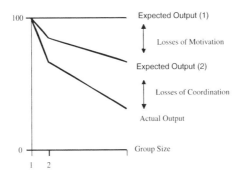

FIGURE 5.11 The Ringelmann effect and steiner analysis.

additive tasks. The group product is the sum of the input of all team members; that it, 2 and 4 is 6. A typical example is rope pulling.

According to the Ringelmann effect, as groups increase in size, they gradually decrease in quantity of output. Steiner then provided an analysis of the Ringelmann effect. The social loafing splits the reduction in output into two segments: motivation loss and coordination loss (see Figure 5.11). However, the productivity effect is better than that of the best member.

In software development, a critical activity is to decide how the whole work can be divided into a number of similar subtasks so that part of development work can be aggregated. For example, how well we can group a number of similar transactions together is so important that subprograms sharing the same coding pattern are grouped together (Figure 5.12). The activity of completing subtasks in the same group is an additive task. However, the activity of dividing tasks into additive subtasks in software development is not aggregated.

5.3.2 2 and 4 Is 4

Problems that require that the truth-wins rule holds are disjunctive. Solving language riddles (e.g., "-gry" riddle) or mathematical puzzles can sometimes

Transaction type	How many tables are involved in this transaction		
	Update	Insert	Select
Sales order	2	3	3
Goods return	2	4	2
Issue invoice	1	1	0

Grouped (Sales order, Goods return)
Grouped (Issue invoice)

FIGURE 5.12 Different transactional operations in the ERP application.

be a eureka task. A "eureka"-type problem has a very limited number of solutions. For example, find an English word ending in "-gry." Two are "angry" and "hungry." What is a third? Thus, in many situations, the highest-performing members of the team are able to compensate for the weaknesses of the other members; that is, 2 and 4 is 4.

Programming involves a number of technical tricks. Harold said he had a number of "aha!" experiences when exploring Java programming tricks (Harold 1997). By common consent, it is difficult to "get" programming problems, but once we have them, they will be either easy or trivial (Bruce 1996).[5]

Many programmers usually take a trial-and-error approach to resolve technical problems. They may take from several minutes to days and eventually discover what the problems really are. Once you know technical problems, you may easily demonstrate both the problems and solutions to your colleagues. Thus, the "truth-supported wins" rule holds, and solving many technical problems is a disjunctive task.

Start a Day

Advances in communications technology now allow us to get help by posting our questions on the Internet. When encountering technical problems, it can be useful to distribute them to each member by email or instant message because many technical questions are disjunctive. Therefore, one recommended practice in agile software development is to have a short, standup meeting before the day starts so that every member can look at problems and suggest quick answers.

5.3.3 2 and 4 Is 3

All members contribute toward estimating uncertainties; this type of task is compensatory, and 2 and 4 is 3. Exemplars of the tasks are the Fermi question: "How many jellybeans fill a one-liter jar?" When each member of a group makes its estimate for the number of beans and the estimates are averaged, the result is more accurate. Thus, the productivity effect is better than most. This case is a bit similar to what we have addressed in the horse-trading problem. The difference is between unnamed and named.

---

[5] "Is there a name for this aha experience?" (http://discuss.fogcreek.com/joelonsoftware/default.asp?cmd=show&ixPost=118430); "Pressing buttons using c#" (http://forums.devshed.com/c-programming-42/pressing-buttons-using-c-322084.html).

Managing software requirements is challenging because in the views of team members they are usually ill-defined. There are three reasons for this: lack of domain knowledge, incomplete requirements, and personal biases.

Domain-knowledge specific is needed to help digest user requirements. For example, ERP developers who have had extensive working experience in retailing systems [e.g., point-of-sales, (POS)] are not considered as being suitable for work as system analysts developing manufacturing applications, although both applications belong to database programming. There is little evidence to suggest that the expertise from one domain (e.g., retailing) is transferable to the other (e.g., manufacturing).

User requirements can be incomplete. Users may have skills to systematically categorize their cases. In addition, the requirements may not be static but changing. Finally, it is possible that the requirements are so fuzzy that there can be many uncertain and exceptional cases to handle.

Requirements are often written in natural language, and hence biases in people can become problematic. This has been mentioned in the horse-trading problem. When it is reframed, the problem becomes a piece of cake.

To some extent programmers have to "guess" what user requirements could be. Thus, in this regard, many tasks in requirements engineering can be compensatory tasks

5.3.4 2 and 4 ≥ 2

Activities that require input from different skills of all team members are conjunctive tasks. Unlike working on additive tasks, each member now performs a different function. When the tasks can be divided into a number of subtasks and each matches member capabilities, the performance of the team is improved. For example, in manufacturing, skilled workers may specialize in particular subtasks on a production line. It appears that a perfect match is difficult, if not impossible, in many cases. Thus, the productivity effect can be said to be only as better than the worst; that is, 2 and 4 is greater than 2.

Once the team decides on the logical separation of a system, we have a problem with whether subtasks are divided in such a way to match individual capabilities or whether individual members are suitably allocated to subtasks. As a result, the overall productivity effect depends on making the right resource allocations.

Often, tasks are not divisible and team performance actually relies on the least competent member. For example, in an assembly line, if one worker works slowly, the whole process is affected. Any assembled component that has been improperly installed will cause the finished product to malfunction. Thus, the productivity effect can only be equal to the worst; that is, 2 and 4 is 2.

The purpose of software integration is to combine two or more programs (or submodules) into one application in which the programs use a common data structure (or database) and interface with each other to exchange data or information. Software integration is similar to the assembly line. Any software module that has a minute defect or is slightly incompatible can crash the system or have hidden errors on it. Thus, software integration is a conjunctive (unitary) task.

Call It a Day

System integration should be done often because the task is unitarily conjunctive. That is to say, the lowest performers have the most impact on overall team performance. Therefore, eXtreme programming encourages continuous integration and throwing away today's code if integration problems cannot be solved before the team calls it a day.

5.3.5   2 and 4 Is Unknown

When the team can decide on how to combine their efforts to solve a problem, the performance accounts for a method they chose (Steiner 1972). For example, how would a team estimate the effort (days) involved in writing an ERP application? Members may determine that programmers who have developed ERP applications before are particularly good at such judgments. An alternative is to average all members' judgments. In either case, judging the programming efforts is a discretionary task. The productivity effect is therefore variable. Thus, two heads are only unpredictably better than one (Kameda and Tindale 2006).

When software teams can decide on how they allocate their resources to design and coding, which is often the case in small teams, this has a tremendous effect on subsequent tasks. For example, software teams can divide a project by system modules or by development phases. In the first case, three application subteams are responsible for sales, warehouse, and finance modules, while in the second case, three development subteams are established for "design and testing," coding, and report writing (see Figure 5.13). The productivity effects in these two cases are different. This kind of task is classified as a discretionary task.

Software development tasks are so complex and interconnected that it is difficult, if not impossible, to strictly classify every programming task into only one or two types of task demand. For example, the tasks of requirements management cannot be easily classified into additive or compensatory. Rather, we discuss key issues and their task demands.

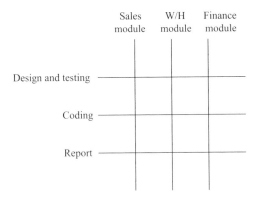

FIGURE 5.13 How we divide development tasks affects structure and productivity of a software team.

Learning real requirements is difficult, and developers may have to speculate about some details in order to develop a model. A divide-and-conquer strategy may seem to accelerate the requirement engineering tasks, but a software team sharing their own opinions stands a bigger chance of correctly identifying real requirements. Because some requirement tasks are compensatory, it is good for all members of a small team to get involved in understanding requirements. In a pair programming study, solo groups and pair groups are often asked to write the same program and to measure the elapsed time. Obviously, the first task is to understand their assignment! Although we do not know how many difficulties there can be between solo groups and pair groups in understanding the assignment at the beginning, assignment interpretation problems do occur in solo groups (Nawrocki and Wojciechowski 2001).

Tasks of design and coding are divisibly conjunctive. Matching people's capabilities to the right tasks is not easy, and hence team productivity is not maximizing. Pair programming with partner rotation compensates for the effect of imperfect matching.

This section helps us understand better why we rarely get 6 from 2 and 4 and when we can organize our team to solve some particular problems according to the task demands.

5.4 PAIR PROGRAMMING IS MORE THAN PROGRAMMING

In software engineering, *formal methods* is a fundamental topic. It provide sets of notations in which to express the initial specification and future design steps toward the final program. Computer-aided software engineering (CASE) software tools help us design, develop, and maintain software. Both are about design. When we have spent a number of hours on working on design using formal methods or CASE, we may wonder how the design can automatically generate executable code, or why we do not design our software just by code so that the design is machine-executable!

5.4.1 Design by Code

Design and coding are intermingled. By *design*, we mean abstraction and semantic algorithm analysis and by *coding*, converting the semantic algorithm analysis into a final executable program in a specific computer language. However, what is programming itself?

The piece of Java code in Figure 5.14 illustrates that the design of an ATM system has had the following four classes: UserSession, User, ATM and Bank, which respectively handle the session's options, user information and security, a menu of possible types of ATM transaction, and bank accounts.

Writing lines 11, 12, 14, and 15 in Figure 5.14 can be compared with solving a deduction problem that requires working out a logical model that describes what we understand about the problem (see Figure 5.15).

Certainly, programming is more than a deduction problem. Looking at lines 01, 04, 05, and 10 in Figure 5.14, we also need to work out a problem of another kind, namely, one about analysis of a flowchart, required in every programming design (see Figure 5.16).

The difference between a deduction problem and a procedural algorithm is a matter of sequential relationships. We may reverse the deduction problems; for example, solving a problem "A B C _?_" is the same as

```
01 if UserSession.checkAlreadyLogin()  return ATM.Error( NOLOGIN );
02 UserSession.selectedOption =
03    ATM.displayOptions(User.authorityLevel);
04 switch(UserSession.selectedOption)
05 {
05    case _ENQUIRY:
06    {
07       ATM.Display(Bank.Balance(User.account));
08       return 1;
09    };
10    case _WITHDRAWL:
11    if ( User.balance >0 and User.requestedAmount <
12      ATM.availableCash )
13    {
14      if(User.balance  > 0 and User.requestedAmount <
15        User.balance )
16      {
17        ATM.processWithdraw();
18      }
19    };
20 };
```

FIGURE 5.14 Automated teller machine (ATM) system.

User.Account.balance > 0 and User.requestedAmount _?_ ATM.availableCash
                                      Or
User.Account.balance > 0 and User.requestedAmount _?_ User.balance

What is ''?''

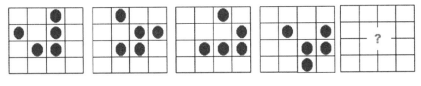

                                      Or
                                  A B C _?_

What is ''?''

FIGURE 5.15 Deduction problem.

" _?_ B C D"; "(statement A) and (statement B)" will be the same as "(statement B) and (statement A)."

However, if we reverse the order of a procedural algorithm as in Figure 5.16 "inquiry → select options → _?_," the possible answer can be "inquiry" again or "withdraw money" rather than "log in." Artificial intelligence tells us that solving both kinds of problem faster is an exploration in a searching space (Luger and Stubblefield 1989) and a pair is able to explore more programming design alternatives than are two individuals working separately (Flor and Hutchins 1991).

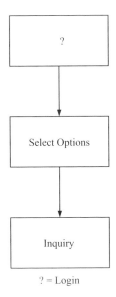

FIGURE 5.16 Procedural algorithm.

If we go ahead doing design by code, programmers are simultaneously thinking about requirement comprehension, deduction problems, procedural algorithms, scripting, code reading, and so on every minute. A team of programmers paired up should rise to the challenge.

Another challenge for design by code is readability. Since there are few design documents for software maintenance, code reading becomes the only way we can maintain the software. In the end, we have to pay the cost for programming source that is hard to read. Scripts written by two persons should be much more readable than scripts written by an individual. Although the term *code readability* is often used in agile software development, what it means in programming is that writing code is better explained by exploiting depictability and consistency. For example, getSalary() is more easily depicted than Salary(). In short, if you are doing design by code, go for pair programming!

Design by code was not so possible in the old days. Many old version compilers do not support us in writing virtual functions or dynamic data structure. Not until the emergence of object-oriented programming in the early 1990s were computer languages developed in a way that we understand in today's world. Class inheritance, polymorphisms, and other concepts have now allowed us to do design by code.

5.4.2 Pair Design

We once paired with a smart guy who acted as an observer. The system we wrote had a variety of business logic, and the guy was lost in what we were doing several times! He blamed himself for his distraction. And we gave him a humorous reply: "You are not Stephen Hawking."

Hawking is a genius mathematician and theoretical physicist but unfortunately suffers from motor neuron disease (amyotrophic lateral sclerosis) and has been severely disabled. How can Hawking have something to do with pair programming? But, surely we are not joking.

Studying physical cosmology involves lots of understanding of advanced mathematics,[6] and your best companion is always pencil and paper. Even though equations are given step-by-step in print, we still need pencil and

---

[6] For those programmers who forgot how difficult the mathematics in advanced physics can be, here is the linearized Einstein equation (Wald ; 1984), and we really need pencil and paper to help ourselves out to understand where it comes from and where it will go:

$$G_{ab}^{(1)} = -\frac{1}{2}\partial^c\partial_c\bar{\gamma}_{ab} + \partial^c\partial_{(b}\gamma_{a)c} - \frac{1}{2}\eta_{ab}\partial^c\partial^d\bar{\gamma}_{cd} = 8\pi T_{ab}$$

paper to understand the logic and work out the calculation. It is very difficult, and for many people simply impossible, to just watch (i.e., read) and think (i.e., do the calculation mentally).

In pair programming, the driver controls the keyboard and mouse and her eyeballs fix on what she writes and she may at any time talk to her partner about what she is writing. It is however, rare, to be writing code and be explaining another part of code finished yesterday that has been on screen. In this regard, the observer may be just doing the same thing that the driver is doing, fixing his eyeballs on what the driver is typing and narrowly thinking about the code on the screen. Anything not on the screen will be out of mind! Of course, this kind of pair programming is not good for design by code. In spite of this, not many programmers can watch the lines on screen but at the same time see a wider picture and strategically think and quest for better ways. In fact, this has nothing to do with their programming capabilities! If we cannot help paired programmers do a better job of pair design, for some paired programmers, design is dead!

Bring pen and paper with you (Figure 5.17). This is our advice. The partner now is more than watching. He will still look at the screen but can now jot points down and sketch a flowchart to strategically look at a bigger design picture. This is an effective way for many programmers who are not yet used to pair programming or are not good at "watch code and think design."

FIGURE 5.17 Bring your pencil and paper with you to pair.

5.4.3 Rhythmic Pair Programming

Well, it seems a bit odd as we have one subsection in this chapter to discuss development rhythms. With a good understanding of what pair programming is, we will have few difficulties adopting pair programming rhythmically. Moreover, software development rhythms are not practices; they reveal when the practices work and when they are used so that the practices deliver value to programmers and software writing in the workplace.

Now let us consider two situations: a team that has just one pair so that the pair cannot exchange its partner, which is referred to as "single pair programming," and a team that has more than one pair, which is referred to as "team pair programming." In fact, team pair programming can become single pair programming when no pair in a team decides to exchange partners.

As for single pair programming, there is no partner exchange, only role exchange. When to exchange role in a pair is less critical as two programmers are working closely together. Either of two programmers in a pair may volunteer to assume a particular role. According to one study, we have a higher length of concentration in the first 30–60 minutes while just listening and watching. Thus, every time a pair has a short tea break, they should consider changing their roles. However, changing roles has nothing to do with the problem that the pair is working on. The pair is still collaborating on the same programming task before or after their roles are exchanged. When the pair has fully shared their ideas and figured out a good solution (i.e., when there is no need to think of an alternative), the driver will be just watching how her partner writes code. Therefore, single pair programming is easy to start but not easy to sustain (see Figure 5.18).

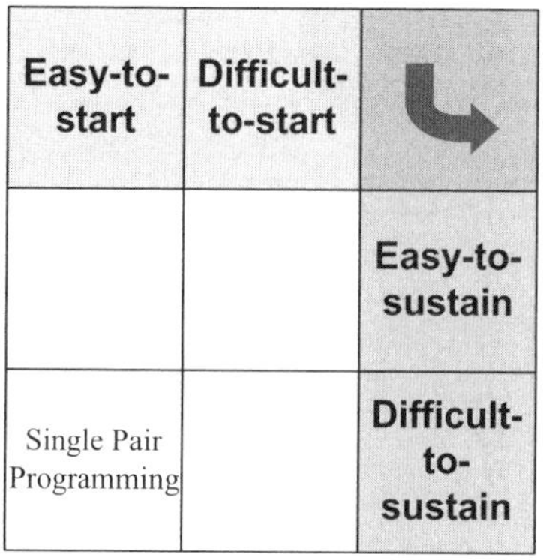

Easy-to-start	Difficult-to-start	⤵
		Easy-to-sustain
Single Pair Programming		Difficult-to-sustain

FIGURE 5.18 Pair programming for a team that has only two programmers.

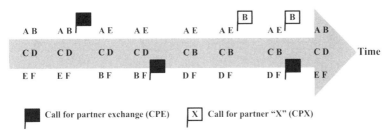

■ Call for partner exchange (CPE)	[X] Call for partner "X" (CPX)

FIGURE 5.19   Walk along time to see the rhythm of partner exchange.

In contrast to single pair programming, team pair programming allows pairs to rotate their partners. In this situation, some programmers will have to think out and work on new problems. As discussed in Section 5.3.5, there is some variation in the productivity effects in pairs that can make their own judgments on how to organize their work. Two and four is unknown. The right timing of partner changes is very important. If we have not rotated the partner for some time, we will simply find ourselves back again with single pair programming. Therefore, to ensure team pair programming productivity, more guidelines should be explicitly given to less experienced, paired teams, in particular, on when to change partners. We do not expect less experienced programmers to organize and do pair programming by themselves.

Pair programming is a way to achieve design by code. The moment a pair has reached a rough design, they should consider partner rotation. This maximizes our chance to let other team members improve our design, thereby removing design defects as early as possible.

A pair that is ready for a partner exchange may have to wait for another pair to be ready. Then, the pair calls for a partner exchange (CPE) by showing a sign card (or a flag, etc.) to the other pair. The idea of signaling to other colleagues or parties where we are is similar to *kanban*,[7] which is the means through which just-in-time (JIT) and "lean" manufacturing are managed. Next, any other pair that has roughly planned out what it will do for its task and is about to exchange partners will rotate its partner with a pair with a sign card displayed (see Figure 5.19).

Often, we may change an agreed-on rough design with a new partner. Once that happens, we have to call our previous partner (CPX) to confirm the

---

[7] *Kanban* is a Japanese word meaning a mechanism using story cards to signal the need for a particular item.

FIGURE 5.20 Rhythmic pair programming.

change (see Figure 5.19). There can also be a situation where two partners agree on the design but a third partner does not. However, your coding should have almost done a lot. Depending on how good the third partner's idea may be, we may either discard the existing code or discuss it in a standup meeting.

If you walk through spacetime, you will see how CPE and CPX interplay in Figure 5.19! Although the diagram looks complicated, the rhythm is simple (Figure 5.20).

Rhythmic pair programming tells us to exchange a partner when a pair has reached a rough design and call for an ex-partner exchange when a pair has revised what has been agreed to by the ex-partner.

This rhythm is good for small software teams and only for team pair programming. When the teams become familiar with this rhythm, it is not necessary to use any sign cards, nor is there any need to mechanically play out the rhythm. Many experienced pairs will know when they should change their partners and when they should pair off with their old buddies again. Rhythmic pair programming is easy to start and easy to sustain (see Figure 5.21).

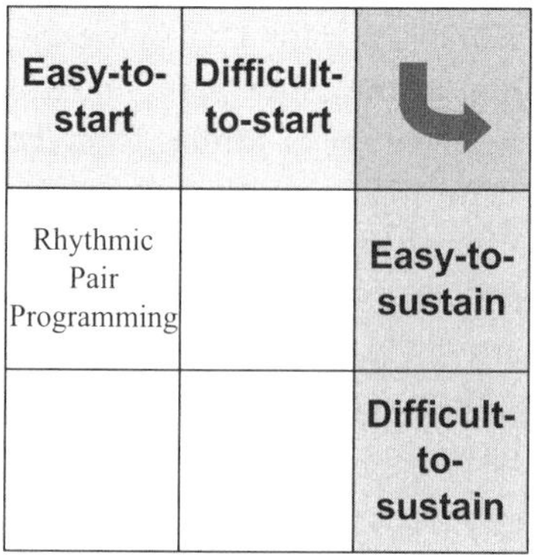

	Easy-to-start	Difficult-to-start	
	Rhythmic Pair Programming		Easy-to-sustain
			Difficult-to-sustain

FIGURE 5.21 In–out diagram for rhythmic pair programming.

5.5   PAIR PROGRAMMING TEAM COACHED

The productivity effect is variable, for pair programming teams as well as for self-organizing teams. Although we should trust that the pair programming team and the members will organize their work best (Schwaber and Beedle 2002), as far as we understand that, the tasks of decisions on design and coding are so discretionary that the team should systematically adopt a way of pair programming.

Here is a summary of some guidelines on coaching pair programming teams:

Principle 1. When adopting pair programming in conventional project management, we have to identify time-critical tasks and shorten them (see Section 5.2.6).

Principle 2. In pair programming, asking your partner open-ended questions minimizes your influence on him/her when you want advice, not consent. For example, how long will it take for others to understand the code? Instead, is it readable? (see Section 5.2.7).

Principle 3. A pair should resolve conflicts by postponing decisions; leave them for a while and let them rethink before deciding to ask for help from others (Section 5.2.7).

Principle 4. Ensure that the requirements are fully understood. Although pair programming results in fewer errors in requirement comprehension, mistakes of this kind will cost much more than in solo programming (Sections 5.2.8 and 5.3.3).

Principle 5. Team members who work in pairs with partner rotation should meet in a short, standup meeting in the morning (Section 5.3.2).

Principle 6. The purpose of the standup meeting is to solve tricky technical problems. Don't rely on each pair to individually work out solutions to them. Remember that 2 and 4 is still 4 (Section 5.3.2).

Principle 7. During the standup meeting, if there is a need to collect opinions from the participants, they should give feedback in descending order of their confidence or experience (Section 5.2.7).

Principle 8. To ensure that paired programmers are making efforts that make the project move forward, continuous integration is necessary (Section 5.3.4).

Principle 9. Bring your pencil and paper with you to pair (Section 5.4.2).

Principle 10. Exchange your partner when a pair has reached a design solution and call for an ex-partner exchange when the design solution has been revised (Section 5.4.3).

We have yet to discuss pair programming productivity, although in looking for software development rhythms, we have come to see that productivity levels for single pair programming and team pair programming are very different. Exploring productivity in *single pair programming* will open more issues than we expect. Will the productivity rise and then drop along the development time if a paired team develops an application with unchanged requirements adopting pair programming practice? Will the productivity of novice–novice pairs be the same as that of expert–expert pairs? Will triple programming (sometimes called *triplet programming*) be just as productive as or less productive than pair programming? Chapter 6 deals with the productivity of single pair programming. Most importantly, we consider the situation in which single pair programming can be productive.

This chapter presents the work in the group's rhythm as a unit. However, we should be mindful of the natural ebb and flow of people's motivation. In addition, groups take time to gel. Once the group reaches its stage of high productivity, provided it is given positive feedback, it can often remain in that stage for a long period of time. Chapter 7 discusses the rhythm of the groups and how they usually go through four phases of productivity, followed by reduced productivity.

REFERENCES

Bisant D and Lyle J. A two-person inspection method to improve programming productivity. *IEEE Transactions on Software Engineering* 1989; **15** (10):1294–1304.

Bruce K. Thoughts on computer science education. *ACM Computing Surveys* 1996; **28A** (4).

Carr NG. IT doesn't matter. *Harvard Business Review* 2003; **81** (5):41–49.

Cockburn A and Williams L. The costs and benefits of pair programming. *Proceedings of First International Conference on Extreme Programming and Flexible Processes in Software Engineering*, Cagliari, Sardinia, Italy, June 2000.

Constantine LL. *Constantine on Peopleware*. Englewood Cliffs, NJ: Yourdon Press; 1995.

DeMacro T and Lister T. *Peopleware: Productive Projects and Teams*. New York: Dorset House; 1987.

Flor NV and Hutchins E. Analyzing distributed cognition in software teams: A case study of team programming during perfective software maintenance. In: Koenemann-Belliveau J, Moher T, and Robertson S, editors. *Empirical Studies of Programmers: Fourth Workshop*. Norwood, NJ: Ablex; 1991.

Gladwell M. *Blink: The Power of Thinking without Thinking*. New York: Little, Brown; 2005.

Gödel K. Ontological proof. In: Feferman S, Dawson JW, Goldfarb W, Parsons C, and Solovay R, editors. *Collected Works: Unpublished Essays & Lectures*, Vol III, New York: Oxford University Press; 1995, pp. 403–404.

Hansen J. Music enhances reasoning. In: Hoffman B, editor. *Encyclopedia of Educational Technology*. 2001; retrieved Sept. 1, 2006, from `http://coe.sdsu.edu/eet/Articles/mozarteffect/start.htm`.

Harold ER. *Java Secrets*. Foster City, CA: IDG Books Worldwide; 1997.

Kameda T and Tindale RS. Groups as adaptive devices: Human docility and group aggregation mechanisms in evolutionary context. In: Schaller M, Kenrick DT, and Simpson JA, editors. *Evolution and Social Psychology*. New York: Psychology Press; 2006.

Keefer G. Extreme programming considered harmful for reliable software. *Proceedings of the 6th Conference on Quality Engineering in Software Technology*, 2002, pp. 129–141.

Luger G and Stubblefield W. *Artificial Intelligence and the Design of Expert Systems*. Benjamin/Cummings: 1989.

Nawrocki J and Wojciechowski A. Experimental evaluation of pair programming, *Proceedings of the 12th European Software Control and Metrics Conference*, 2001, pp. 269–276.

Nosek JT. The case for collaborative programming. *Communications of the ACM* 1998; **41** (3):105–108.

Robert M. *Agile Software Development: Principles, Patterns, and Practices*. Upper Saddle River, NJ: Prentice Hall; 2003.

Schwaber K and Beedle M. *Agile Software Development with Scrum*. Upper Saddle River, NJ: Prentice Hall; 2002.

Stasser G and Dietz-Uhler B. Collective choice, judgment and problem solving. In: Hogg MA and Tindale S, editors. *Blackwell Handbook of Social Psychology: Group Processes:* Oxford: Blackwell; 2001, pp. 31–55.

Steiner ID. *Group Process and Productivity*. New York: Academic Press:1972.

Tan G, Gallo PB, and Jacobs GM. Using cooperative learning to integrate thinking and information technology in a content-based writing lesson. *The Internet TESL Journal* 1999; **5** (8).

Wald RM. *General Relativity*. Chicago: University of Chicago Press; 1984.

Williams L and Kessler R. *Pair Programming Illuminated Reading*. Reading, MA: Addison-Wesley; 2003.

Williams LA, Kessler RR, Cunningham W, and Jeffries R. Strengthening the case for pair programming. *IEEE Software* 2000; **17** (4):19–25.

6

REPEAT PROGRAMMING

One day to build a piccolo, and two days for two.
One minute to cook an egg, and one minute for two.
One week to write a piece of code, but never think
of writing the same twice?

A shocking experiment, known as the *Stanford prison experiment*, which was terminated when it went out of control 6 days into its planned 2 weeks, was designed to investigate what happens when good people (students) are put in an evil place (Zimbardo 1971). After three decades, two professors, Haslam and Reicher (2002), re-created aspects of the same experiment to investigate how decent people (nonstudents) in a mock prison could behave with malice. Ultimately, some may express surprise that people could behave as badly as they did given such trivial stimuli. Although there were many differences between two experiments in terms of mock prison conditions, interrupts for TV confessionals, and known being videotaped all the time, both experiments appear to entail that, rather than arising from anything inherent in the individual personalities involved, it is the situation that dominates the participants' bad behavior. Every angel in the hell[1] becomes a sort of Lucifer—and it does not matter how you run the prison experiment. The prison experiment will always cause good people to act in evil ways.

The prison experiment stimulates our thinking about the relationships between experiments, software practices, and programmers. How can we

[1]The term *Lucifer effect* was coined by Professor Zimbardo (2007).

Software Development Rhythms: Harmonizing Agile Practices for Synergy
By Kim Man Lui and Keith C. C. Chan
Copyright © 2008 John Wiley & Sons, Inc.

reproduce programming experiments of a particular type and reach consistent findings regardless of individual human capabilities, team cultures, and human emotions?

In pair programming, some people support pair programming productivity by controlled experiments. Others question whether pair programming productivity is still valid in the workplace as such experiments by students in academic environments never cross the line between writing to study and working to live.[2] Later, we will realize that either pair programming or solo programming is too extreme. As so often happens, the truth lies in between. Thus, alternatives of pair programming could be side-by-side collaboration on a software maintenance task (Flor 1998), side-by-side programming (Cockburn 2005) and reviews (Müller 2004), and some experiments conducted to juxtapose them with pair programming.

Now no one needs to scratch one's head over pair programming (PP) against solo programming (SP); everyone is comfortable, at least psychologically, to say that pair programming is good but side-by-side programming (or reviews) is even better (see Figure 6.1 for all three types). To celebrate our achievements, everyone gives a yell of delight and opens a bottle of whisky. While swirling the hooch and before saying cheers, there is a collective expression as everyone recalls the last time we drank to forget troubles. Does whisky "always" mean celebration? We are unconsciously brought to another maze: Is pair programming (or side-by-side programming, reviews, etc.) "always" better than solo programming?"

"When does pair programming work best?" is not a good question. The challenge is to demonstrate to people who have never tried and/or have been skeptical about pair programming when pair programming can be significantly productive. More importantly, it helps synthesize one interesting rhythm:

$$PP \sim SP \sim PP \sim SP \cdots PP$$

This chapter could be a little academic! To unlock the secret of pair programming and to discover that rhythm, we have to adopt a much more rigorous approach to pair programming. We will come back to the practical applications in Section 6.3. Bear in mind that pair programming in this chapter means *team pair programming* in general and *single pair programming* in particular.

---

[2]As the students know that they are being studied, their tendency may be to act differently. This is the *Hawthorne effect*.

FIGURE 6.1 The evolution of solo programming, pair programming, and side-by-side programming.

6.1 CONTROVERSIES IN PAIR PROGRAMMING

The basic idea of pair programming rests on a time-honored and superficially straightforward assumption—two heads are better than one. However, pair programming has always been controversial. In reality, pair programming is simply a way of teaming in which two programmers collaborate on the design, coding, and testing of a piece of software. It's an approach that supports skills transfer, job rotation, and more creative approaches. On the surface, it seems as uncontroversial as any type of teamwork. So why is it controversial?

Well, like so many things, it's all about money. Many people question the economy of pair programming: Why pay double to do just one job? Interestingly, pair programming is much more than our intuition tells us. It is a problem with passion and belief. We shall discuss three questions that we think have been pretty heavily challenged on the Internet and, surprisingly, none of them is about money.

6.1.1 Is Programming a Unique Work?

Many adherents of eXtreme programming (XP) push to try pair programming, to become familiar with its advantages and its practices. But project managers and inspectors who know little about programming or have not programmed for a long time won't understand why pair programming is better. It will be apparent to them that it would increase the cost of a project. To determine whether pair programming is good, such managers can only listen to other people's comments. Supporters will say "pair programming is effective, and people have proven it by experiment! But, if you're still not sure, they may at last recommend that the simplest way is to have a try!"

It's a very interesting phenomenon that the nature of programming seems to be overemphasized—it's so challenging that we need two people to do the same work (i.e., design, code, test, and integrate) together! Is there any work in the world that has the same characteristics as computer programming?

If not, then is there any work besides programming that is best done in pairs? Teaching—team teaching—may be one area, and we note that students can learn better and faster if they are paired. But are teaching, learning, and working three different things?

Who else works in pairs? Police and pilots work in pairs for *safety*, and in this they do the same work but play different roles—good cop–bad cop, driver and navigator/observer, for example. But the pair work of physicians, teachers, and engineers is not necessarily *better* than their individual work. And why are there only pair programmers, but no pair engineers, pair managers, or pair editors? Is programming more challenging than the tasks of these other jobs?

6.1.2 Are Three Minds Better than Two?

If two minds are better than one, are three better than two? We have discussed the antigroup phenomenon in Section 5.2.7. When two people of a group of three firmly believe that they have worked out a good solution, the third person may just either follow them or be persuaded into favoring that solution, even though that solution is in fact the worst. However, this cannot be used to conclude that triple programming is antiproductive as triple programming does not mean three programmers sitting together to vote on how to program!

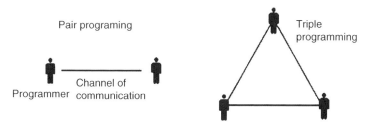

FIGURE 6.2 The number of communication channels increases to 3 when the number of programmers is increased by 1.

In education, research into the effectiveness of pair learning relative to group learning has shown that group learning could be more effective than pair learning. Well, if it makes sense to place two people on one computer, why not put three or four people on one computer? The defense of pairing relies on certain hard-to-prove claims about better quality, knowledge sharing, and collaboration. All of these claims support tripling and quadrupling in addition to pairing.

Intuitively, the argument that triple, quadruple, or quintuple programming is relatively unproductive is too obvious to need proof. Oddly, Williams and Kessler (2003) mentioned triple programming—the collaboration of three very experienced, mature, responsible programmers (using a single computer) can provide a solution to a very tough problem. An effective triplet was once used at Bell Labs; one person who represents the customer thinks out aloud, one at the whiteboard works on design, and one controls the keyboard.

Stephens and Rosenberg (2003) then argued that two or more people results in slower communication and decisionmaking because there's more than one channel of communication. Increasing the number of communication channels decreases the productivity of programming (Figure 6.2).

The argument that pair programming is more productive than solo programming and other multiple programming arrangements has yet to be proved experimentally. However, if we assume that there are relationships between pair programming and triple programming, then an experiment that can show that pair programming is efficient should also validate triple programming.

6.1.3 Unreplicable Experiments

The best way to deal with these controversies would be to conduct an experiment. It should be a simple matter to compare the productivity of a pair of programmers and a solo programmer. Just invite some programmers to take part in an experiment, divide them into a pair programming group and a solo programming group, and then ask them to write the same program so that their results can be directly compared. Such an experiment appears at least intuitively valid and would also appear to be easy to conduct. But that isn't so.

People have done these experiments, but they have clarified little as different people have conducted similar experiments and produced very different, apparently incompatible results (Nosek 1998; Williams et al. 2000; Nawrocki and Wojciechowski 2001; Arisholm et al. 2007). Yet the results are far from being in agreement and sometimes contradict each other. It may well be that pair programming is productive under some conditions and not under others, but that the difference in the conditions was not accounted for or made explicit.

Interestingly, despite the uncertainty around these results, proponents and opponents on every side have tried to exploit them. Supporters of eXtreme programming claim that pair programming is a practice proved by academic experiments. Naturally, their opponents challenge it by pointing out the discrepancies between those experiments.

If all of these experiments were conducted with care, seriously, and without artificial error, then only two assumptions would be left to us: (1) either the productivity of pair programming measured by controlled experiments is always uncertain[3] or (2) we have not yet looked at the right variables that can produce consistent results.

Before there was any detailed research into pair programming, the only controversy was over cost, because it meant paying for two programmers. Research into pair programming raised more issues than it solved, issues beyond money, such as unique work, multiple programming, and unrepeatable experiments. The more research we've done on pair programming, the more controversy we've seen.

6.2 REPEAT PROGRAMMING

Many experimental situations in software development are not representative. Even using the same assessment method for different subjects and problems may produce a variety of results. Often, time alone can be deceiving.

---

[3]We feel that there is nothing wrong with the existence of uncertainty in our world, although Einstein said that God does not play dice.

Different programmers might solve different problems at different speeds so it is hard to convince anyone to select 10 or a 100 programmers out of millions of programmers around the world and put them in front of low-complexity problems in straightforward development environments.

That is not to say that programming situations do not have certain common features. There exist certain intrinsic properties regardless of the complexity of the problem, the profession, the personnel, or environments, in the same way that the sum of the internal angles of a triangle is 180 regardless of the triangle's size and shape.[4] These intrinsic properties are what we set out to test as we sought to answer one fundamental question: How can we demonstrate when pair programming is most productive?

Many project managers will be familiar with the following experience. A new programmer comes onto the team. This guy is new to the problems that the team is working on and has not written anything similar before, so initially he takes a week to complete a program. He continues to work on other problems of that type, and soon he can write them faster and better even starting from scratch and without looking back at his previous code. After 3 months he is a master at coding that problem and he can finish a program of that type in one day, but that is the limit of his improvement, that is, there is a point at which it is nearly impossible for him to finish the job sooner.

We now look at a slightly more complicated case. In pair programming, we have two scenarios: novice–novice and expert–expert. A novice–novice pair, two newcomers working as in pair programming, may complete a program in less than a week. In this scenario, we assume that there will be $x\%$ time reduction. By intuition, we know that 50% is the breakeven point since there are two people.

In another scenario, after three months of these two people working on the same kind of problem, we put one of them with an experienced colleague as in pair programming for collaboration. This is an expert–expert pair, at least with regard to the kind of problem they have already mastered. Hypothetically, as a pair they should work $y\%$ faster.

We do not think that we can differentiate the values of x and y. Therefore, the figures are meaningless. Well! Nothing interesting can be found until we put x and y together! Relationships like dx/dy[5] could be something

---

[4]Strictly speaking, the sum of the internal angles in a triangle is 180 in space whose intrinsic curvature is 0. Whether the intrinsic curvature is 0 constitutes the difference between Newton mechanics and relativism.

[5] To ensure accuracy, we should be interested in d^2x/d^2y, which measures the change of curvature.

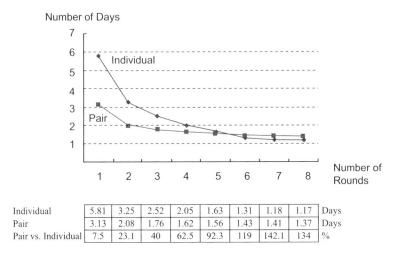

Number of Days

FIGURE 6.3   Repeat programming: a pair versus an individual.[6]

Individual	5.81	3.25	2.52	2.05	1.63	1.31	1.18	1.17	Days
Pair	3.13	2.08	1.76	1.62	1.56	1.43	1.41	1.37	Days
Pair vs. Individual	7.5	23.1	40	62.5	92.3	119	142.1	134	%

that throws a light on answering when pair programming can be adopted for the maximum of its productivity or when a pair outperforms two individuals.

An experiment called "repeat programming" examines how pair programming performance varied when measured along an axis in which developers become more familiar with a programming problem by repeatedly writing the same program several times. By holding some variables in each situation relatively constant, we can see variation in others. We keep one aspect of the human variable constant so that we can see how task solution time varies with problem repetition.

Figure 6.3 shows how long the individual and the pair took to write the same program on each occasion. The two curves are similar as both are hyperbolic descending. The trend is far more noteworthy and meaningful than the values indicated by the curves. It is a little unrealistic to claim to have three programmers with nearly equivalent skills, knowledge, and ability. There has to be a certain amount of variation between them. Programmers with different abilities can produce different sets of results. However, it makes less difference whether a value is 5.8 or 6.8 days on any one round because what we are interested in is the pattern in each round, which is

[6]The percentage in the table is calculated by

$$\frac{(finish\_time\_of\_pair) \times 2 - (finish\_time\_of\_individual)}{finish\_time\_of\_individual} \times 100\%.$$

illustrated in the slope of the curves and how they cross. In short, the trend of the curve remains consistent. The characteristic is conservative and is independent of whether they are fast or slow coders, or talented or weak programmers.

To apply repeat programming out of the laboratory with confidence, we have to fully exploit the rigor of repeat programming. Here are several major issues in human–computer studies:

- *Human Intelligence*. The theory of multiple intelligences by Gardner (1993, 1997) states the fact that people can be intelligent in various ways. So often, we are more competent in one task or ability than in others. This suggests that intellectual strengths are not faithfully reflected in high intelligence test scores. Thus, experiments can be much more controlled to observe how people can master the same programming task in different situations rather than to measure them in pairs writing different programs. This is compatible with our current understanding of the theory of human intelligence.

- *People Distribution*. During the early 1990s, the MIT Blackjack Team beat the casinos by card-counting techniques that allowed the team to know when there were more high-value cards than low-value cards left in the deck(s). It worked as long as they knew how many kings and queens were in one deck and they could track every hand. In the same way, knowing how many novices and experts are in a group of programmers is essential in pair programming. We have to take a combination of people skills into account; otherwise, we are just finding the average of the productivity of the most frequent pairs among novice–novice, novice–expert, and expert–expert.

- *Born to Program*. When it comes to pair programming, there are at least three kinds of combinations: novice–expert, novice–novice, and expert–expert. Understanding how the last two work is more difficult. The reason is that, on the basis of our total of 25 years' experience, novice programmers may never become experts. They may only become better mediocre programmers. On the other hand, experts may already be experts during their student days. Thus, "repeat programming" does not merely refer to an experiment but to a model for understanding how people who are new to programming become expert at it. More precisely, we are modeling novice–novice and experienced–experienced pairs, rather than expert–expert. We presume that experienced programmers able to select a best solution from other solutions that they already knew before, while expert programmers not only are experienced but also have the ability to improve a solution from nothing.

BOX 6.1

EXPERIMENT (2004): REPEAT PROGRAMMING

The repeat programming experiment is conducted in two steps: select "nearly capable" subjects and write the same program repeatedly.

By choosing "nearly capable" subjects, we minimize a disparity in programming ability that, between the best and the worst, can greatly vary. In 2004, from among 63 candidates we selected *three* whose abilities were the most nearly capable. This was done by testing the candidates on several programming exercises. Whether their programs were good or bad was not an issue.

We split these three into an individual and a pair. To get a taste of how pair programming works for them, they were asked to write warmup exercises. We also suggested that in cases where conflicts arose they should be resolved by the decision falling to the one controlling the keyboard/mouse. The subjects fully understood that dispute and self-assertion would reduce productivity and run counter to the objective of the experiment.

The subjects, the individual and the pair, were asked to write a first-in first-out (FIFO) warehouse application in our laboratory. The tasks were standard—they had to create tables in SQL 2000 and code in JSP. The subjects worked 8 hours a day. The time was measured in day units in order to avoid confusion over nonstop working hours. The subjects worked on consecutive days. In Figure 6.3, one day is 8 hours.

In the experiment, subjects' programs had to pass 756 test cases. The cases included (1) application requirements, (2) load tests, and (3) exceptional handlings such as power-off during a long transaction. These three types of measurement were appropriate because (1) we could objectively measure the quality by testing rather than by relying on human graders and (2) from a customer perspective, users (i.e., customers) would be more satisfied with software products that had been extensively examined by these three types of test and would regard the products as being of a high quality. Developers and customers tend to see software quality differently.

All the programs submitted by the subjects had to pass 756 test cases. It was unlikely that subjects would be able to pass all 756 test cases at the first attempt. The more test cases, the less likely would it be for one program to be of very high quality, while the other would be merely good enough to pass the tests. Thus, the subjects needed to test the cases in an iterative manner in order to get through them. This way, software quality could be maintained constant.

On the first round of programming, the individual completed the program in a bit less than 6 days (5.8 days). Predictably, the second round he did it much faster. The result is shown in Figure 6.3.

6.2.1 Variances

Repeat programming (Box 6.1) confirms the results of past experiments that independently reported that pairs require 15%, 42% or 100% longer than individuals (Nosek 1998; Williams et al 2000; Nawrocki and Wojciechowski 2001). It does not matter what the value we get each time by experiment but how those values are correlated. According to the descriptions of their experiments, the difficulty of programming problems for subjects was different in each experiment. In Nawrocki's experiment, subjects were asked to write programs for finding the mean and standard deviation of samples of numerical data. This is regarded as an easy job for university students with majors in computer science. Thus, the result of this case can be reflected in the late round in repeat programming and shows that pair programming is inefficient.

STOP! Repeat programming appears to be too academic to be practical. It is neither a software practice nor a management theory; it is just a controlled experiment. We are keenly interested in which agile practices deal with rapid changing requirements or how we can avoid pitfalls of developing software so that we do a better job, rather than in the psychology of programming and empirical software engineering! You really think so, and we cannot agree with you more. But please hold on!

One day, we have another experience-based principle, namely, eXtreme programming tells us not to work on tomorrow's design, and we always anticipate changes. This sounds like the opposite of what we learned in the past. On second thought, eXtreme programming emphasizes dealing with rapid changing requirements; our adoption for projects without fixed requirements makes sense.

Unfortunately, before project managers meet eXtreme programming, they may be unaware of changing requirements and rigidly apply the old principle for every project. It is expected that these managers will complain about the users who changed the agreed-on requirements. There is no experience-based principle for all software projects. Along with bad things comes good news. New lessons and enhanced principles from experience put software development into perspective time after time. All we need to do is sacrifice more of our family time for reading and differentiate them from our old principles.

Principles deduced from experiments can be different. Ideally, they should be widely applicable as long as certain conditions addressed in the experiments are met. They are proved by scientific experiments with statistically accurate results. Perhaps we just do not realize that many experiments in software engineering are merely good for reference. Reproducing the previous results may not be so straightforward owing to inherent complexity and changes of technology. Thus, we should always bear in mind that references are from Mars and principles are from Venus. What we have learned can be just experiment-based references!

The characteristics of repeat programming utilize matching instead of randomization, and time-series analysis. In this sense, repeat programming is a quasi-experiment; not a true experiment. However, the experiment is rigorous as mentioned before and it is reproducible. In 2005 we were able to reproduce repeat programming with a large sample size (Lui and Chan 2006).

Well, we should not have kept you waiting so long. But we have to learn to walk before running fast and jumping high. It is philosophically essential to understand the nature of principles in software engineering. Then, it makes sense to focus on when they can be actually applicable.

6.2.2 Principles

To be essentially pragmatic and broadly applicable for pair programming in real development, we must first resolve the question of when a pair outperforms two individuals. Thus, from the interpretation of the people performance along time series in repeat programming, we establish the first principle.

> *Principle 1*: A pair is much more productive in terms of completion time and can work out a better solution in terms of software quality and maintenance than can two individuals when the pair is new to a programming problem and more effort is required for design, algorithm, and coding of that program.

This principle says that pair programming works well when a pair encounters challenging programming problems. Although few people will define what the term "challenging programming problems" actually means, for us it simply means solving problems that make greater demands using more complicated (i.e., less straightforward) computer algorithms. Rarely is it related to the skills of any particular computer language.

Usually, if a principle is in connection with human behaviors, the reverse may not hold. This is well exemplified by Herzberg's (2003) motivation theory—job dissatisfaction is not opposite to satisfaction, but is simply no dissatisfaction.

> *Principle 2*: The productivity of pair programming can substantially drop when a pair has had previous experience with the same task.

This principle does not address any change in software quality. It simply states the fact that in terms of time, solo programming can definitely beat pair programming when programmers are working on solutions they have already met. As long as a pair knows a programming solution well enough, it is effective for the writing of programmer A, who controls the keyboard and mouse, to not be interrupted even with the risk of making small mistakes such as typos. On the other hand, programmer B probably feels less challenged by watching the known solution that programmer A is writing.

Clearly, two principles suggest pair programming before solo programming. Assume that there are three submodules in ERP (e.g., Internal purchase requests, purchase quotation, purchase order) in which the programming logic patterns are somewhat similar for A and B. Principle 1 tells us to do one of three in pair and principle 2 tells the rest of two in solo.

6.2.3   Triple Programming Unproductive

Triple programming was once mentioned as an efficient approach to solving extremely complex problems. However, this does not mean that it is a productive way of programming. How triple programming can be adopted in real applications is a matter of myth. More questions like time-to-market, productivity per worker, and cost should be separately understood in comparison of solo programming and pair programming. Moreover, the case of better than solo but worse than pair is possible.

Here, we analyze triple programming with repeat programming. The purpose is not to prove that triple programming is unproductive. Rather, we would like to introduce the patterns discovered in repeat programming.

It is easily observed that there are two conservative patterns in Figure 6.4. They can be used to explore the efficiency of triple programming.

> *Pattern 1*. The curves are degressive, and the slope decreases along with the axis of rounds and finally is near to zero.
> *Pattern 2*. The curve for pair programming is relatively flat, so there may be a breakeven point, before which pair programming is better and after which solo programming is better.

As repeat programming involves modeling the skills development of programmers, early rounds and late rounds, respectively, represent the performance of novices and experts. Thus, we will investigate triple programming from these two aspects. For the late rounds, it is straightforward. Referring to pattern (2) in Figure 6.4, solo programming is optimal when the programmers are quite familiar with the problem. It is expected that the curve of triple programming there is flat and definitely above the curve of solo programming.

As in the early rounds, we suppose that triple programming is better than pair programming when programmers have no knowledge of the problem at all. The curve will appear as in Figure 6.4a. The curve becomes a rather straight line. This appears to contradict pattern (1). To match our pattern (1) as shown in Figure 6.4b, we can see that triple programming compared with pair programming is less productive.

Now that pair programming and solo programming are understood better, we continue to move forward in our efforts to design a rhythm using these two software practices.

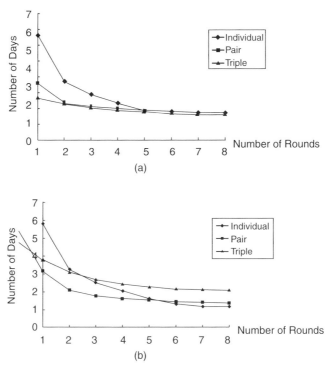

FIGURE 6.4 Speculated curves for (a) productive and (b) unproductive triple programming.

6.3 RHYTHM: PAIR–SOLO–PAIR–SOLO

In eXtreme programming, all production code must be written by pairs of programmers. Individuals can write prototype code for a feasibility study. However, in eXtreme programming, any code not written in pairs must be discarded. This approach appears to contradict what we did in software development in 1996. At that time, we were asked to pair to explore the functions of PowerBuilder 1.0. After 2 weeks, we learned the tool well enough, knowing the best way for us to manage a database and develop graphical user interfaces (GUIs). Everything then got back to normal and we returned to working in our own cubicles. Occasionally, we paired when we were haunted by hard-to-kill problems.

Not all work is pair programming. *Pair programming* is a heteronym. In eXtreme programming what pair programming does has a rhythm: test first–code–refactor, whereas the rhythm we normally beat out is design–code–test. Two or more rhythms are often playing simultaneously. We will talk about how to compose the pair–solo rhythm with the usual method of programming: design–code–test. Although combining rhythms may produce different effects, the principle behind how we compose the pair–solo rhythm (i.e., when a number of software practices work) can still be applicable to many others.

6.3.1 Persistence

Anyone who has learned how to play the piano knows that touching the right key at the right time and continuing to do it right are two separate things. Understanding whether pair programming is productive, we also need to consider the difficulty of sustaining pair programming implementation.

As mentioned in Chapter 1, the in–out diagram helps us analyze how easily we can adopt a practice or rhythm. However, starting them does not mean that we can easily continue to do so. Often, this requires a discipline. How difficult it is for the team to sustain is very important for rhythms. The in–out diagram in Figure 6.5 illustrates that single pair programming is easy to start practicing. However, to sustain it depends on more factors.

Most of us will talk to a driver while they are driving. When a driver has just learned how to drive they will probably tell you that they need to concentrate. But an experienced driver on a routine path is happy with an entertaining traveling companion. Driving is a piece of cake. Their minds are now doing two things: chatting and driving.

Among many other things, the problem with sustaining pair programming can come from a program itself. It is rare that every part of a program is

Easy-to-start	Difficult-to-start	↳
Solo Programming		**Easy-to-sustain**
Single Pair Programming		**Difficult-to-sustain**

FIGURE 6.5 In–out diagram for analyzing solo programming and single pair programming.

equally challenging; there are always easy portions. When a pair is working on easy parts, the observer may get bored and can be easily distracted to chat with his partner about something else. Focus is lost. The pair is doing two things: chatting for fun and programming for work. In many cases, the driver will not mind the observer taking his own break. Thus, pair programming is then practiced intermittently, and this is why all-the-time single pair programming is hard to sustain (see Figure 6.6).

The program task is not the only problem with sustaining pair programming. It also depends on the working environment, project pressure, and software development leadership. It is interesting that pair programming can often end up as pair programming at will (or in need)—programmers pair up when they need support.

In an empirical study, two novice programmers in a company, TCMS, were selected to produce portions of an application for the verification of payload hardware at TCMS in the Kennedy Space Center (Poff 2003). The study lasted one month, and the data collected were compared with historical data. Instructions were given to programmers that the successful and timely development of the application was of primary importance; the experiment was a secondary priority. Therefore, the programmers were *left to decide* how often they would actually work together but were required to work as a pair at

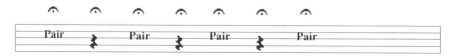

FIGURE 6.6 Hard-to-sustain all-the-time single pair programming.

Easy-to-start	Difficult-to-start	↳
Pair Programming in Need		**Easy-to-sustain**
Single Pair Programming		**Difficult-to-sustain**

FIGURE 6.7 Pair programming in need.

least 33% of the time. If they wished, they could work as a pair all the time. The result was that this single pair worked as a pair around 50% of the time.

Figure 6.7 shows that pair programming in need is both easy to practice and easy to sustain. However, we do not consider it a good software practice. It is ad hoc. Most importantly, it is not a rhythm. Moving from one practice to another without planning is counterproductive. Without rhythms, the alternating pair–solo programming appears to be uncontrolled and chaotic (see Figure 6.8).

We would like to compose a rhythm that tells us when to change between pair and solo for better programming.

6.3.2 Connection

On real-world software development projects, many programmers may pair up at will (or in need) to seek assistance or to manage personal stress. This cannot be considered a disciplined practice as there is no planning or guidelines to say when they should pair up and split off for better performance.

Repeat programming has shown us that the less experience a pair has, the better the pair performs relative to the two similarly inexperienced singles (see cartoon in Figure 6.9). A programming task can normally be divided into a number of subtasks, and many subtasks share a similar logic. It makes sense

FIGURE 6.8 Pair programming in need is not a rhythm.

FIGURE 6.9 Using repeat programming to solve a puzzle.

for us to adopt pair programming to pilot the best breakup of a task and solo programming to work on any subtask in which its logic has been well tested in pairs.

It would be impractical to attempt to identify all such similarities and complementarities of all subtasks at one time in pairs. To be effective and pragmatic, programmers pair up to discover a few patterns and test them all. Then they split off to work on subtasks with those tested patterns. This pairing up and splitting off is repeated until the task is done. The following case, albeit simplified, shows how to move with the pair–solo rhythm.

TABLE 6.1   Master Data Setup for an ERP System

GUI	Creation	Maintenance	Inquiry
Product	Insert into product_table values *data* Insert into price_table values *data*	Update product_table set *data*	Select *data* from product_table
Customer	insert into customer_ table values *data*	Update customer_table set *data*	Select *data* from customer_table
Price	Insert into price_table values *data*	Update price_table set *data* Update product_table set *data*	Select data from price_table, product_table

In an ERP project, we were assigned to develop a module that had a number of graphical user interfaces (GUIs) setting up several master data including products, customers, and prices. We paired up and quickly learned that each GUI involved specific tables (see the pseudo-SQL statements in Table 6.1).

Having patterns allows us to manage software complexity so that we can apply the same logic to different GUIs. This helps us expedite our overall software development because it makes little difference for either a pair or two individuals to work on subtasks relevant to any pattern(s) that the pair has discovered and tested. Nothing is given up for this movement. Bearing this in mind, we as a pair notice that price GUI is required to retrieve data from and update two tables; and product GUI involves inserting data into two tables. They are two-table manipulations whereas the others are merely one-table (see Figure 6.10). Aha! We make our first attempt to build product GUI for creation, price GUI for maintenance, and price GUI for inquiry. The real challenge is to develop not only the three work products but also the patterns for building the other GUI with one-table logic such as a customer GUI.

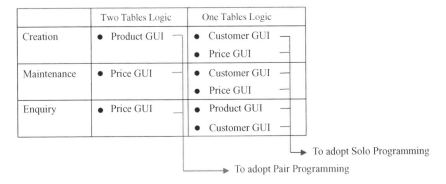

FIGURE 6.10   Analysis of similarity.

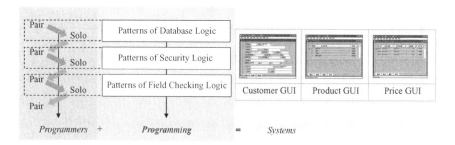

FIGURE 6.11 Pair–solo rhythm at work.

After having completed these three programming subtasks, we feel excited about our little achievements. We are confident of working on the rest in solo programming. We split off and code subtasks alone. On the basis of your own experience, you may like to do unit tests in solo or in pair, but a quick review in pair is a must. Once we have finished the subtasks, we pair up again and continue to work on other things such as security logic and field checking. Figure 6.11 illustrates how the alternation of pair and solo moves on for building the GUIs.

The pair–solo rhythm directs our movement of collaboration. The rhythm chart shown in Figure 6.12 describes the pair–solo rhythm. We start with pair programming in which pairs work on design and identify patterns of logic that demand more effort, and pair programming is a right approach to adopt. The pair then split off to work on subtasks that are similar to the subtask that they have previously worked on in pairs. To metamorphose into solo programming depends on the contributions from pair programming. Next, programmers pair up to review their work products. More effort is needed for design and pilot execution. Thus, it should be achieved in pairs. Less challenging jobs are then left to two individuals.

Consider a case in which the pair work out all the patterns and implement each of them and then split off to work alone on the rest. In this case, there seems to be just pair–then–solo rather than a rhythm as shown in Figure 6.12. Pair–then–solo can be possible when the pair documents their work. Human programmers can easily forget what they have done and need to refer to some

FIGURE 6.12 Pair-solo rhythm.

documentation; otherwise, two individuals will have to talk to each other intermittently.

The pair–solo rhythm has not yet been played simultaneously with test-driven development (TDD). We will explore the TDD rhythm in Chapter 9.

6.3.3 Motivation

The performance of a committed team is a product of ability, self-efficacy, and progress demonstration. In certain situations when problems and solutions are well known to programmers, pair programming can take as much time as solo programming does; this doubles the effort. Fortunately, pair programming in any case does not seem to produce lower-quality software than solo programming does. Thus, two programmers in a pair offer a combination of the experience of two people, and this undoubtedly increases their ability to do the work. Self-efficacy is the expectation of performing well. Pair programming facilities self-efficacy through pair pressure; a pair member does not want to disappoint a partner. Pair pressure encourages the pair to plan their time more wisely (Williams et al. 2000).

As for progress demonstration, people are better motivated when their efforts can be physically seen as early and often as possible.[7] Sadly, work products are invisible during software development. In pair programming, we do not metaphorically interpret that early work progress is shown by the participation in a pair's discussion. Effective communications can indicate the work progress, but it can be apparently irrelevant to how often or long a pair talks.

Inherently, a rhythm through its beat (i.e., movement) "visualizes" work in progress. For example, as in the pair–solo rhythm, the change from pair to solo can be considered an intermediate target signaling that a pair has managed to develop design patterns and to implement them once in pairs. Each change is the completion of the intermediate target. This kind of progress demonstration fosters a very positive attitude toward job achievement.

On day 1, a team leader who walks through spacetime (see Figure 6.13) will see pairs talking about their assigned tasks. Again, depending on their cultures and means of communication, the leader may hear them laugh or dialectically talk, whisper, kvetch (complain habitually), "hai"[8] or similar. As

---

[7]The claim is supported by the observation that "virtually every individual learns at an early age that you perform better on a task if you pay attention to it, exert effort on it, and persist at it over time than if you do not do so" (Locke and Latham 1990, p. 11).

[8]In Japanese, "hai" means not only "Yes" but also "Uh-huh," "I see," or "Hmm." Therefore, Westerners are frequently confused by Japanese saying "yes" all the time (Hiroshi 1997).

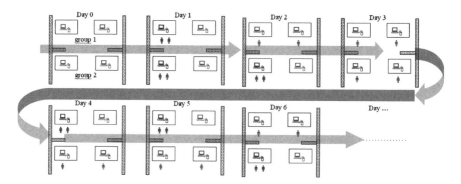

FIGURE 6.13   Walk along time to see the rhythm of splitting off and pairing up.

long as the team does not lose their focus, the leader should not bother about this. The team leader strolls away and on day 2 the team may see one pair split off. The leader thinks "Looks good!" The programmers are applying their reusable patterns. On later days, the team will pair up to continue their work. Their progress beats out the rhythm. After a month, the team leader has caught the rhythm of the team and is now able to notice unusual cases if the rhythm is out of beat: pairs are not split a long time or solos are working unexpectedly long. This could be a signal that the team needs more support.

It is clear that paired programmers are glad to move on to solo programming as their separation shows their achievements not only to others but also to themselves. To master the complexity of problems through the understanding of "similarity" and "complementarity," they develop reusable patterns of their own. The time when programmers are splitting off is a moment to enjoy a cup of coffee after their hard work. It is also a time to share their experiences with others and even their supervisor on how, working in pairs, they have killed many birds with one stone. Perhaps, working with good software practice without seeing anyone around does not encourage programmers.

An example of pair–solo rhythm in software development is illustrated in Box 6.2 (see also Table 6.2).

TABLE 6.2   Experimental Project in Southern China

		Huida Programmers		
Item	Measurement Description	Pair	Pair	Single
1	Number of GUIs developed	7	6	2
2	Number of stored procedures written	15	9	5
3	Ratio	1.7	1.9	N/A[a]

[a]Not applicable.

BOX **6.2**

CASE STUDY (2005): SOFTWARE DEVELOPMENT IN CHINA

In southern China, Huida Technology Ltd. had seven technical staff providing ERP solutions to their local customers. Two had 4 years' experience and the other less than one year. To better manage less experienced programmers, the company was piloting the pair–solo rhythm on their Web-based CRM project.

After a month, the company provided their measurements to us (Table 6.2). As the project was not an experiment, it is a matter of happenstance that there were five staff available, so the use of a single programmer was not intended to serve as a control group. The programmers appeared to develop more (sub)modules in terms of stored procedures and GUI. From an academic perspective, we are interested in a ratio, defined by the total time in solo programming over the total time in pair programming which can be used to compare with other team's adoption of the pair–solo rhythm. For example, Poff's experiment on pair programming, which ended up with pair programming at will, was about 1 (Poff 2003).

Supervisors' Comments

The supervisors worked with those five programmers daily and knew them well. Their comments on the process are of interest:

1. They found that they were able to spend less time supervising the pairs as they tended to support and monitor themselves.
2. Coding standards were much better.
3. The pair–solo rhythm encouraged junior programmers to actively seek design patterns for reuse. This has rarely been seen before as the programmers just wanted to complete the program on time, rather than considering software reuse. Hitherto, it was common to see duplications of logic in the junior programmer's code as they had the habit of simply cutting and pasting code.

We should be aware that superimposing another rhythm may break the harmony. But it may also produce a synergy. The principle by which we compose the pair–solo rhythm may be implemented flexibly so as to develop a new rhythm for your workplace. In eXtreme programming, exchanging partners with another pair supports "collective code ownership." Unfortunately, the timing of partner changing is an unresearched topic. On the basis of pair–solo rhythm, we may replace splitting off with exchanging partners, and the rhythm will be "pair–pair with exchanging partner–pair with exchanging partner." In this way, once a pattern is discovered by a pair, they need to rotate partners with another pair to facilitate knowledge sharing. Looking at a single rhythm for all development situations is not wise. Readers should be careful to compose their own rhythms.

6.4 AN EXCEPTION THAT PROVES BROOKS' LAW

According to the Brooks' law, adding manpower to a late project makes it even later.[9] This is not too difficult to understand as adding new members to a team often means an increase in communication costs, the need for additional training time, and time to reassign responsibilities and/or repartition a task. All these factors together can outweigh the productivity gain from the additional team members.

During the course of software development, a project team may encounter problems relating to variables such as product quality, budget control, and project planning. Among these different problems, schedule slippage is most easily noticeable. While it requires rigorous testing to identify defective quality, every member of a team can tell how long a project has been late. It probably is not difficult to convince anyone that, of all the problems, schedule slippage is the problem most commonly encountered when managing a project. In fact, the problem is more of how late a project is rather than whether it is late. There is, as yet, no easy solution to such a problem. Consciously or subconsciously, many project managers hope that Brooks' law does not hold true in their projects. They hope that they can add people in their team in exchange for a shorter completion time.[10] What is truer than Brooks' law is the preference for believing what we want to believe!

There have been studies on how an increase in manpower may impact factors such as communication costs and productivity showing that communication costs can be asymptotically proportional to the square of the number of programmers[11] or, if there exists an optimal number of people, above which project time can be decreased only marginally. These studies are concerned with communications, productivity, design complexity, optimization, and people management. Here, we suggest a different way to look at Brooks' law.

---

[9]A study shows that adding manpower to a late project can be very costly, but it does not necessarily make it later (Abdel-Hamid and Madnick 1991). This statement is not very relevant to our discussion here as long as it is held that adding manpower to a late project does not shorten the completion time.

[10]Men and months are not interchangeable units because partitioned tasks are not totally independent in software development (Brooks 1995).

[11]The number of communication paths of channels for N programmers can be computed as $[N \times (N-1)]/2$, that is, this is of order $O(N^2)$.

To explain our observation, let us consider a simple example. Suppose that an outsourced programmer in India promises to submit a program to her manager in the United States in 4 weeks' time. The project manager, Ralph, would naturally plan to start the user acceptance testing in week 5.

One lovely morning, although the project has been a week behind schedule, the programmer, Sita, is relaxing in a Mumbai café, when her phone rings. Ralph, who is very worried about the progress, tries to explain to Sita the terrible consequences of a late submission. Ralph would like to introduce another developer there to speed up the work. This idea is rejected as Sita thinks that it will only delay the project further.

By committing to the original one month schedule, Sita was only guessing as to how long she would need to complete the program. Taking a number of risk factors into account, a probability distribution function can be developed (see Figure 6.14). There may be a 50% chance that she will complete the work in week 4, and the chance of completing by week 6 may be 10%. The cumulative probability that Ralph will receive the work by week 6 is therefore 95%. In this case, adding an additional developer may not make it faster as there is already a 95% chance that the work will be finished by the following week as long as all risk factors can be kept unchanged.

If Ralph knew the probability distribution, he would probably be willing to wait another week for the program. Even though he might still be concerned, he probably would only ask whether the probability distribution function is still valid. If there were no other uncertainty factors and if all known risk factors were managed, things would be regarded as under control and the schedule would be regarded as more or less predictable!

What this story intends to convey is that all late projects are different. In fact, there are two different ways of classifying late projects. There are late projects that are *simply late* and there are late projects that are *troubled and late*. In case of the former, risk factors originally anticipated may materialize. In

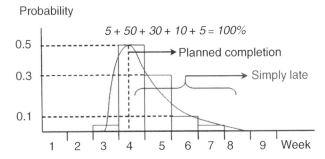

FIGURE 6.14 A project plan says that a task will be done by week 4; this actually might mean that there is a 50–50 chance of completing it by then.

such a case, the probability distribution function of the project being on time may remain valid. As long as a project team can keep their morale up, adding manpower is just not of any value. The team may just need a pat on the back, and everything can continue as planned.

For troubled–late projects, however, lateness (tardiness) may be the consequence of something that is more serious. For example, changing of requirements, insufficient user involvement, lack of executive support, unrealistic project goals, and other factors can all be hidden behind the noticeable result of *lateness*. In the most serious cases, these could lead to project abandonment. Thus, a troubled–late project can radically change the original probability distribution. Often, in such a situation, a project manager is under great pressure and would like to do more than just add additional manpower.

6.4.1 Low Morale

Troubled–late projects, as one can easily imagine, usually accompany low morale and high stress. The low morale is a result of negative outcomes despite a team's hard work. Team members can be very worried and frustrated about what might happen to both themselves and to the project as a result of possible drastic actions that may be taken to alleviate problems and ease difficult situations.

Although Brooks' law is generally accepted by most people, many programmers probably will admit to having been helped by some very experienced developers at some point in time. In fact, this is particularly the case when one finds oneself overwhelmed by the work on hand and experiences low morale at work and is under great stress. A study on CRM implementation reports that a project team with low morale, with overall satisfaction graded at 2 out of 10, can quickly jump up to a rating of 5 or 6 whenever a new member joins the team (Anton and Petouhoff 2002). If emotional support has such an impact on a CRM implementation's success, we believe it to be particularly important for troubled–late projects.

Adding manpower is a way to boost morale. If team spirit can be kept up, the team can work faster and better. However, is this something that is in direct contradiction to Brooks' law? No, probably not. With a team of such low-morale members, a troubled–late project can be doomed for termination in the minds of these team members. Adding new members to a late project may mean that the management is still interested in rescuing the project. Even though it can complete the project even later, *late* is better than *never*.

6.4.2 Communication Costs

Brooks' law assumes certain relationships between people and their communications. One may wonder if there is an ideal situation in which Brook's law does not hold and in which we add manpower without adding to the costs of training and of repartitioning tasks. Of course, project managers don't consciously follow laws. They are concerned only with making sure that their projects are successful. Under pressure to perform and weighing up adding new members as opposed to being removed from the project, many managers of troubled–late projects would probably opt for the former. To minimize any possible damage to an already late project, it is important that new members be added to the project in the optimal way.

In eXtreme programming, there its a truck number criterion. If a project fails when just one member got hit by a truck, then all members of the project team are critical to the successes of a project. This is a very risky situation that should be avoided.

However, a truck number is influenced by how programmers are organized and how tasks or responsibilities are assigned. To decide whether progress can be made on a project, we need to know how many developers can quickly take over each task. Here, we define the smallest such number to be an extended truck number.

Tasks in software development are rarely independent. In Figure 6.15, even though Liz is working on task D, she needs to find out, from other team members at times, how other tasks such as task B are related to task D. Since task B is assigned to one person only, Liz can talk only to John. If John is busy, she has to wait.

Liz can continue to work if she does not need immediate answers to her questions. However, if Liz has joined the team only recently, a quick response

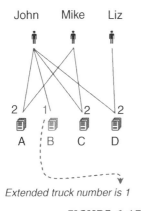

The way we look at truck number is people allocation!

The way we look at *extended truck number* is task allocation!

FIGURE 6.15 Extended truck number.

to her questions can be critical. Communication costs including calling time and waiting time can be minimized if anyone in a team can give Liz answers to all the questions she has immediately. To reduce the slope of a learning curve, old team members must allocate time from their original schedule to train new members. Thus, the higher the extended truck number, the less likely we are to get information flow bottlenecks.

In pair programming, the extended truck number is at least 2. Imagine that a new but experienced member is assigned to a pair. While an observer discusses with the driver, he can spare time to brief a new member on necessary background and progress to date. This should be seen as a factor in calculating training costs and mentoring burden.

Adding more staff may require reorganization or reallocation of tasks. As repartitioning an original task involves rework, effort previously made will unavoidably go into the trash. Straightforwardly, dividing existing subtasks into smaller ones appears to make sense if a subtask is divisible. Otherwise, on repartitioning, you have to balance the time you need to rework the previous task with the time you gain from the shorter completion time.

If all these issues can be dealt with, we stand a better chance of over-throwing Brooks' law.

6.4.3   Rhythm for Late Projects

Everything has its day. Briefly speaking, triple programming could be unproductive when compared with pair programming. However, out of the shadow of pair programming, triple programming has its place in real-world applications. In triple programming, as more people are involved, there will be a corresponding increase in communication overheads. In particular, the number of communication channels would raise costs exponentially. Intercommunication, in fact, can be considered the bottleneck of triple programming.

Pair programmers who have not practiced triple programming may think that there would be three communication channels (or paths) (Figure 6.16a). This, in reality, may not be the case. The driver can be substantially distracted by the two observers' discussions and or by conflicts between them. If three people are to work together, they have to work rhythmically; that is, their activities should be planned and coordinated.

In triple programming, we introduce a new role for a programmer, called a *moderator*, who coordinates the communications between the driver and the observer, who, basically, do not talk to each other. The moderator, like a bridge across two heads, not only communicates to the driver and thinks strategically, but also discusses ideas with the observer sitting beside her.

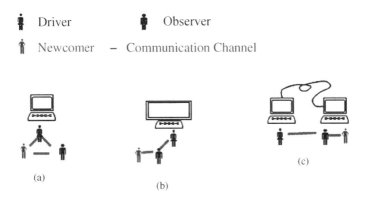

FIGURE 6.16   Communication channels (or paths) in triple Programming: (a) unfeasible; (b) feasible but crowded; (c) feasible.

In the case of adding a new person to a pair, the pair will be either the driver or the moderator and the new member can only be the observer. This can ensure that there are just two communication channels (see Figures 6.16b and 6.16c), and this can help reduce communication costs. Physically, to facilitate their working together, a larger liquid crystal display (LCD) can be used to enable the three people working together to more easily view the screen contents (see Figure 6.16b). From an ergonomic perspective, three people sitting close to each other, talking and working together for a prolonged period, can feel quite uncomfortable. Technically, Figure 6.16b is feasible, but it could be too crowded for the programmers to work comfortably.

With remote desktop technology such as terminal servers, it is better for a triple to sit in front of two machines (see Figure 6.16c) so that the driver can work on a single machine, with the other two sitting in front of another machine accessing the driver's computer. These two programmers can talk very quietly so as not to distract the driver's attention from programming. The driver and the moderator can talk as usuals.

With the communications moderated, adding new members to pairs can be pragmatic. Triple programming facilitates the transfer of necessary background knowledge so that the third programmer can become a contributing member in a shorter time period. Adding new members in such a way can have a smaller impact on task repartitioning.

Despite these advantages, it should be noted that triple programming cannot be made very productive if it is adopted from the very beginning. However, this is not the case if it is adopted to counter the negative impact of introducing new members to a late-project team. By adopting triple programming as described here, we can at least be sure that productivity will not

FIGURE 6.17   Rhythm of triple programming.

decrease. In fact, if *splitting*, a technique we propose here, is introduced to turn triple into solo programming, productivity can be increased.

The idea of splitting is fairly simple as it is the same as the pair–solo rhythm (see Figure 6.17). The triple, together, are looking for patterns of logic and ways to break up remaining tasks. They share necessary background knowledge with the new member, and therefore, Figure 6.18, which is a chart showing a development rhythm for troubled–late projects, can apply.

The rhythm of triple programming may actually save a troubled–late project and can allow Brooks' law to be overcome to some extent. To manage troubled–late projects, one may have to "burn the boat" even though this could be an expensive thing to do. In addition to adopting this strategy, determination and encouragement are also essential. One does not have to be bothered by Brooks' law. A project manager can ask for the necessary human resources but should not practice anything ad hoc. Instead, she should focus on a rhythm of her own and keep moving on towards the project goals.

Software development rhythms are not development methodologies. Unlike eXtreme programming, the development rhythms won't tell you how to build software from beginning to end. This also cannot be done for software principles. For example, one may have mastered practices in eXtreme programming that are useful in one's organization and know how these practices are interrelated. But, one may wonder what practices should be adopted under a particular development rhythm.

Every software methodology has it own rhythm, and software development rhythms are a way of understanding them all, regardless of whether they are heavyweight, lightweight, rigorous, adaptive, static, dynamic, just-in-time, schedule-based, fast-paced, slow-paced, people-focused, or

FIGURE 6.18   Rhythm for late projects.

process-driven. A particular method for managing software projects will work only for some of us. It is better for us to develop our own unique situation based on some guiding principles:

Fair is foul and foul is fair.

REFERENCES

Abdel-Hamid T and Madnick S. *Software Project Dynamics: An Integrated Approach.* Upper Saddle River, NJ: Prentice-Hall; 1991.

Anton J and Petouhoff NL. *Customer Relationship Management: The Bottom Line to Optimizing Your ROI.* Upper Saddle River, NJ: Prentice-Hall; 2002.

Arisholm E, Gallis H, Dyba T, and Sjøberg D. Evaluating pair programming with respect to system complexity and programmer expertise. *IEEE Transactions on Software Engineering* 2007; **33** (22):65–86.

Brooks FP. *The Mythical Man-month.* Reading, MA: Addison-Wesley; 1995.

Cockburn A. *Crystal Clear: A Human-powered Methodology for Small Teams.* Boston: Addison-Wesley; 2005.

Constantine LL. *Constantine on Peopleware.* Englewood Cliffs, NJ: Yourdon Press; 1995.

Flor NV. Side-by-side collaboration: a case study. *International Journal of Human Computer Studies* 1998; **49** (3):201–222.

Gardner H. *Frames of Mind.* 2nd ed. New York: Basic Books; 1993.

Gardner H. *Extraordinary Minds.* New York: Basic Books; 1997.

Haslam A and Reicher S. *The Experiment (videorecording).* London: BBC Worldwide; 2002.

Herzberg F. One more time: How do you motivate employees? *Harvard Business Review* Jan. 2003; pp. 87–96.

Hiroshi K. *The Inscrutable Japanese: 41 Cultural Puzzles that Foreigners Have on the Japanese.* Tokyo: Kodansha International; 1997.

Locke EA and Latham GP. *A Theory of Goal and Task Performance.* Upper Saddle River, NJ: Prentice-Hall; 1990.

Lui KM and Chan KCC. Pair programming productivity: novice-novice vs. expert-expert. *International Journal of Human Computer Studies* 2006; **64**:915–925.

Müller MM. Are reviews an alternative to pair programming? *Empirical Software Engineering* 2004, **9** (4):335–351.

Nawrocki J and Wojciechowski A. Experimental evaluation of pair programming. *Proceedings of the 12th European Software Control and Metrics Conference* 2001. pp. 269–276.

Nosek JT. The case for collaborative programming. *Communications of the ACM* 1998; **41** (3):105–108.

Poff MA. *Pair Programming to Facilitate the Training of Newly-Hired Programmers*. MSc thesis. Florida Institute of Technology; 2003.

Stephens M and Rosenberg D. *Extreme Programming Refactored: The Case Against XP*. Berlin: Springer; 2003.

Williams L and Kessler R. *Pair Programming Illuminated*. Boston: Addison-Wesley; 2003.

Williams L, Kessler R, Cunningham W, and Jeffries R. Strengthening the case for pair programming. *IEEE Software* 2000; **17** (4):19–25.

Zimbardo PG. *Quiet Rage* (videorecording, 1971): The Stanford prison study/Stanford Instructional Television Network; production services provided by Stanford Center for Professional Development Publisher: Philip G. Zimbardo, Inc., The Board of Trustees of Leland Stanford Junior University, 1992.

Zimbardo PG, *The Lucifer Effect*. London: Ebury Press; 2007.

7

AGILE TEAMING

One step by 100 people is better than 100 steps by one person.
                                                    —KOICHI TSUKAMOTO[1]

A college rugby team from Uruguay flew to Chile for a match. The plane crashed into the frozen Andes Mountains. Of the 45 passengers on the plane, 27 survived the crash but now they faced the problem of surviving in the freezing mountains. The most important survival decisions were made by the group, so it was a collective decision when the group decided to eat the flesh from the bodies of their dead friends. And it was a group brainstorm that produced an insulated sleeping bag to keep them alive through the cold nights. On December 22, 1972, after 72 brutal days, they were rescued, but only 16 had survived (Parrado and Rause 1998).

The group was isolated from the outside world. They had to reach consensus with little time to test and evaluate their ideas. The group members, as human beings, were instinctively motivated to survive, but that does not mean that they shared a common belief. For example, although everyone wanted to survive, some did not think that they would be rescued while some firmly believed they would just survive.

When a group of people share a common belief, they can be totally devoted to the group. In fact, it can be less important whether the belief is understandable to the outsider. Depending on how a group is established,

[1] Quoted in Eppler.

Software Development Rhythms: Harmonizing Agile Practices for Synergy
By Kim Man Lui and Keith C. C. Chan
Copyright © 2008 John Wiley & Sons, Inc.

motivated, and led, the team members could be totally committed to achieving it. Let us look at another story.

In 1997 there were 39 people who belonged to a religious group and together they ran a successful Website design company. One spring morning, the team all put on brand-new running shoes and gathered in a rented house in a suburb of San Diego. These people passionately believed their group leader's claim that extraterrestrials from the "kingdom of heaven" were monitoring Earth with a view to taking a select part of humanity away to salvation. The group had long been preparing for the day when a spacecraft, concealed by the Hale–Bopp comet, would come to take them off to heaven. But the only way to get a boarding pass for the aliens' craft was to free their souls from the bodies. So on March 27, 1997 all 39 of those educated and otherwise average people took overdoses of sleeping pills and very soon after they were indeed freed from their bodies (Giddens et al. 2006).

Whenever we hear this kind of news, "teaming" comes to mind. We can see that the team has goals, resources, plans, and timeframes; it is just like running a project. It involves member motivation (i.e., what they are looking for in a team), team organization (i.e., how the group interlocks different roles played by the members that guides the group behavior), a disciplined methodology (i.e., how to die or survive), and so on. It also includes one significant element at the group level: a can-do attitude.

Software teaming is multidisciplinary, involving psychology, sociology, group dynamics, project management, and software engineering. Experts in different areas on team collaboration, however, are exploring more or less the same things. Psychologists and sociologists have reported their studies on the behavior of software project teams (Sonnentag 2002; Yeh and Chou 2005). Unfortunately, teaming is an area less popular in software engineering, although this topic is almost as old as the first Unix system by Ed Thompson.

When software products can be produced only by more than one, we have to deal with teaming. An early study of software teaming is Baker's *chief programmer teams* (1972), a model of teaming in which developers are divided into chief programmers who are responsible for all development tasks, backup programmers whose role is to act as assistants to the chief programmers, and a librarian whose job is to support all the clerical functions associated with a project.

Yet, although teaming may have been soft-pedaled, issues of group dynamics are always addressed in traditional software methods/models [e.g., team software process (TSP) and CMMI]. A wall of project management books have discussed the establishment of a "project charter" at the inception of a project that is designed to define roles and responsibilities.

Agile software development also emphasizes people, and claims to bring concerns with accountability, responsibility, and transparency (Beck and Andres 2005) back into the discussion of software development. How do TSP, CMMI, and so on, differ from what agile software development tells us? Are they (i.e., agilist and nonagilist) just saying the same thing from different perspectives? Our answer is "No."

A *process* is a collection of specific activities that together can be used to achieve the process objectives. Many software processes have been practically structured with the idea that developers are well coordinated so that activities for acting, planning, doing, and checking are controlled. As such, software processes should be designed to coordinate a number of activities and to assign responsibilities to developers.

Agile software development realizes that it is not possible to execute plans with perfect accuracy because of the uncertainties that will arise within a team and working on a software project. Therefore, people in a team should closely collaborate on the same set of tasks to ensure a more accurate estimation of the whole team's performance and software capability.

In short, the emphasis in traditional software development is more on task coordination, with allocation of the right amount of tasks for each developer, while agile software development focuses more on people collaboration for completing tasks. Now that people over process (i.e., focus on how people collaborate) or process over people (i.e., focus on how tasks assigned to people are better coordinated) are different approaches, two thorny issues are arising: when either one works better and when either can be better used. Let us look at a simple example.

Assume that you are running a project that can definitely be completed much earlier before deadline. In this case, process over people or people over process does not matter. You have plenty of time to manage any inaccuracy and risk that may materialize.

Yet, if the deadline is suddenly brought forward, how do people react? Process over people is inflexible, as the order among processes or activities is established under an assumption of no change. It is people over process that could handle the problem of this kind. When will there be such unexpectedly dramatic events during software projects? Our opinion would be that many software projects that have been changing from promising to failing always occur unexpectedly. Later in this chapter, when we are dealing with failing software projects, we will manage troubles better using a people-over-process approach.

Unfortunately, teaming is a difficult topic and it is difficult to put its theories into action. In *Winning,* Jack Welch, CEO of General Electric for 20 years, argues his preference for a flat organization (see Figure 7.1) because it

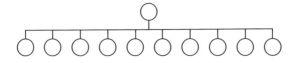

Large Flat versus More Layers

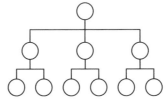

FIGURE 7.1   "Managers should have 10 direct reports at the minimum" (Welch and Welch 2003).

allows for more talented subordinates to be directly involved in decisionmaking. This is an example of people over process (or people *before* process).

Nowadays, software projects are so large and complex that they are beyond an individual's efforts alone to complete. As long as development and implementation requires more than one person, there is the need for teaming. Excellent teaming is just *sufficient* to successfully run a software project. When we intend to rescue troubled–late projects, teaming plays a dominant role in dealing with such projects. Teaming with a sponsor from top management is a necessary condition.

7.1   PROJECT TEAMS

Some software managers who are merely interested in project data and deliverables may consider themselves result-oriented persons. However, it is people not project data who do the job and get the result. Failing to understanding people and the development paradigms that they adopt will not provide any proven evidence that the same team always delivers quality software on time and within budget. Both people and results should be equally important. However, when people are working as a team to deliver the results, there is the need to first learn more about how the team works. Obviously, software development will never make teaming dispensable.

One of the authors attended a Hewlett-packard (HP) industrial seminar in 1997 and talked to a person who was the head of the IT department of a retail chain. Since the author was working as project leader in a large supermarket chain in Hong Kong, he talked to and shared project experiences with this IT person who said it was good to be a department head. Certainly, as far as money is concerned, the salary package for the head of IT can be 2 or 3 times higher than that of a project manager. But what this IT guy was trying to say was that heading a departmental team would be much *easier* than running a software project.

When members are in a permanent team according to an organizational chart, its manager (e.g., department head) has absolute power and can manipulate rewards and penalties in the work environment.

A project team can be temporarily established to achieve specific goals, and teammates are often selected from different departments within an organization, or from two or three software vendors. With that kind of project team, there are two problems: (1) the project manager is expected to exercise more personal power than positional power because he/she is often regarded as one highly competitive person and should provide a good role model for his/her team members, and (2) the project manager may not have much power to take disciplinary action against problematic members from other departments or companies. Such differences between managing permanent teams and running project teams are where conflicts come from.

In addition, while we may want to educate a project development team and establish some sort of team culture, we must consider the project schedule. Teams that are more permanent such as departmental teams are easier to control, and longer timelines and greater team stability mean that team development is not necessarily in conflict with work progress.

Even in a software company, a project team is established by selecting programmers from different specialties in the company. Such a heterogeneous team will introduce conflicts as there are many ways to build software. When the company is sizable, team members may not know each other well. It takes time for us to understand them. It is not easy to manage the heterogeneous teams with their differences in personalities and to resolve conflicts among people's ideas. In some cases, some programmers, particularly experts, are often involved in many projects rather than just one. In a worst-case scenario, they may just show up in a project meeting to report their work progress. For sure, the team members hardly establish a close rapport with one another and they become increasingly coordinated to achieve their assigned tasks. The team ends up practicing process over people.

In a project that involves partnership, it is not unusual for project team members to be drawn from two companies. In this case we should be cautious about cultural differences between the two organizations. Potential team members should not assume that the way things are done in their organization must be the way things are done in the combined team. In particular,

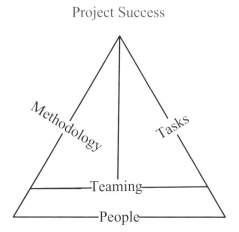

Project Success

FIGURE 7.2 People are the foundations of software projects.

people from different areas should take the time to agree with practices that should be adopted before tasks are undertaken.

Project teams have their own dynamics and lifecycles. People are the most fundamental layer of program tasks and programming paradigms. A project must be built on the base of a strong team (see Figure 7.2). The path to success involves a series of tasks that the team must finish. However, it is not enough just to get the tasks done. Methodology and tasks are interrelated. The team must use good methods to complete all the tasks. By "good methods", we mean that there should be working rhythms that are right for the team to ensure that values to people and software are delivered.

7.1.1 Self-Organizing Teams

The software requirements can be written in a stack of user stories, each of which has one or a few features. A small software team can pick up some user stories that can be completed within 30 days. These 30 days constitute a noninterrupted iteration that is called a "sprint." During the sprint, the team is totally self-organizing and can do whatever is necessary to get the work done. When the sprint ends, they give a presentation to their users of what they did. The users may change the features after a review. Afterward, the team picks up more features and enters another sprint of 30-days. This iterative process continues until the application is done. But it is not without problems.

Self-organizing teams can be a risky practice if the team members do not know how to organize themselves to maximize productivity. Team decisions

FIGURE 7.3 A rhythm of 30 days—review.

as to how to combine their efforts to solve a problem are a discretionary task (see Chapter 5). To play it safe, there should be a coach to guide the self-organizing teams.

Fortunately, the risk can be lower when the iteration is short. Even if a user is not satisfied with the work or wants to make substantial changes leading to a total loss of all work done to that point, the team will still lose only 30 days (Schwaber and Beedle 2001).

During a sprint, users cannot interrupt the team. The user can change their requirements only after the 30 days. Team organization in the first sprint is risky. However, if we look at each sprint flowing as a rhythm, it is not. We can see the rhythm after two or three sprints. The rhythm of each sprint tells us what the team will achieve. When the team runs into difficulties and needs help, a short daily meeting, a scrum (scrummage) meeting, is a good problem-solving device.

Such a self-organizing team is normally small and very rhythmic (Figure 7.3), which fits well with agile teaming. Later we will discuss agile teaming in which the structure of a team is dynamic so as to respond easily to project issues and changes. We will see that a self-organizing team can achieve agile teaming as long as the team can organize itself to react to changes.

7.1.2 Teams in a Team

A traditional team structure is like a tree diagram (see Figure 7.4). Team members often possess complementary skills. Mutual education and skill-sharing is a possible outcome. In many real situations, to make a team productive by skill sharing is challenging. For example, one is in finding ways to promote the sharing of knowledge and experience. Sharing experience that does not help meet a project's deadline around the corner can be time-wasting. Another problem is in ensuring that theoretically complementary team member skills do in fact work together in a complementary way. Complementary skills are not freebies. There are associated communication overheads as team members need to understand one another.

As pointed out in our earlier discussion of pair programming, two people can work together as a single unit to collaborate on the same task (see Figure 7.5). This practice not only sets the scene for complementary skill use

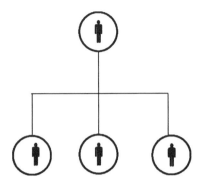

FIGURE 7.4 Traditional team structure.

but also reduces the associated communication overhead. The structure (see Figure 7.5) must be dynamic because the sharing of knowledge and experience is an outcome of well-timed pair rotations.

This is a team-in–team approach, which is different from arrangements where a team is composed of subteams. Each team in a team-in-team approach exists for just a short period and exchanges partners with other teams. Teams can organize their own partner rotations, but this doesn't always produce ideal outcomes. It is not reasonable to expect that all teams will perform equally or ideally.

When members of a team rotate their partners with "right" timing, they will soon feel their rhythms (shown Figure 7.6) and get an idea of the strengths of each pair. But this depends on how long the self-organizing team takes to get its timing. In some cases, it may just create an arrhythmic atmosphere in the workplace (see Figure 7.7).

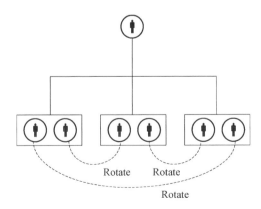

FIGURE 7.5 Dynamic team structure for team pair programming.

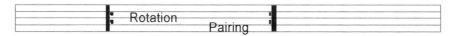

FIGURE 7.6 Rotating makes team structure dynamic.

7.1.3 Project Team Composition

Any project must start with the establishment of a project team in which the members are selected from different positions in major functional units of the company. Such heterogeneity in a team will, on one hand, contribute to a staff member's functional expertise in reengineering a business process and designing an integrated system, and, on the other hand, cause conflicts of interest among different functional departments, which to some extent may lead to scheduling slippage, failure to keep costs within budget, and low morale among team members (Yeh and Chou 2005).

Suppose that we won a CRM contract. CRM applications are a bit more company-oriented than industry-driven. Where one company sees attractive customers, another may see only the ugly. The Gartner Group says that many CRM applications are tailor-designed and are built in-house. This kind of project needs technical programmers and different staff.

We may need to form a project team to build a CRM system by finding the right people from one (probably more) organization so that the whole team have good domain knowledge for that industry, the company's unique operations, and technical programming. There are two simple ways to compose our team: functional diversity and positional diversity.

Functional diversity is when team members are selected from different functional areas (e.g., sales and marketing, finance, distribution, information systems). Functional diversity has been negatively associated with team performance because people from different backgrounds may bring irresolvable viewpoints to a team and a project manager will have to manage their conflicts.

Positional diversity is when team members are selected from different ranks within an organization. Positional diversity has a positive influence on team performance because people at the junior level appreciate the opportunity to engage at the level of strategy and planning with more experienced

FIGURE 7.7 Arrhythmatic pairing.

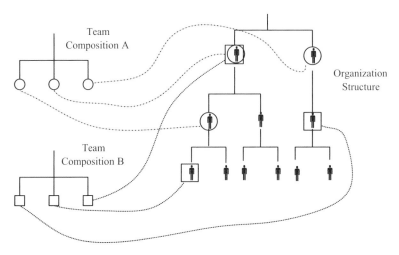

Team Composition A

Organization Structure

Team Composition B

FIGURE 7.8 Team B is better than Team A!

staff, while senior staff are exposed to issues related to more operational problems. This way may lead to lower levels of conflict within a team and greater effectiveness.

We might want to try to use positional diversity to lessen conflicts caused by different functional perspectives (i.e., functional diversity), to get people at different levels from different divisions (see Figure 7.8).

7.1.4 Team Lifecycle versus Learning Curve

A project plan that shows the tasks of a project team and project charter also records roles and responsibilities. But this may not address one critical point: how productive a team can be. The productivity of a group of people, even though they form a team with common project goals, relies on communication and respect to develop its structure. This grows over time. Let us start with a rhythm for team formation.

Once a project team has been established, it moves through four stages to reach its optimal level of productivity (Figure 7.9). In the *formation* phase, group members start to orient toward one another. Then *conflict* emerges. It subsides when the group becomes more structured. Norms and cultures emerge in the *structure* phase. Finally, in the *production* phase, the group moves beyond disagreement and concentrates on the work to be done.

Strictly speaking, the Tuckman model can be arrhythmic if we don't get the right timing for a team we are building. Each team may take a different amount of time to pass through the cycle regardless of whether it is a big team

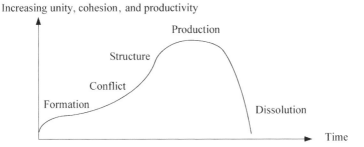

FIGURE 7.9 A Lifecycle of a project team by Tuckman's model (1965).

or a team of just two members. Thus, the model alone does not give us the details of how to build a productive team. The team has to get its rhythm at each phase (see Figure 7.10).

For example, expecting two people to sit down and immediately make pair programming productive is unrealistic. Even a team of two requires time to communicate on how to collaborate. As in pair programming, this period is referred to as the "pair jelling" time (Williams et al. 1965).

The Tuckman model has a relationship with a project cycle. When the project lifecycle is shorter than the time that a project team requires to reach its optimum productivity (i.e., the production phase of the Tuckman model), the project manager will have to deal with more teaming problems than project issues. This is not good at all (see Figure 7.11). It is preferable to select the right members so that the team will reach their productivity in the fastest possible time. In addition, we should also try some warmup exercises and cooperative games to facilitate team building.

In many software projects, a newly established team needs to learn new skills, such as software tools, development languages, and domain knowledge. Depending on the team's experience, its learning curve can vary. Suppose that a learning curve over project time for a team can have three possible scenarios as depicted in Figure 7.12.

No team has complete knowledge about any software project. Often, they have to learn new skills or acquire project-relevant knowledge. Throughout a project cycle, we may expect that project tasks will demand different skills

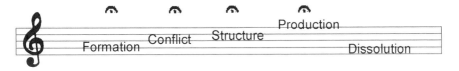

FIGURE 7.10 Rhythm for Tuckman's model.

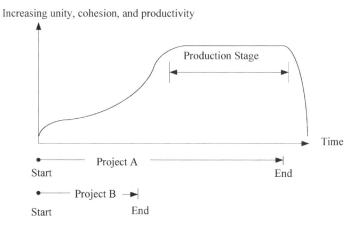

FIGURE 7.11 The worst-case scenario would be project B's lifecycle being much shorter than the time to reach the team's production stage.

over time, and so the learning curve–project skill demand curve will not rise regularly and irresistibly but will rise and fall over time.

Learning speed varies with each team and project. Ideally, a team gains the necessary skills quickly and is capable of performing the most challenging time- and skill-demanding development tasks well before they arise, at the apex of the project cycle (see learning curve A in Figure 7.12).

If the learning pace lags behind the project cycle, team productivity will not reach the level required by the project cycle until the end of the project, resulting in a waste of resources (see learning curve C in Figure 7.12). This is the worst–case scenario, and the project is not expected to go smoothly.

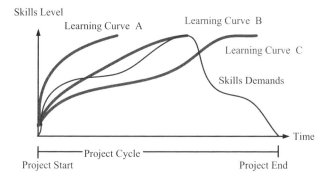

FIGURE 7.12 Learning curves versus project skills demands.

Training is not the same as learning. We can provide extensive training to our team, but when or whether they acquire the skills and knowledge to contribute to a project is another story. For this reason, teams should start with enough experience rather than trying to train everybody on the job. Reliance on the learning curve should be avoided.

Despite the importance of all of these factors—team performance, learning curve, and project cycle—they are never reflected in a project plan.

7.2 PRODUCTIVITY

Low or below-target productivity is always a problem in software development, yet it is not always easy to identify its sources, in part because the factors of productivity are often intangible and hard to measure. Even if a factor has been identified, there are difficulties in isolating and influencing it. Productivity in software development is not, as in manufacturing, a relatively simple matter of machine capacity and labor-hours. Programmers rarely complain that their tools—the computers, for example—affect their programming speed. Rather, productivity in software development is a function of factors that are difficult to identify, measure, or motivate; for instance, human intelligence and human experience.

The productivity of creative workers can be captive to personal factors. Some work well in the day and others at night. Similarly, over an 8-hour day, some may be more productive in the first four hours and less productive thereafter. Imagine that two *independent* programs of the same amount of workload need to be written. When one of the two is done in 4 hours, there is the expectation that the other will take no longer so that the whole task will require a total of 8 hours. But experience tells us that this is not necessarily so. Any programmer who has worked hard for the first four hours can be expected to be less productive for the next four hours. However, two programmers may complete the two tasks in 8 man-hours. This is because human productivity of writing code varies along working hours—and this can be far more complicated for team productivity.

Team productivity in software development relates to how a team makes use of their intelligence and experience so as to produce high-quality products with less rework effort. A team's organisation definitely affects productivity. Although it is hard to tell how to reach the maximum productivity of a software team, we surely know of some teaming issues that will hurt a software team's productivity.

7.2.1 The Illusion of Productivity

Members of teams working on collective tasks generally think that their team is more productive than other teams. Team members also feel that they are doing more than their fair share—even those who are loafers. These two individual illusions produce the group illusion of team productivity. At the same time, people performing simple tasks often work harder over any period when they are being watched and evaluated and do less when they are not being evaluated.

We can show the relationship between anonymity and social loafing by the shouting test. There are large differences in how loudly people will shout in pairs, shouting alone, and as part of six-person groups that shout at the same time. In pairs and six-member groups, individuals worked at only 59% and 31%, respectively, of their individually expressed capacity. But when their individual contributions were to be identified, their loudness increased by 69% for individuals in pairs and by 61% for individuals in six-person groups. The identification of a contribution encouraged people to make a contribution.

When teammates work anonymously and their contributions are not easily identified or recognized, individual contributions fall. Even in a self-organizing team, the efforts and contributions of individuals should be appreciated and evaluated.

7.2.2 Collective Code Ownership

Team members can do less than their share of the work yet still share equally in the team's rewards. When people's contributions are combined into a single work product and it is difficult to measure individual contributions, some will try to "free-ride." And the more free riders there are perceived to be, the more other team members will hold back, for fear of being "suckers" (Forsyth, 2003). They will only get the average team reward, so why should they make more than the average team effort? If we were writing "the 10 laws of teamwork," law 1 would have to be:

> Workers in a team-rewarded team will eventually try to match their efforts
> to the average of what they think their workmates are doing.

It is important to be able to identify contributions to collaborative work. Therefore, collective code ownership, in which any programmers can make any change to any part of the source code at any time, should not be anonymous. We should be able to identify who has fixed bugs and updated the system. If this is difficult in small software teams, have a day-end meeting to let team members claim credit for their work.

It is somewhat difficult to quantify individual contributions in pair programming as two programmers sit side-by-side and collaborate on the same task. Williams and Kessler 2000 suggested peer appraisal to provide a clearer idea of whom to reward. This can provide valuable feedback, although peer appraisal doesn't always work well (Peiperl 2006).

Another straightforward way to quantify individual contributions is to measure the pair's effort by achievement. For example, A and B pair up and spend a morning finishing nine function points, while C and D complete another eight function points. Then in the afternoon, the pairs rotate and exchange partners. This time A and C finish seven function points while B and D finish six points. Each function point will be different but in the long run such variances should be averaged out. A simple calculation will measure the individual's contributions:

$$A : 9+7 = 16$$
$$B : 9+6 = 15$$
$$C : 8+7 = 15$$
$$D : 8+6 = 14$$

If these ratios remain consistent, we may conclude that D is a free rider or simply that the programmers have different abilities. This measure, albeit less subjective, can just be one part of a diagnosis.

7.2.3 Accountability, Responsibility, and Transparency

The difference between responsibility and accountability is not that clear. For example, a program was written by Colleen. Its testing was assigned to Jason, so he had the responsibility. Jason tested the system and picked up all the software bugs for Colleen to fix. Later on, when a customer called about a hidden bug that had caused data loss, the boss may wrongly blame Jason for doing nothing. This is an accountability issue.

Accountability is about holding people responsible for their actions. We always need to improve accountability for results as in Jason's case. In software development, it is not enough to fully take responsibility for our work tasks. Accountability is a connection between the responsible party and a given outcome.

To deal with this situation, we have to consider another element, transparency. This helps us understand what others are doing and vice versa. We should communicate obligations and expected behavior in a team even in collective tasks. Let the team know how their efforts are recognized on one hand and what is known about social loafing on the other hand.

It is important to be proactive in identifying and preventing teaming problems. Accountability, responsibility and transparency provide the foundations to make teams more productive.

7.3 PROBLEMS AND PROBLEM OWNERS

As early as 1998, and before the "agile manifesto," Metes et al. had already talked about agile teams. They are virtual teams that are trained to quickly adapt themselves and their processes to change. Metes's agile teams can also be quickly formed and just as quickly disbanded when an initiative ends. In addition, the team members collaborate in a distributed manner. Metes' definition described it as teaming on demand (Metes et al. 1996).

Software teams that adopt agile practices and thereby embrace changes are closed to Metes' definition, except that they may not be virtual at all. The teams can be collocated and face-to-face in the workplace.

Here agile teaming is a little bit different. Agile teaming is a practice that restructures a software team so as to maximize team performance or to respond to serious project issues. While the project is ongoing, many things can happen. There is no reason to think that the original team structure is always suitable for solving every problem throughout a project's lifecycle.

As agile teaming is considered to be a software practice, we may say that any group that adopts agile software practices is an agile team. But this is not to say that an agile team adopts the practice of agile teaming.

It is difficult to generalize about the root causes of many problems in software projects. What appear to be causes of one problem may simply be the symptoms of another. However, it is relatively easy to group an event or a problem by type rather than to identify its cause. In this way, we can identify a problem by its type and as having two dimensions: a process area dimension and a functional module dimension. For example, a problem such as a user disagreement with new report formats may correspond to three functional modules but will correspond to only one process area: report writing development.

The process area and the functional module can link up with two types of team structure. A team can be established according to the functional model as shown in Figure 7.13. The drawback is the main source of task conflicts. A team can also be structured with process areas. Many software development teams are formed in this way; this team is usually composed of three or more subteams, each of which is responsible for business requirements, development, and testing.

A two-dimensional matrix of process area and functional module can be formed. Problem types can be identified in the matrix. For example, problem A, as shown in Figure 7.13, involves both user acceptance test and report development; problem B involves three functional modules.

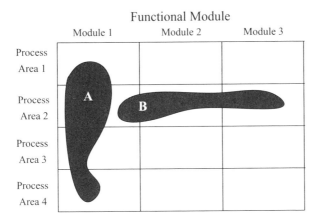

FIGURE 7.13 A matrix of process area and functional module.

When project problems are oriented to more functional modules than process areas, the team structure should be organized by process areas so that each problem will be managed by one subteam. For example, in problem B in Figure 7.13, a team structure by functional module says nothing about which subteam is responsible for dealing with problem B. However, when a team structure is formed by process area, problem B belongs to the subteam of the user acceptance test. The team and its subteams can concentrate on their commitment to accountability, responsibility, and transparency in the way the team manages and operates software projects.

For instance, consider the scenarios unfolding in Figure 7.14. The message here is to avoid "nobody's business" and "everybody's business"; and make sure that each project issue has just one owner.

7.3.1   Rhythm: Trouble–Restructuring

When a software project is making slow progress, sometimes even halting for a while, and finally slipping behind schedule, that project is in deep trouble. This trouble often comes with reworking something, as shown in Figure 7.15; the team has lost its development rhythm.

Arrhythmic software projects have problems concerning either no owners or too many owners. Agile teaming deals with this by restructuring the teams so that they match the problem sets (see Figure 7.16).

There are limits on how often we can use agile teaming. For those teams that are sizable and have been well-structured, we may be restructuring them only once or twice. In this case, agile teaming is not considered as easy to sustain.

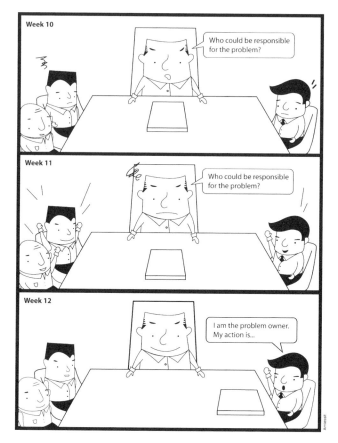

FIGURE 7.14 Problem ownership.

Although agile teaming can be used to resolve serious problems, as in troubled–late software projects, some project leaders commonly use agile teaming to maximize team productivity and to facilitate job rotation in an iterative development method, tuning their team structure in review meetings between two iterations. As we can see, for a self-organizing team it is possible to change team structure to react to problems encountered previously in the review (see Figure 7.3). In this case, the practice is easy to start and easy to sustain in the in–out diagram (see Figure 7.17).

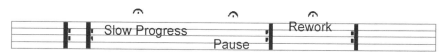

FIGURE 7.15 "Trouble" rhythm.

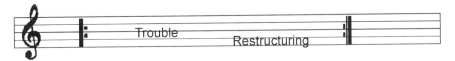

FIGURE 7.16 Agile teaming rhythm.

Kent Beck said that we should keep a team workload constant but gradually reduce the team size until there is no more wasted effort (Beck and Andres 2005). What Beck advised was actually about agile teaming adopted for a self-organizing team, to enable it to reach an optimum structure and size that can lead to a highly productive team.

We know when to beat out the rhythm; but our next question is how to beat the rhythm: agile teaming.

7.3.2 Teaming Principles

Agile teaming involves changing team structures in troubled projects, is not without costs, and is best reserved for serious problems. The following are some principles for executing agile teaming.

The importance of root cause analysis has been addressed in agile software development management (Beck and Andres 2005), but learning from software projects is just as challenging as managing them. Project problems can be rooted in a different combination of factors, such as programming issues, domain knowledge, and human factors. Causes that are multifactorial and difficult to define are not going to produce problems that are easy to fix.

Overcoming the temptation to think in terms of cause and effect is very difficult for software managers who combine technical skills with an understanding of the organization across all functions from problem solving to

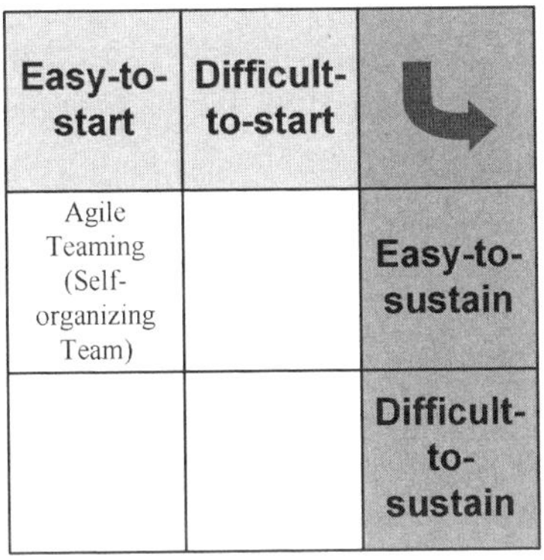

Easy-to-start	Difficult-to-start	
Agile Teaming (Self-organizing Team)		**Easy-to-sustain**
		Difficult-to-sustain

FIGURE 7.17 Agile teaming for self-organizing teams.

strategies. Instead of doing a lot of analyses, taking some exploratory action such as agile teaming is suggested.

Principle 1: Exploratory action over heavy analysis.

Project managers seldom know much about technical implications. Drawing incorrect conclusions about problems in IT projects can be dangerous. Executives who have stronger programming backgrounds tend to prefer determining causality in a troubled software project and then immediately taking remedial actions to rescue the project.

> *Rescue practice (1)*: In a troubled software project, executives should concentrate on the process areas and functional modules where the (technical/non-technical) problems show up rather than on where the problems actually come from.

Many people focus on stepwise solutions. But we should find the right problem owners for problems. Many software projects in the commercial sector involve users over more than one department (e.g., writing ERP applications) and/or sometimes over several organizations (i.e., supply chain management). Thus, we have another principle behind agile teaming.

Principle 2: Problem owners over problems.

Many companies are in trouble with their supply chain systems. Most difficulties stem from an uncoordinated and fragmented allocation of responsibility of the various supply chain activities over a number of functional areas. But we often overlook a simple problem when in trouble. This is because no one in the company is responsible for solving each supply chain problem (Taylor 2002).

Similarly, we should ascertain who owns a problem rather than what the problem could be. It makes sense that the project structure has gone wrong when many project issues have no owner or more than one owner. It is therefore important to fix the project structure in order to rescue a troubled software project.

> *Rescue Practice (2)*: In a troubled software project, if there is no owner or more than one owner, restructure the team so that for each problem there is always one owner of each problem.

Management that ignores the complexity of software projects may replace the project manager. They then need to be sure to put the right person in charge because removing team leaders and members late in the life of a project can be counterproductive as it means losing valuable experience.

> *Principle 3*: Change people responsibilities as needed over their titles responsibilities as planned.

Rather than asking a team leader to leave a software project, management should continuously motivate the project manager but, meanwhile, narrow that person's responsibilities to a few particular areas.

> *Rescue Practice (3)*: In a troubled software project, senior management should narrow down the responsibilities of the driving staff (e.g., project managers) so that they could focus on only one or two process areas (or functional modules).

Management should assign a person of a senior rank to take over the functional title of the project manager. The superior will be the project owner (e.g., senior management). This resolves or relieves existing conflicts.

> *Principle 4*: Collaboration over organization hierarchy.

To deal with a troubled project, it is advisable for management to sit in on all regular meetings. This has three major benefits: (1) rebuilding team spirit, (2) resolving any politics among team members, and (3) improving team effectiveness by providing positional diversity.

> *Rescue Practice (4)*: In a troubled software project, management should assign a person of a higher rank than the project manager to take the chairperson role for each project meeting.

These principles conform to those of the agile manifesto. This is no accident. Agile thinking provides a way to solve problems that are uncertain and changing. Table 7.1 juxtaposes each principle with its related expression in the agile manifesto.

7.4 FAILING PROJECTS RESCUED

High failure rates have long been associated with software projects (Ewusi-Mensha 1997), even though there are a number of postmortem studies on abandoned software projects, key lessons learned from the successful software projects, classifications of troubled projects, and advice on how to avoid project failures by using risk management. However, these are of little help

TABLE 7.1   Principle for Agile Teaming Related to the Agile Manifesto

Principle for Agile Teaming	Agile Manifesto
1 Exploratory action over heavy analysis	Work product over document
2 Problem owners over problems	People over process
3 Change people responsibilities when needed over their position responsibilities as planned	Change over planned
4 Collaboration over organisation hierarchy	Collaboration over contract

for dealing with failing or troubled late projects because we not only have to take corrective actions but must also respond in a timely manner to many project-related problems that we do not really know much about or how they were developed. In fact, once the cause of a problem is understood, half the battle is won, and solutions will be found.

In 2006, we were giving a presentation on rescuing software projects in Finland. In the question/answer (Q/A) session, one audience member suggested investing in project management tools, techniques, and training, in the areas of teaming and risk control, saying that these would produce substantial benefits in dealing with runaway projects. One woman in the audience was very keen to share her experience on this and spoke up, saying, "I have done lots of things, including risk management and project management, to monitor and control my projects, but there are times where things can still go unexpectedly wrong. I don't know why."

This is true. Sometimes we just don't know why things won't go according to plan. These situations call for corrective action, which can be very different from either preventive or detective action. All three of these are part of a rhythmic problem management cycle: detection–correction–prevention. When we are dealing with troubled late IT projects, bear in mind the following;

- *Don't play Sherlock Holmes.* The famous sleuth had a prodigious eye for detail and never missed a clue. But saving a failing project is a race against the clock. You don't have time for the unlikely and the obscure.
- *Don't believe everything project members tell you.* Project members may speak out of self-interest, rather than with the goal of identifying real problems.
- *Bad news always comes late.* People are reluctant to report bad news in a runaway software project.
- *Project data may not be correct.* Since software is intangible, measurements for building software may not be used as reliable tools in assessing the real status of a software project.

- *No one wants to be fired.* When the problem is a conflict of interest between two parties, the situation can create political infighting. Every one is afraid of bearing all the responsibilities at the end.

Teaming helps us act quickly. What is important is not what caused a problem but who owns it.

7.4.1 Project Traffic Light Reporting

Managers may typically use any of a number of approaches to identify a troubled project. One simple and useful project status reporting technique is "traffic light reporting," where status is reported as "green," "yellow," or "red," according to whether the project has met three basic project objectives of being within budget, on schedule, and achieving function/performance ratios as planned (Snow and Keil 2001).

Traffic light reporting has been used to rate business partners for many Y2K readiness tracks. It provides a simple and intuitive way of communicating project status. However, what constitutes a green, yellow, or red state can be variously defined in different organizations.

For any project, a review meeting will be held on a regular basis and a project manager will report on the status of the assessment of the above-mentioned three project objectives:

A green light means that all three objectives have been substantially met to date. The project is on track.

A yellow light means that two of the three basic project objectives have been substantially met to date; management involvement or resources may be required to handle the problems before the next review.

A red light means that only one objective has been substantially met to date. Senior management involvement is needed to deal with the project problems. Projects that get a red light are defined as failing projects rather than as "simply late projects." A red light project may eventually be abandoned, or it could be partially complete.

Traffic light reporting is intuitive for senior management. However, it is not without problems. Suppose that every new project starts with a green light. If there is a long gap between meetings, it is possible for the traffic light to change from green to red without passing through yellow. Therefore, we have to carefully define the satisfaction of objectives in percentage terms to avoid a sudden leap from safety to danger without getting yellow warning signs.

Now let us look at a real case rescued by agile teaming.

7.4.2 A Business Case

Jespersen was the managing director of KuDrink*, an international beverage company with a presence in more than 100 countries. His background was in law and he had taken part in many mergers and acquisitions in Laos, Thailand, and China. He knew little about IT, but he knew that KuDrink's current IT project was in deep trouble.

In the beer industry, the use of "customer fund/outlet promotions" and "free beer/discounts" constituted nearly 40% of the total annual costs, implying that there should be a proper control over how these resources were allocated, in particular to high-repeat customers.

The legacy application on IBM A/S400 in KuDrink could not provide an analysis of past performance (e.g., profitability of operational transactions of customers), which would provide a rational support for decisionmaking and would serve as a baseline for judgment, so the KuDrink senior management established a project goal that used a new application that could handle rebates, customer sales contracts, logistic costs, promoter bonus, and other requirements. This application would produce a profit-and-loss statement for each customer. This would allow KuDrink to better allocate its resources and determine the right level of service, pricing, and distribution.

7.4.3 Steering Committee Meeting

The project was running okay and was reported as green and yellow. Jespersen did not attend any meeting until the traffic light turned red. The original plan shown in Figure 7.18 (where the asterisks * denote time needed to revise a project plan) indicated that the project should have been completed

	2001				2002								
	9	10	11	12	1	2	3	4	5	6	7	8	9
Original Project Plan													
1st Revision by Project Manager					*								
2nd Revision by Project Manager						*							
3rd Revision by Project Manager						*							
Proposed Revised Plan by voting							*						

FIGURE 7.18 Project schedule.

*KuDrink is not the company's real name.

in 7 months, from September 2001 to March 2002. The system was to go live on April 1, 2002. The project schedule was revised several times: in January, early March, late March and May 2002.

The reported reason for extending the length of the project was that users could not complete their assigned tasks on schedule, yet the users complained about their heavy workload in producing lengthy documents and drawing flow diagrams, and had also encountered unknown technical problems during testing. Often the users reported that previous cases tested okay but the same cases failed after the consultants fixed other problems. They felt frustrated and lost confidence in the system.

The company's finance director accused project managers of making confusing and misleading comments relating to the potential issues of "overexpectation of finance functionality and overused accruals."

However, what stunned Jespersen was the idea of "project management by democracy." The project manager reported that she had asked all project members to vote for the date of the system going live. She told everyone in the team:

> Before we move forward, I would like to have opinion polls. My role is to set up the achievable goal for the project team; therefore, you must agree on it. Our consensus is crucial. My philosophy is that we are our own enemies. Many of us have lost faith in this project and we are losing our team spirit. Quality must not be sacrificed for productivity. I will not give up quality. However, you can make your own choice. Please select one of the go-live dates and send it to me by email.

Here are their date candidates:

1. August 1, 2002
2. September 1, 2002
3. October 1, 2002
4. I cannot say, as it is unforeseen at this moment

Jespersen thought that this sounded more like a spiritual speech than project management. And it seemed to be just a technique to galvanize senior management into accepting the difficulties. Evidence and data were presented, but how could Jespersen make a ruling? Defendants and prosecutors had their reasons. Jespersen only knew that he was not a judge to decide on these issues. Nevertheless, none of the so-called reasons would be good enough for the board of directors.

7.4.4   Agile Teaming in Action

Jespersen applied a sort of development rhythm of agile teaming. He thought of problems and problem owners and decided to put this thought into action. He knew nothing about IT and hence did not bother to try to understand the causes of the problems. What he looked at was not remedial actions but the connection between the team structure and problem domains.

On June 1, 2002, Jespersen announced a restructure of the project team from functional modules to process areas. The finance director was appointed to assume all the responsibilities of user acceptance testing. The project manager would be responsible only for data migration, but she still held the title of project manager. One MIS guy would be in charge of all other technical problems.

Surely, before the announcement, Jespersen already talked to those key project members about his concept of team flexibility and personal adaptability. He further explained that the project methodology was inflexible to cope with unexpected challenges, and hence the project team had to be restructured to overcome such inflexibility. Moreover, he praised the hardworking project manager and asked her to support his decision.

These three team leaders reported directly to the general manager. With this structure, the team leaders managed their resources with the direct support of the top management. A weekly meeting chaired by the general manager was held as usual to report and monitor the progress of the project.

A month later, Jespersen and the general manager further restructure the team by splitting the technical area into two. A more experienced person was fully responsible for the report writing, and the MIS programmer was responsible just for technical server problems. Now four team leaders reported to the general manager in the weekly meeting.

Agile teaming was adopted in this case to match the team structure with the problem areas. The system with the original planned functionality went live on September 1, 2002. After a month, the legacy system A/S400 stopped production.

7.5   BEWARE OF IAGO

We would like to end this chapter by another real case to illustrate that some software project failures are not because of development rhythms, team structure, management support, software complexity, risk management, or rapid changing requirements, but just one kind of person. We call him or her "Iago." Unfortunately, we have no hints as to how you can tell whether Iago has joined your software team.

On December 1, 2004, Brian, a senior IT manager with 10 years working experience, joined a well-established pharmaceutical company in Asia. After 6 months, he and his subordinate, Dennis, were dismissed from their posts as IT managers and an analyst programmer, Yvonne, was promoted to system analyst.

Yvonne was around 30, was sociable, and got along with the other seven colleagues except her supervisor, Dennis, who was in his late 30s. Other staff thought Dennis was not really qualified to be the IT manager because they knew more new technical stuff than he did. But, they did not conspire against him.

On the first day, Brian could smell some problems with the team that was made up of analyst programmers. There was no system analyst levels between the IT manager and the programmers. As Brian was new, Yvonne came to him and they talked about jobs and the company's culture. Yvonne did not mention that she did not get on well with Dennis. On the contrary, she said Dennis was a nice guy.

The bomb started with a meeting in which company directors got together to discuss project difficulties. Two analyst programmers absented themselves from the meeting. This situation immediately embarrassed the two IT managers. The human-relations (HR) manager was instructed to interview every member in the department.

Yvonne managed to convince other colleagues to speak ill of both Dennis and Brian because Dennis had given a list of names to Brian as part of a plan to replace some staff in the department. They all complained about the two IT managers when HR interviewed them. Meanwhile, Yvonne almost won a chance to be promoted to project manager instead of system analyst. One programmer who realized that he was being used for her promotion said to Brian after he left the company: "Yvonne was manipulating the whole game."

Not all project team members positively contribute to a project or help make it a success. At the worst, someone like Yvonne acts as an Iago in a project, winning the friendship of a manager and offering advice but with only his or her own interests in mind or perhaps even out of some animosity. An Iago in a project is sly and acts like a friend but is not. In the end, we should remember that not all project problems are to be found in the programming code or the team structure.

O, beware, my lord of jealousy; It is the green-eyed monster which doth mock The meat it feeds on.[2]

— *OTHELLO*, ACT III, SCENE III

REFERENCES

Baker FT. Chief programmer team management of production programming. *IBM Systems Journal* 1972; **11** (No. 1):56–73.

Beck K and Andres C. *Extreme Programming Explained*. 2nd ed. Boston: Addison-Wesley; 2005.

Eppler M. *Management Mess-ups*. Franklin Lakes, NJ: Career Press, 1997.

Ewusi-Mensha K. *Software Development Failures: Anatomy of Abandoned Projects*. Cambridge, MA: MIT Press; 2003.

Forsyth DR. *Group Dynamics*. 4th ed. Belmont, CA: Thomson/Wadsworth; 2006.

Giddens A, Duneier M, and Appelbaum R. *Introduction to Sociology*. 2nd ed. New York: Norton; 1996.

Metes G, Gundry J, and Brahish P. *Agile Networking: Competing through the Internet and Intranets*. Upper Saddle River, NJ: Prentice-Hall PTR; 1998.

Parrado N and Rause V. *Miracle in the Andes: 72 Days on the Mountain and My Long Trek Home*. New York: Crown; 2006.

Peiperl M. Getting 360-degree feedback right. *Harvard Business Review* 2001; **79** (No. 1):177.

Schwaber K and Beedle M. *Agile Software Development with Scrum*. Upper Saddle River, NJ: Prentice-Hall; 2002.

Sonnentag S. High performance and meeting participation: An observational study in software design teams. *Group Dynamics: Theory, Research and Practice* 2001; **5** (No. 1):3–18.

Snow AP and Keil M. The challenge of accurate software project status reporting: A two-stage model incorporating status errors. *IEEE Transactions on Engineering Management* 2002; **49** (No. 4):491–504.

Taylor D. *Supply Chains: A Manager's Guide*. Reading MA: Addison-Wesley; 2003.

Tuckman BW. Developmental sequence in small groups. *Psychological Bulletin* 1965; **63**:384–399.

Williams LA, Kessler RR, Cunningham W, and Jeffries R. Strengthening the case for pair programming. *IEEE Software* 2000; **17** (No. 4), 19–25.

Williams L and Kessler R. *Pair Programming Illuminated*. Boston: Addison-Wesley; 2003.

Welch J and Welch S. *Winning*. New York: HarperBusiness; 2005.

Yeh YJ and Chou HW. Team composition and learning behaviors in cross functional teams. *Social Behavior and Personality* 2005; **33** (No. 3):391–402

---

[2] This was the villain Iago's persuasive warning to Shakespeare's Othello against the very jealousy, but it was just a means to hide Iago's real intentions.

8

INCREMENTAL DESIGN

> Programmers don't design software; they make the computer work for users.

In the early 1990s, many commercial PC applications such as accounting packages and point-of-sales (POS) systems were written in Clipper or FoxPro. They are standalone applications with facilities for data exchange. For example, in the POS system, sales data were exported into a file, which would be transferred from stores to the office over phone lines. The reverse flow would be used to update price and product files from the office to stores. Data exchange was not automated, so end users had to complete their day-end operations to initiate data transfers. In practice, some end users may have forgotten to do so, and the price and product masters on the POS became outdated. The business operations could be in a mess. To secure our job, we had no choice but to say that even a well-designed system needs user cooperation.

Before long, the advance in Transmission Control Protocol/Internet Protocol (TCP/IP) networking lowered the costs of data communications and made system data transfer simpler. This led many management information system (MIS) heads to think about how their information systems could facilitate workflow collaboration, information sharing and real-time availability. Software was modifiable. Now the only question would be how much they had to pay to modify their existing systems that enabled multiuser operations over a network. Their bottom line would be to pay nearly 50% more than the original investment. Then, MIS guys picked up phones and asked their vendor the amount. Straightforwardly, the vendor said, "I am

Software Development Rhythms: Harmonizing Agile Practices for Synergy
By Kim Man Lui and Keith C. C. Chan
Copyright © 2008 John Wiley & Sons, Inc.

afraid that it is nothing about money. We will have to redevelop the system for you!"

It was a bit hard to imagine why the vendor had to rebuild the system, just because the system was not designed flexibly from the beginning! Some of customers may have expressed disapproval of rebuilding as there should be virtually no limitation to software modifications. But the vendor said that "programming multiuser systems technically involves data locking, deadlock handling, timeout to release resources, and user authorization." Thus, we have to change almost every part of the existing code related to data manipulations. Besides, success in redesigning the system also very much depends on the tool that we used to build it. If Clipper supported modularizing of crosscutting concerns as aspect-oriented programming suggests, it would be easily to modify the system for the multiuser authority. In fact, Clipper was dying rather than evolving.

Finally, concerning the application, the user interface should display information differently depending on the role of the users. Many people just did not quickly see that "multiuser" actually means that a system has different authorization levels or roles to retrieve and update records. MIS managers need to review their existing user requirements from A to Z.

It became clear that the interplay between programming issues, technology availability (or constraints), and changes of user requirements dominates our success in redesigning an existing system or developing a new system. To meet the challenge of changing requirements, we should build software in such a way that we are able to shorten the time our users take to go from imagining what they want to understanding what they need by seeing a prototype product.

8.1 MODELING AND PLANNING

Many software architects have given a number of slightly different definitions of software design. For software teams, software design means two things: modeling and planning. Software design can be described as the general arrangement of the different parts of software logic — what and how it will be implemented and tested. Basically, we cannot complete our design tasks without understanding the requirements. For example, in database applications, user requirements affect what and how we define the data model, business mapping, screen layouts, and systemwide procedure calls.

Software design is also a process of deciding when different parts of the system should be built. We can carefully plan our activities in order to optimize our resource allocation in the whole project cycle. As mentioned in Chapter 1, modeling and planning in developing software are not as tightly connected as in building engineering products.

Now let us look at incremental design. As its name implies, this means to design and develop software in a highly evolutionary manner. Incremental design ties in with the first semantics of software design (i.e., modeling) as we can always build new components, add on some features, modify old components, or integrate them with others. However, incremental design by nature should be highly iterative. It does not seem to follow traditional project planning, in which, as best as we can, activities have been prioritized far in advance so that resources will be optimally allocated.

8.1.1 Agile Planning

Traditional software project management tells us that we should try our best to understand task dependences and estimate time. In addition, we should be cautious about allocating resources: who will be responsible for a particular task. All these elements would be reflected into a project plan. Furthermore, we could calculate the critical path among all the tasks that must be completed on schedule (see Section 5.2.6 on CPM).

When user requirements can be continuously collected for implementation, it may not be possible to develop a full plan for construction at one particular stage as we did in the waterfall model. Moreover, in traditional project management scheduling, the duration of each task is more complete and less split over different time periods. Tasks are longer (days to weeks, but not hours to days) and are less frequently repeated. When adopting incremental design, the tasks become much shorter and highly repetitive (see Figure 8.1).

Irrespective of the programming implementation, the amount of business functionality is defined and then measured in a unit of logical user function, which can be referred to as *function points*. When user requirements can be divided into a number of blocks, each of which has few enough function points that it can be done in a few days, we may easily prioritize these blocks and incrementally build them.

More precisely, in agile software development, we briefly record user requirements in a stack of cards (called "story cards" in eXtreme programming or "product backlogs" in scrum) so that customers can prioritize the story cards by moving them around and programmers can incrementally build the system according to the order of the story cards (see Figure 8.2).

In order to estimate the programming effort required to build each story card, we use an index scale ranging from 1 representing minimum effort to 5 representing maximum effort. The software team will pick up some story cards to develop, and we can calculate the team's velocity by the elapsed time

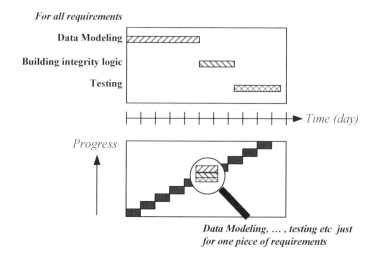

FIGURE 8.1 Traditional project planning versus incremental design.

over the sum of the indices as follows:

$$\text{Velocity} = \frac{\text{elapsed time}}{\text{sum of indices}}$$

Think of software development as a journey and each story card as a road segment. Then the index will be a measurement of the segment. To monitor the team's progress along the journey, we have to know how quickly the team drives forward. Figure 8.3 illustrates this idea—the total development time is the sum of the indices of each story card over the team velocity.

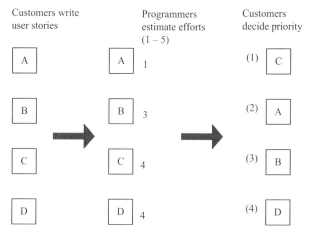

FIGURE 8.2 Planning as part of software design.

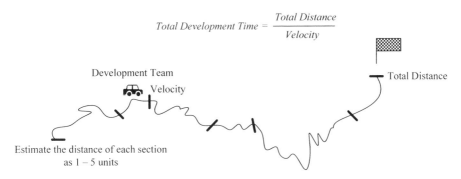

$$Total\ Development\ Time = \frac{Total\ Distance}{Velocity}$$

FIGURE 8.3 Software development journey.

The team certainly has different development speeds. Thus, we may prefer to set our iteration as a fixed short interval, say, a week. Our project progress can then be easily tracked. At any moment, our customer may change or add new features to the project and therefore the stack of outstanding story cards does not always shrink. In addition, we may reestimate our index for some story cards. As far as we can track the change in velocity, we should be confident in managing the project and can predict more accurately when we are likely to complete the project on the basis of our team velocity. This management methodology, called *agile project planning*, is suitable for incremental design (see Figure 8.4)

Incremental design, however, differs from what we know as traditional software development by module although both involve building a system by dividing a whole system into smaller ones.

8.1.2 Design by Functional Modules

In the 1990s, enterprise resources planning (ERP) was introduced to integrate all core business functions into a single database so as to streamline the

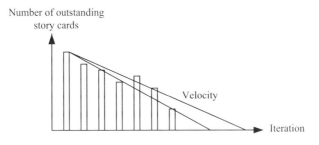

FIGURE 8.4 Agile project progress.

workflow across each different department within the enterprise. For such a fully integrated system, it seems logical to design a database model covering all necessary functions at the beginning. In fact, many early versions of the ERP package had just a few complete modules that most companies could implement for their business needs. Take MFG/PRO (an ERP package) as an example. The early version included manufacturing resources planning, rough-cut capacity planning, and other modules but, it did not support sales quotation or customer relations management. Another example is Exact's ERP. The system had strong features in accounting and e-commerce. But until 2005, the Exact's ERP package had only enough functionality to support midsized manufacturing operations.

No doubt, software can always be divided into a number of modules. A module-by-module approach is characterized by the construction of the software in modules, and normally concentrates on the implementation of a few related functions across modules at any one time. This approach however is not considered as incremental design here, for the software requirements are logically broken down into a few modules that are then built by a chain of complete development cycles instead of a number of story cards that are small enough to be done in a slot of a few days (see Figure 8.5).

In reality, we may adopt a hybrid approach by dividing the system into modules. We take a top–down strategy to estimate the effort and resources required to build each module. Each is then built incrementally. The team velocity can be used to adjust our early estimate of the effort required to develop the module. This is a bottom–up approach. The new estimation based on velocity can be used to monitor our overall project plan.

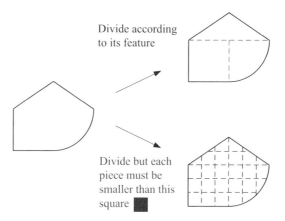

Divide according to its feature

Divide but each piece must be smaller than this square

FIGURE 8.5 Divide by module or divide by slot.

So far, we have seen how incremental design is related to the software modeling and project planning. In the following, we will discuss two important concepts in software design: simple design and total cost concept.

8.1.3 Simple Design

In general, eXtreme programming encourages doing the simplest thing that could possibly work and discourages building features not requested by customers; in a word: "Just in need." Building things for future use is unwise. We do not know exactly what features will deliver business value to our customers. To ensure that our design can cope with unpredictable future requirements, we should make things simple.

Simple design is also where art and engineering come from. In software development, the quality of being *simple* cannot be measured just by lines of code or the number of classes or other variables. Although *small is beautiful*, modeling our relationships among objects is the beauty of contemporary software design. Let's consider an example. Figure 8.6 illustrates a simple design competition in which you need to find the simplest design for a story card saying that the general manager assigns a quota of customers to each account manager. Are you ready to win? In other words, software design is

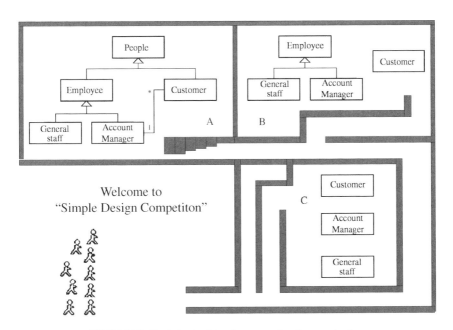

FIGURE 8.6 Labyrinthine Pattern of software design.

like a maze or labyrinth; it is easy to lose one's way. For example, which design shown in Figure 8.6 is leanest and simplest?

If we consider only that story card alone, we don't need the employee class and/or the people class. Therefore, we will just go for "C." In practice, we are working on many story cards, instead of one. They are always intertwined and interrelated; we may not easily tell which design is simplest.

In any case, we should not implement any function that is not yet requested. However, we should have a thinking-forward mindset for design. From an incremental design perspective, the purpose of simple design is to make sure that any late functions added do not force a substantial redesign of the system.

8.1.4 Total Cost Concept

To many of us who work in the commercial world, the purpose of software applications is to virtually simulate behaviors or processes or to model business systems. Unfortunately, business processes can be partially ill-defined while programming logic allows no fuzziness. Worse yet, ill-defined things often represent a gray area for which users have their own interpretations.

Therefore, from the viewpoint of programmers, user requirements become ambiguous, inconsistent, and incomplete. However, the user often fails to understand why programmers or programming cannot cope with business operations that they can manually carry out without advanced computer technology. This means that we need a platform on which the user and the programmer can easily communicate.

When building a system, we should start with something less ambiguous that we can explore further with our users. We need to talk to them often throughout the development cycle instead of just at the user requirement phase. The best strategy is to have the users involved in the software design! Therefore, invite the users to review your design. But to do this, we have to illustrate our design in a visual presentation that the user can understand.

To bridge the perception gap of system requirements between users and programmers, we need pictures that can represent thousands of programming commands. These pictures show us how real-world events are mapped to software functionality (see Figure 8.7). Such visual software design documents complex business processes. It also assists us in continuous and ever more detailed modeling of the target system. As we see in Figure 8.7, both customers and programmers can communicate with each other through a diagram that shows relationships among different events.

OMG, a nonprofit computer industry consortium, has already set up a standard for drawing diagrams in software engineering, the universal

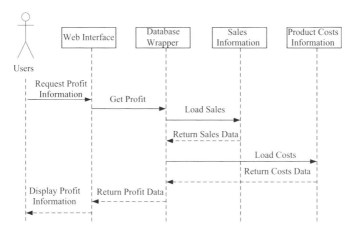

FIGURE 8.7   Customer–programmer communication.

modeling language (UML), a visual tool for user specifications, documentation, and software construction.

We may design our programs using diagrams, code, or both. Even though we practice design by code, we can still quickly write UML diagrams to communicate with our teammates and customers. As for incremental design, completing every UML diagram before coding is not necessary. What we may suggest are "code" to build software and "UML" to communicate with people. When we are stuck with code, it may be time to stop and draw a diagram that clarifies our understanding and ask others to review it.

"Visual software design" (i.e., design by diagram) or "design by code" involves two kinds of cost. Software practitioners are seldom alert to the total cost concept. Since reducing costs and waste in one area could drive up costs and waste in other areas, we have to be aware of total costs, not only one or two cost drivers.

On one hand, if programmers merely do design by code in which the programming activities include code and user interface, the cost of noncoding related work is low because the source code can be compiled for the end product but communication costs go up because the source code can be easily understood only by other programmers, needless to say not by customers. Using communication or explanation only through conversations or short descriptive texts (e.g., email dialogs and story cards) may not be enough.[1] Our customers may misunderstand us. Customers are just like us.

---

[1]In eXtreme programming, real user involvement consists in coping with that limitation.

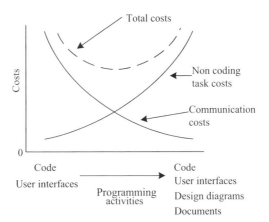

FIGURE 8.8 Costs in software development.

They also need both time and visual tools (i.e., diagrams) to think about their requirements.

On the other hand, drawing any design diagram to allow ideas to be shared with others reduces communication costs but increases non-coding tasks costs because the diagram cannot be automatically converted into computer instructions. Figure 8.8 illustrates the total cost concept, in which we should balance our communication costs against the costs of non-coding tasks.

8.2   REWORK OR REUSE

Good design often evolves from bad designs. If we think so, then we have one big problem haunting almost every programmer: rework! The ability to do less reworking in getting a program done is a great talent. Some programmers code with amazing speed. Some build programs with few bugs. Some are well versed in language skills. Some can write code that can be easily understood by others. However, if we were asked to seek gifted programmers, we would judge them by the amount of rework on design.

There are many scenarios that result in "rework." Some are quite preventive. For example, rework that arises from miscommunications with users about requirements could be avoidable. Many of us have a fairly negative attitude to rework. However, in some situations it can be positive.

In order to examine and reconstitute an existing system into one that is built from more reusable components, we rework (or refactor) program code (Mens and Tourwé 2004). We are eager to encapsulate the right features into the right classes, associate the right inhabitant relationships between parent and child classes, and so on so that our code can be truly reusable for other systems as well. In this case, rework, maintainability, and reusability are connected.

This seems to be telling us that we are not able to get things right at the beginning. Obvious solutions today were not so obvious yesterday. Let us have a look at some cases.

8.2.1 Unpreventable Rework

The BodyBuilder Gymnasium chain allows clients to work out on their own program and training schedule. It has attracted many busy people. Its customer base almost grew by 30% in one year to a total of 30,000 clients. The gym owner was a very customer-oriented person who thought of many special promotions to target the right people. He gave drink discounts *randomly daily* for those customers who spent 3 hours in the gym and did not buy a drink or snack. He gave no coupons to those who regularly bought snacks. The wisdom of "torment your customers (they'll love it)" seems applicable here (HBR, 2002). Let those who got the discount feel lucky and those who did not be envious!

In order to execute that special promotion, the gym needed a bidaily (twice daily) operation report from the computer system showing them which customers spent 3 hours in the gym without buying a drink. The logic may look like this:

```
if(staying>=3hours and buying_drink=no)then print
          customer_name
```

The report, albeit easy, took hours to run and the users were not happy at all. The problem was that we did not consider the data distribution when the report was being developed. We knew from the past that 90% of customers spent 3 hours in the gym and that 20% of customers brought water with them and so would not buy a drink at the gym. For performance purposes, we should rewrite the code as follows:

```
if(buying_ drink = no and staying >= 3 hours) then print
          customer_name
```

In this way, we can filter 80% of customers using the first condition, thereby reducing workload in the second condition as shown in Figure 8.9. This case demonstrates the necessity of reconstructing the programming code to reflect the distribution of data. Certainly, there was little we

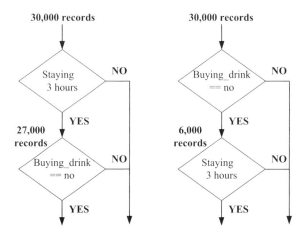

FIGURE 8.9 Performance tuning.

could do before the system was implemented. Often, we have to denormalize a database in order to meet the performance requirements. This is usually done by adding summary tables and/or deliberately introducing redundancy. When data volume grows exponentially, the code definitely needs reexamining. Having highly maintainable code is a strategy for future success.

8.2.2 Improvisation

> *Romeo* It is my lady.
> Two of the fairest stars in all the heaven
> do entreat her eyes
> to twinkle in their sphere till they return.
>
> *Juliet* Ay me!
>
> *Romeo* She speaks. O speak again bright angel.
>
> *Juliet* O Romeo, Romeo, wherefore art thou Romeo? ....What man art
> thou that thus bescreened in night so stumblest on my counsel
>
> *Romeo* By a name I know not how to tell thee who I am
>
> *Juliet* Art thou not Romeo, and a Montague?
>
> *Romeo* Neither, fair maid, if either thee dislike.
>
> *Juliet* By whose direction found'st thou out this place.
>
> *Romeo* By love. He lent me counsel, and I lent him eyes.
>
> —ROMEO AND JULIET: ACT II, SCENE 2

Playwrights edit their work thousands of times. The modifications could vary from trivial to substantial. No matter what changes have been made; the theme, actor and actress should remain much the same.

Take a look at a counterexample of what would happen if the Bard felt like swapping the role of Juliet and Romeo. Juliet was strolling in Montague's garden and heard Romeo sighing heavily on his balcony. The revision would mean rereading and rethinking each word and sentence. Besides issues of syntactic correctness fixing gender-specific pronouns (e.g., he and she), there are changes for semantics, for example, the expression "bright angel"[2] could become "brave hero." Obviously, play writing needs a plot (i.e., a plan). The actors' roles were well thought out; there would not be any role alteration. Thus, play rewriting needs a plan. The same goes for program rewriting.

When programmers prefer an experience-driven approach to code and software development has few planning activities, we call this *improvisation*. In the working environment of a small software house, requirements may even be written down in keywords. In addition, programmers may very quickly deliver a small prototype, but the increase in the amount of rework becomes obvious as the software complexity grows beyond a certain point.

Improvisation is different from incremental design, in which developers practice simple design, small lot-size-like user requirements, and agile project management to plan and to control their development. Improvised developers may not even bother to ask their customers what they really need. Their experience guides their minds. Improvisation might work well, depending on the complexity of user requirements and the programmer's individual talent and experience. However, improvisation makes it difficult to team up with others.

Another problem with improvisation is that when customers ask for any change, the improvising developers may be required to do a tremendous amount of rework because their design has not been thoughtful or their experience fails to predict what customers want now. In reality, improvisation is extreme and only a few gifted programmers can write by ear. In conclusion, improvisation is easy to start, but sooner or later the team will encounter lots of stupid problems. It isn't sustainable (see Figure 8.10).

---

[2]Angels are not "female" or "male" in theology. Although early Renaissance artists would prefer to cultivate this gender ambiguity commented by Dr. Frank Vigneron in the Department of Fine Arts at the Chinese Hong Kong University, angels are often depicted as female. Examples are *The Virgin of the Rock* by Da Vinci, *The Virgin with Angels* by Bouguereau, and *Lost and Found* by van Gogh.

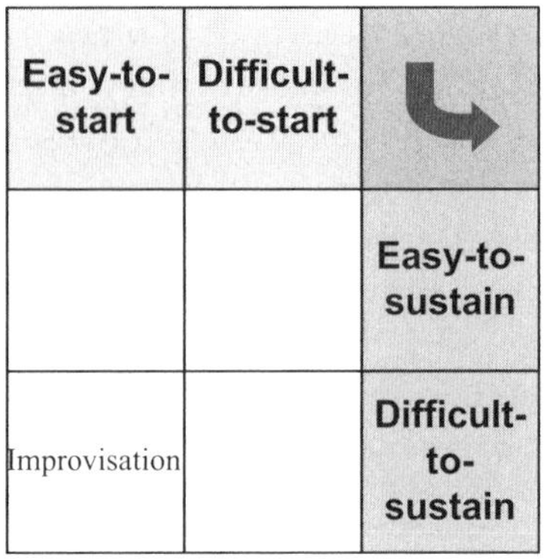

Easy-to-start	Difficult-to-start	⬏
		Easy-to-sustain
Improvisation		Difficult-to-sustain

FIGURE 8.10 Improvisation is not sustainable in software development.

8.2.3 Up-Front Design

The purpose of up-front design is to establish a process in which developers work on the what, how, when, or even the why of constructing and implementing a software system. As expected, a formal, well-organized design process will guide the whole team as to what to do almost for the rest of the project. From a management perspective, building things as planned is good. Furthermore, programmers from a project team who have more experience can contribute more in the areas of both user requirements and design. Allocating the right people experience to the right tasks optimizes a team's performance.

What makes up-front design different from incremental design is that we deliver a plan that should be well-documented for software construction, team collaboration, people communications, and task execution. The team is committed to following the plan and the design accordingly. Doing anything outside the plan could have uncertain negative impacts on the whole development and on the team. We would ruin the previous effort that was put into developing the plan and damage the team commitment and collaboration. The team may need to rework previous tasks. However, when the user requirements are stable, up-front design is easy to start and easy to sustain (see Figure 8.11).

Separating design and construction as two big phases is less workable when user requirements are changing. In this case, a software team needs constant feedback. Design guides us how to code, and the program being coded provides us with feedback to a better design. The values of incremental design seem to have nothing to do with design from a technical perspective

Easy-to-start	Difficult-to-start	↳
Upfront Design		**Easy-to-sustain**
		Difficult-to-sustain

FIGURE 8.11   In-out diagram for upfront design for stable user requirements.

but everything to do with communication and collaboration. This paradigm is more acceptable in a changing world. Information has been much more available than before, which keeps driving the world getting flatter (Friedman 2006)! Therefore, our world is always changing and changing faster than yesterday. So are user requirements.

Before we discuss incremental design further and understand when incremental design can be best used, we have to understand the just-in-time concept. Here is a review in one sentence of how we understand incremental design so far:

> Incremental design lies somewhere between big up-front design and improvisation.

8.3   JUST-IN-TIME SOFTWARE DEVELOPMENT

In the mid-1970s, responding to the global oil crisis, the manufacturing and logistics costs of the Toyota Motor Company increased sharply as the company imported almost everything they needed to produce cars. To remain competitive, the company had to eliminate any kind of waste such as idle time, storage, transportation, workforce imbalance, quality defects, linking production cells, equipment downtime, labors, and product backlog. The company invented the Toyota production system (TPS).

The philosophy behind TPS was just-in-time (JIT). There is no generally accepted definition of JIT. It is an approach to manufacturing that, in the ideal, attempts to meet demand with zero delay (Schonberger 1982). Womack et al.

(1991) coined the term "lean production," placing emphasis on the removal of all sorts of waste rather than just time. Perhaps the term *just in time* has misled many programmers into thinking that it deals with time only. JIT is about eliminating anything that is wasteful and does not add value to the manufacturing and customers (Harrison and Petty 2002). In fact, JIT and "lean" are almost exchangeable in manufacturing (Black 1991; Black and Hunter 2003).[3]

Manufacturing is about the production process. Therefore, JIT met *kaizen*, a Japanese term meaning "continuous improvement." It is clear that techniques should be designed to help minimize unnecessary work by continuously improving the production processes. Wait a minute! This sounds like the capability maturity model (CMM) or CMM integrated (CMMI) developed in the early 1990s, which concerns software process improvement (Paulk et al. 1995). The association is not accidental! The main idea of "eliminating waste" is to achieve production excellence, which cannot be done in a single reengineering project, but only through continuous process improvement.

8.3.1 The CMM Rhythm

Neither CMM nor CMMI explicitly addresses waste elimination, but the model appears to be useful in understanding lean (i.e. JIT) production. We can even adopt some CMM principles for "lean manufacturing" to eliminate waste in manufacturing production. CMM recommends that after basic project management techniques (i.e., CMM level 2) are in place, we have to clearly standardize our working process so that we can tailor our process to suit unique features of each software project (i.e., CMM level 3). According to the standard process, we quantitatively measure the performance of those tailored processes, and use these measurements as the basis for continuous process improvement (i.e., CMM levels 4 and 5). The assessment helps us improve our process. Undoubtedly, the method of "measure to improve" is fundamental in JIT.

In software development, we borrowed principles from lean manufacturing for lean software development (Middleton and Sutton 2005). However, a few agile zealots may turn a blind eye to the value of CMM. For example, some may say that with CMM the task is to follow a process. This shifts the focus to process rather than single project success, while lean focuses purely on the work products and continual improvement. Software development rhythms

---

[3] Black, in his early book *The Design of the Factory with a Future*, explains JIT by a flow diagram; 12 years later, the same diagram in Black's book on lean production was used but only the term JIT was replaced by *Lean Production*.

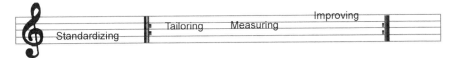

FIGURE 8.12   The CMM rhythm.

will help us understand CMM[4] and agile software development from another perspective.

As we see things as being about rhythm rather than where they belong, CMM has a strong rhythm (Figure 8.12) for managing a set of software projects: (1) *standardizing* our organization process, which is an important step for assessment, enabling us to define different measurements; (2) *tailoring* a standardized process for a single project; (3) *measuring* the tailored process; and (4) *improving* our standardized process in order to better manage future projects through tailoring an even better standardized process.

Adopting a full set of CMM practices demands a lot of effort to sustain the rhythm. In a word, to sustain the rhythm using CMM practices is another story. However, the CMM rhythm is useful for both agile software development and JIT manufacturing. Here is an example: standardize generic lean practices to eliminate waste, tailor (and/or select) the practices that are most beneficial for the project we are running, then measure how much waste has been reduced and improve the generic practices on the basis of the previous assessment. As illustrated in Figure 8.13, agile practices also need continuous process improvement.

Now, we have a little confusion over JIT software development because improving software process and eliminating development wastes can be strongly associated, in the same way as light is a coin of two sides: particle and wave. To clarify what we could learn from JIT for software development, we had better go back and ask what the Toyota production system has suggested to achieve manufacturing excellence. This kind of relationship has something to do with incremental design!

To avoid confusion so far, here is a short summary:

> JIT software development entails developing software by incremental design and implementation in small steps in a way to reduce both preventable rework and unnecessary work.

---

[4]Although some may argue that there is massive expense and waste in the CMM accreditation process to satisfy the examiner rather than the customer, let us look at the basic idea of the CMM model. It is about process improvement, as shown in Figure 8.12.

FIGURE 8.13 Agile and CMM.

The CMM rhythm is related to about managing software projects by standardizing, tailoring, measuring, and improving software processes and/or practice.

We had years of personal experience in working in different production plants in China. Honestly, we did not enjoy working there much. The shop floors were filthy, the air was polluted from the smoke and dust coming from

other neighboring factories, and the dormitory had few entertainment facilities. The bright side was that we could gain rich, hands-on experience of JIT
assembly lines. Sections 8.3.1 and 8.3.2 will give a fast-track route to JIT
practices in the manufacturing process. Afterward, we will return to our
discussion of JIT software development.

Now let us visit a factory that makes clocks. Enjoy your journey.

8.3.2 A Factory Tour

Walking into a factory of the classical manufacturing system, we quickly
see that machines are functionally grouped together according to the
manufacturing process. For example, the drilling department will be responsible for all kinds of drilling tasks such as tube bending, hole drilling,
and punching operations. The layout shown in Figure 8.14 is intuitive,
particularly when doing mass production.

We often use forklifts or handcarts to move around work-in-progress
(WIP) components that are being worked on or are waiting between different
operations in the factory. For example, we move subassemblies from a work
center for spraying to another for welding. After welding, we may have to
move some product components back again for spray finishing. Such transportation has been regarded as unnecessary work.

A simple assembly line promotes efficiency by dividing labor. Each
worker is repeatedly doing a type of single-skilled task such as drilling a
clock spindle. Workers need not move between different stations. They are
organized to perform a single operation in a repeatable manner at fixed

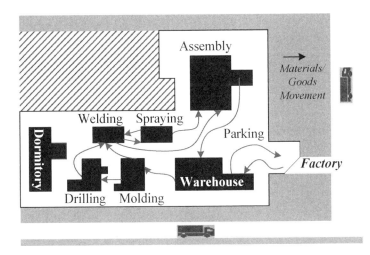

FIGURE 8.14 Where is the waste in traditional manufacturing plants?

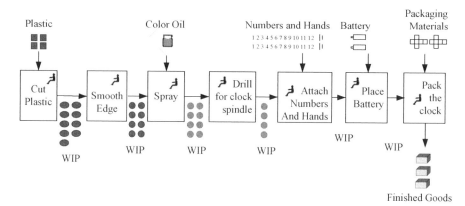

FIGURE 8.15   An assembly line for producing clocks.

locations as illustrated in Figure 8.15; the assembly line shown in this flowchart is somewhat analogous to the traditional software development method (e.g., the waterfall model).

Because of lack of communication and varied speeds of production, the worker who sprays the clockworks much faster than does the one who drills spindles. This leads to work-in-progress (WIP) inventory accumulation of semifinished goods. Those inventories are not ready-to-sell goods. There are costs of waiting time for WIP and stock storage.

Worse yet, defects not caught at an earlier stage will accumulate lots of WIP with the same defects at later stages. For example, it will be too late if the worker at the fourth stage discovers the defect. He or she will have to return the goods to the earlier work area for rework while colleagues at the earlier work area are continuing to make defected parts.

An assembly line is a proven technique for the industry to produce a large quantity of products of a standardized design. However, there is the potential for many kinds of waste along the line.

8.3.3   Walking Worker

If our raw materials are less plentiful, "make to stock" is not smart. Moreover, what we have made may not be exactly the same as what customers order. For example, if the customers prefer red instead of green clocks, the manufacturer will have to rework the finished products. Clearly, we may prefer producing things only when they are needed!

We can arrange our manufacturing production layout as in Figure 8.16. Unlike a traditional layout, the production line is organized as a number of

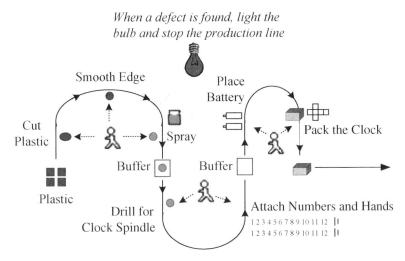

*When a defect is found, light the
bulb and stop the production line*

Smooth Edge

Place
Battery

Cut
Plastic

Spray

Pack the Clock

Buffer

Buffer

Plastic

Drill for
Clock Spindle

Attach Numbers and Hands

1 2 3 4 5 6 7 8 9 10 11 12 |I
1 2 3 4 5 6 7 8 9 10 11 12 |I

FIGURE 8.16 Just-in-time manufacturing.

U-shaped cells. In each cell, equipment, machines, and tools are placed in process sequence. The workers move around within the cell to perform multiskilled operations. The last processing step is in close proximity to the first step so that workers can quickly move to the beginning point of the next cycle.

To avoid accumulation of WIP inventory, a small lot buffer (i.e., small lot size) is used as a signal to workers when to manufacture particular items. The worker will produce only when the buffer is empty or drops to a certain level. This mechanism can also be implemented using cards to signal the need for an item (i.e., recall the Japanese term *Kanban* from Chapter 5, footnote 7).

Any worker who encounters a defect, abnormality, or tool malfunction switches on a light, may find production halted both upstream and downstream. Work does not continue until the problem is corrected. On the surface, this may sound counterproductive because the whole assembly line must stop even though a defect is found at only one point on the line. However, it is meaningless to continue to produce semifinished products that are defective and that will be subject to reexamination and rework to remove the defects later on.

It is easier to implement the JIT methodology for repetitive product manufacturing,[5] in which the skill set is low, the equipment is highly

---

[5]Some of the key tools of JIT are appropriate and valuable for any kind of production, from repetitive to highly customized.

TABLE 8.1 Traditional Assembly Line (Push) Versus Just-in-Time (Pull) Manufacturing

Parameter	JIT	Traditional Assembly Line
Lot size	Small	Large
Skilled environment	Multiple	Single
Quick action for any serious defect found	Stop production line	N/A
System	Pull	Push
Production	Good for repetitive products	N/A

specialized, and flow of work is highly defined and fixed. A short summary of traditional assembly line and JIT is presented in Table 8.1.

8.3.4 Just-in-Time Software Development

Just-in-time software development makes use of many ideas from JIT practices. Handling small-lot-size user requirements parallels organizing user requirements in a stack of user story cards in eXtreme programming or backlog items in scrum, each of which has one or a few features. Small-lot-size user requirements (i.e., story cards) allow customers to give a software team prompt feedback. Customers can add or remove story cards or reprioritize their order. This can reduce avoidable waste as feedback is provided on a JIT basis. In addition, small-lot-size user requirements allow the measurement of a team's velocity and the closer tracking of the progress of a project (see Section 8.1.1).

In traditional software development, we always see that, regardless of the size of a team, programmers are assigned to different dedicated jobs, such as collecting requirements, designing databases, or writing interfaces. In contrast, JIT demands that workers perform a variety of functions within a process. This versatility makes them more valuable to their teams. As discussed earlier, coding gives feedback to design. When we adopt design by code, programmers will no longer do just one task, but all of them.

Many programmers, however, have specialized in only one or two task areas such as UML or programming in C. They really need continuous training. Unfortunately, in reality, 52% of programmers receive less than 2 days of training annually (Harrison 2005). In this case, pair programming becomes a solution. Even though the JIT practice never addresses paired workers, JIT emphasizes the need for multiple skills in each individual.

The purpose of an alert system in JIT is to ensure that defects are fixed promptly so as to reduce the costs of rework. Software teams should integrate software daily to ensure that errors are not perpetuated. If a problem is found, the team should either fix it before going home or discard the day's work.

Software applications seem to operate as a pull model because they are responsive to customer requirements. Yet we may also say that customers actually push their requirements at the system analysts and the analyst pushes them at the programmers. As a consequence, many programmers do not fully understand what their customers want and need. This kind of collaboration is unsatisfactory. The better way to eliminate waste due to misunderstanding is for customers to generally describe how they expect the system to help their business and for the programmers to study the descriptions to confirm their understanding and then clarify the details with customers. This is the philosophy of a pull model. The "pull" comes from the actual customers directly communicating with the working programmers, and the programmers incrementally get the detailed requirements to build the system.

Just-in-time practices in manufacturing are appropriate (i.e., easier to implement) for repetitive products. Therefore, when we adopt JIT thinking for software development, programmers must have relevant experience. For example, a team of programmers that specializes only in point-of-scale (POS) applications may not be able to develop airport resource management using JIT software development. In a word, the more relevant the experience, the more effective is JIT software development.

8.3.5 Incremental Design

There are at least two approaches to incremental design: divide–conquer–integrate and evolution through prototyping. For the first method, the requirements are divided and recorded. At any time the customer may add new features. We incrementally build them while the work product is continuously integrated.

Evolution through prototyping places emphasis on completing a prototyping system, from which developers collect feedback from the customer and continue to enhance the functionality on that prototyping system. Since there is virtually no physical law to govern relationships among logical software components, they do not contradict each other. We are able to combine these techniques to various extents for our incremental development model.

Incremental design is something between big up-front design and improvisation. In fact, anything within the circle shown in Figure 8.17 is incremental development. This gives us the flexibility to choose our own way to incrementally develop software. There is a dimension where

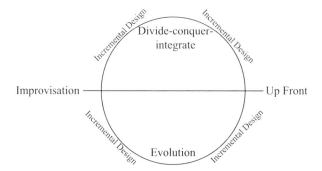

FIGURE 8.17   Software design methodology.

divide–conquer–integrate is on one end and evolution through prototyping on the other end. We may like to have up-front design that just covers a database model and a rough plan of what we do in 2 months and then during that period, we incrementally build the system. It is still possible that we have up-front design covering the details of our prototyping development. A premise tells that a complex system must start with a successful simple system and then evolve (Lowell 1992). Afterward, customers may add features on the basis of the prototype application and we further develop the application.

Software teams using incremental development may not immediately see its associated difficulties. It is relatively easy to start. The team will realize that the design methodology is inappropriate for their software project only when they cannot sustain (or are exerting much unexpected effort to sustain) the original incremental design of that software. In a word, we cannot easily judge whether incremental design is easy or difficult to sustain (see Figure 8.18). This leads to our final question. What component has been missing that has made it

Easy-to-start	**Difficult-to-start**	↳
Incremental design		**Easy-to-sustain**
Incremental design		**Difficult-to-sustain**

FIGURE 8.18   In–out diagram for incremental design.

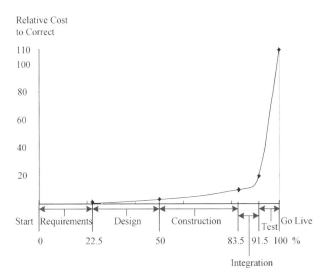

Relative Cost
to Correct

110
100
80
60
40
20

Start | Requirements | Design | Construction | Test | Go Live
0 | 22.5 | 50 | 83.5 | 91.5 100 %

Integration

FIGURE 8.19 Relative cost to correct a requirement defect (meta-analysis).

so difficult to determine whether our incremental design is easy to sustain for a particular software project? An immediate answer is requirements complexity!

8.4 REQUIREMENTS COMPLEXITY

No software product is designed without user requirements. Their importance cannot be overemphasized. Changing the requirements or having defective requirements will drive up our development costs. Wiegers (2006) summarized previous findings and reported that the relative cost of correcting a requirements defect in operation can be as high as 110 times. During 1993–94, Blackburn et al. (1996) surveyed over 150 software projects and conducted a number of follow-up field interviews to learn about the development stage as a percentage of the total software development time. As a rough estimate, we get the relative cost to correct a requirement defect by combining two studies: Wiegers' and Blackburn's data. The relative cost curve shown in Figure 8.19 resembles the cost of change given by Beck (2000).

Cost of change is significantly affected by both requirements and software design. Consider a case in which programmers design an ordering processing module comprising four classes (Figure 8.20). Hence, one more class may create more channels of object communications as the number of messaging units is a factorial of the number of classes. Clearly, it may be riskier to produce a design that is difficult to manage. As shown in Figure 8.20, by

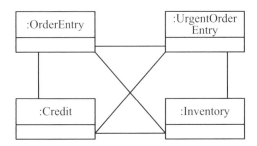

FIGURE 8.20 Design complexity.

combining `UrgentOrderEntry` and `OrderEntry`, the system has fewer classes. Unfortunately, things are not black or white. We cannot judge a design by the number of its classes. Our experience just tells us that more features added to a "bad smell" design could result in spaghetti messages passing among lots of objects. Therefore, design and requirements have a strongly coupled relationship that affects our costs of change.

There is a fuzzy line between requirements and design (Wiegers 2006). In a serial process model like the waterfall, the cost of change can sharply increase (Figure 8.19). In incremental design, the cost of dealing with bad-smell design can also make our software complexity grow exponentially to unmanageability and require redesign of parts of the system.

Another problem with user requirements that affects incremental design is the number of users contributing to requirements. In the case of building a small system, the requirements can be collected from and confirmed by just one customer. We call this type of communication for requirements "one to one" (i.e., one programming team to one user or one programming team to a few users in the same department in an organization).

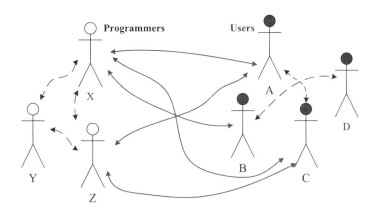

FIGURE 8.21 Communication burdens.

Very often, as illustrated in Figure 8.21, three customers, A, B, and C, are responsible for different departmental functions in the same company. To build an integrated system across their functions, they all need to provide their requirements. Thus, each user talks to our programmer X. In the end, programmer X sees their requirements as both overlapping and contradicting. Just as eye-witnesses to a crime tell different stories, users do not provide consistent requirements. This type of communication is called "one to many" (i.e., one team to many users from different domain types).

Internal communications on the user side may be noticed only when problems arise. For example, for some reason users B and D rarely talk to A and C. There is a gap in their internal communications.

In addition, programmers may have a profoundly different understanding of the same requirements. For example, user A may separately talk or write to both X and Y but they interpret A's requirements differently. In this case, some may suggest that we put effort into formal or semiformal specifications. However, not all user requirements will lead to different interpretations between X, Y, and Z. Writing specifications for clearly understood requirements is unnecessary work. The best strategy is to have an effective communication mechanism for software development in place.

In the following sections, let us learn about three situations of software requirements given by our users in the commercial world: forgotten requirements, conflicting requirements, and rapidly changing requirements.

8.4.1   Forgotten Requirements

A beer manufacturing company in Laos planned to phase out its legacy system and move forward to an Internet-based ERP application so that their retail customers could place orders themselves and thereby the average order cycle could be cut by 20%. Gary was a hands-on marketing manager there. He was a systematically thinking guy and knew the ins and outs of the sales and marketing operations. Gary could tell us exactly what he wanted and explain when certain conditions were true, what results the system should produce, and what quality his sales team wanted.

Gary could roughly draw the system modules (Figure 8.22). When a customer places a sales order, the system immediately checks the available stock in our finished goods inventory for fulfillment and reserves the stock for the customer. In addition, the credit control helps us manage the customer credit status. For customers who are far from the warehouse, the delivery lead time may be days. Therefore, the invoice can be issued only after the customer has received the goods.

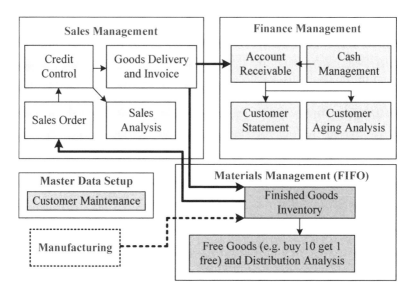

FIGURE 8.22 Typical sales and distribution application for beer.

The system should not delete any data that the users have typed in so that the finance department could audit the data. Gary also suggested that sales supervisors could create new customer accounts and the system would assign credit limits by default. This would expedite sales processes for new customers.

Everything seemed to be covered. However, Gary forgot to mention one thing. During the Christmas holiday season, each sales order should expire in one day. Some customers might wish to place an extraordinarily large order several days before Christmas, but it was not possible for the company to hold stock for them for more than 2 days as they would become monopoly customers. This would prevent the company from serving others and would adversely affect product distribution and availability in the market place. This had happened only rarely in previous years but it was a problem to be avoided.

> Gary forgot to mention one critical requirement: every sales order issued
> 7 days before the holidays should automatically expire just in one day!

8.4.2 Conflicting Requirements

After meeting with the sales manager, we met another key user, the company's financial controller, Szeto. One of major duties of the finance department is to monitor not only the cash flow control but also the company's performance. Szeto repeated much of what Gary told us, but he talked from a finance perspective. And there were apparent contradictions in the two descriptions.

According to generally accepted accounting principles, the company should issue invoices to the customer when goods have left the warehouse. This differed from Gary's version of events. What is more, all customer accounts, including their credit limits, should be maintained by the finance department. Szeto understood that new customers would have to wait longer to process their first orders. But he did not want to write off a huge amount of uncollectible invoices in accounts receivable.

> The financial controller disagreed with the sales manager about many operational practices.

We should talk to every key user before we start our development; otherwise, we will have to rework our system later. Conflicting requirements will exist across functional departments, and the situation can become political.

8.4.3   Rapidly Changing Requirements

The CHAOS report from the Standish Group in 1994 reported that three major causes of software project failures regarding user requirements were lack of user input, incomplete requirements, and changing requirements. The CHAOS Chronicles report (2003) reflected some major improvements. As computer systems have become indispensable business tools, today's users, like Gary and Szeto, are more IT-enabled, process-literate, and experienced with commercial computer systems and are therefore much more willing to participate than before. But this is not to say that they can provide complete user requirements.

Incomplete requirements are different from forgotten requirements. Incompleteness could mean exploring requirements in which users lack a vision or knowledge of how a future system could help them. For example, new business applications such as CRM in early 2000 could trouble many users to give their CRM requirements because CRM applications were just new to them. Forgotten requirements are a kind of incomplete requirement. Less experienced programmers who have not yet gained domain-specific knowledge may not easily realize that the requirements have defects due to some missing pieces.

Changing requirements could partially result from adding forgotten requirements and resolving conflicting requirements. What users say may not be what they want. Users could realize their needs only from product experience. We can lessen the extent of this problem through frequent feedback from peers and users.

Changing requirements are still a constant factor, and this is not expected to change soon in our work. As organizations evolve and change existing practices, merge or partner with competitors, and share information with their suppliers for supply chain management, requirements will change rapidly, and this has scared many of us into going agile!

For the 2002 FIFA World Cup, the beer company created the slogan "Without fresh beer, no real live match." To support the million-dollar campaign, senior management decided that the distribution center would temporarily take a last-in first-out (LIFO) method to ensure that fresh beer would be delivered to major cities in Lao and would use a first-in first-out (FIFO) approach for small towns in the countryside. When the world cup campaign was over, everything would get back to normal. As expected, the logistic department immediately called the MIS to support.

> Experience tells us that users would demand new features in days or weeks because business opportunities never wait!

8.4.4 Requirements and Design

Our case presented many challenges about user requirements in the real world. Table 8.2 provides seven situations in which we consider different design strategies. The recommendations listed in the table serve as a simple guideline because our real situation could be more complicated as other factors such as size, complexity, or risk profile are not fully considered. Table 8.2 does, however, provide an overview of where we may consider a development strategy for each software project.

8.5 REFACTORING

The term *refactoring* in software development was first used by Opdyke in 1992 in his PhD dissertation, where it was defined as a process of changing an object-oriented software system in a way that the internal structure of an object-oriented program is restructured to improve reusability but the external behavior of the code is not altered. The restructuring may include redistributing classes, variables, and methods across the class hierarchy in order to facilitate future adaptations and reusability (Opdyke 1992). There has

TABLE 8.2 Considerations for Software Design Strategies

This Has Been What Our Team Knows So Far. The Commercial Project:—	Up-Front Design	Divide–Conquer–Integrate (DCI)	Incremental Design	
			Incremental Design between DCI and ED	Evolutionary Design (ED)
1. Has stable user requirements	Good	Good	Good	Good
2. Is to replace a legacy system with some extra features that the old one could not fulfill	Try	Better	Good	Good
3. Seems to have stable user requirements but one-to-many communication for user requirements	Good	Not Suggested	Try	Good
4. Is new, but the software team has worked on the same type of application before	Try	Try	Good	Good
5. Is a new project, and the team has no domain-specific knowledge of the application	Good	Not Suggested	Good	Better
6. Seems to rapidly change user requirements, and the team has worked on the same type of application before	Not Suggested	Try	Better	Good
7. Seems to rapidly change user requirements, and the team has no domain-specific knowledge of the application	Not Suggested	Not Suggested	Try	Better

not been much change in the definition of refactoring, except that it may not be a process. It can be a practice of changing the internal behavior of programs in small steps (Fowler 1999). Readability is now emphasized in refactoring.

For some simple programs, it is not difficult to guarantee the preservation of system behavior after modification. For complex systems, this could be guaranteed only by blackbox testing. Given the same set of input values, the resulting set of output values should be the same before and after the refactoring (Opdyke 1992).

Refactoring has been closely connected with design in general and incremental design in particular. Adding features requires changing the structure of a program, but external behaviors for existing features are, of course, preserved. Doing refactoring can be more than readability and maintainability of the existing code. In practice we do refactoring and performance tuning at the same time. However, we may still sacrifice performance for readability and maintainability, the objectives of refactoring.

Refactoring comes with costs:

1. To ensure behavior preserved and correctness of recoding, we have to retest our program.
2. Testing cannot show the absence of fault, and the part being revised might often be connected to others; more test cases may be needed after the system is refactored. Otherwise, only when we encounter problems with some part of code that is related to our modifications do we realize that we should have changed it as well.
3. It is not easy to estimate the amount of effort involved in refactoring a program. Often, an expected hour of effort turns out to be a day.

There is always room for improvement. Refactoring is not a way to produce perfect code. We must know when to start and when to stop. Time, however, is precious. Considering that constraint, we have to prioritize our refactoring tasks. Some experts have recommended a number of techniques called "bad smell" that can be used to spot where to refactor. As it is difficult to judge the time required to do refactoring, we offer this advice: *Refactor only those parts that you may think are most likely to be the first to have new features added.*

There are at least three levels of refactoring: within-classes, among-classes, and class-relationship-restructured. By *within-classes*, we mean that programmers refactor the structure and logic only within classes, for example, variable naming, method accessibility, or method addition. Even though the logic of the variables or methods that we have restructured could be accessed or called by other classes, the programming complexity is limited.

We may use a refactoring browser to help, which can allow a programmer to rename variables or methods and then all other logic related to it will be automatically changed.

By *among-classes*, we mean that we move variables or methods from one class to another. Clearly, this will be more complicated than within-classes in terms of programming logic, even though a refactoring browser has a graphical user interface (GUI) that allows us to simply drag among classes instead of having to use text editor commands.

Class-relationship-restructured is the most complex and is most prone to having bugs that won't manifest until the program is used in a particular way. Programmers redefine relationships between classes by introducing new classes, merging class relationships, or changing class inheritance relationships. Restructuring classes helps us better model objects for real-world problems. Figure 8.23 provides a simple illustration of three types of refactoring.

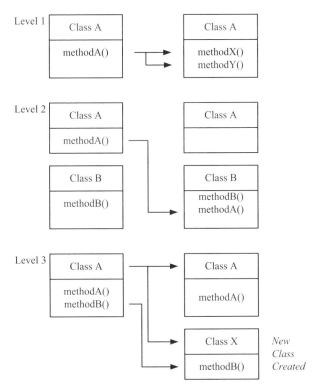

FIGURE 8.23 Within classes, among-classes, and class-relationship restructured changes.

Here is some more advice: *Don't refactor any code at the third level when the product is going to be released next week!* Try to refactor programs at the third level at the soonest. This is like something called *prefactoring*, in which programmers should pay attention to their refactoring experience so that they get the design right as early as possible (Pugh 2005). Prefactoring does not mean that we do not need refactoring. It emphasizes the value of the refactoring experience we have had.

8.5.1   Refactoring Activities

This section discusses refactoring activities. At the beginning, we have to identify where to refactor. Beck (2000) and Fowler (1999) introduced 22 kinds of bad smell where code should be fixed for both readability and maintainability. This bad-smell concept has been identified for decades; we were all taught not to write a long procedure. Long methods, long classes, and long parameter lists are the same—small is beautiful. Some bad smell is concerned with software design; for example, an object class not sufficiently responsible enough to be recognized as a class should be considered for refactoring.

Another approach to spotting where to refactor is to take an economical perspective. Refactor bad-smell code that is more likely to have features. This is not to say that we guess as to future requirements. We don't need to know exactly what the new functionality is; we only need to consider where it may be added. We should talk to our customers, understand their business, think about the user experience, and use your intuition.

Now we have to think about which refactoring techniques should be applied. This is more important when we plan to do level 3 refactoring. Various techniques are explained in Fowler's book 1999.

We should guarantee that we have unit tests on hand to ensure that the applied refactoring preserves external behavior. We may need to roll back to the previous version at any time. Since extreme programming tells us to discard our unfinished refactored code before calling it a day, a version control system should be in place before we start refactoring.

After refactoring, it would be good to have some sort of assessment of whether we have reached a certain level of software quality. Unfortunately, this can be a time-consuming activity as there is no direct assessment. To make evaluation objective, we have to adopt quantitative evaluation, which may include peer review, grading, and statistical analysis. To go agile, we may consider adopting pair programming in which the characteristics of software readability and maintainability are assessed constantly.

Finally, we have to maintain consistency between the refactored program and other software artifacts such as data models, class diagrams, and any test cases added for refactoring. Here is a summary list (Mens and Tourwé 2004):

1. Identify where to refactor.
2. Determine which refactoring technique(s) to apply.
3. Guarantee the preservation of external behavior.
4. Make sure that a version control system works for refactoring.
5. Apply the refactoring.
6. Assess the effects of the refactoring.
7. Maintain consistency between the refactored program code and other software artifacts.

8.5.2 Refactoring by Challenging

Our program has been done and tested. Later on, we may devise a better design solution. This is referred to as *code-driven refactoring* (see Box 8.1). If coding tasks are assigned to different programmers, then the biggest problem

---

BOX 8.1

CODE-DRIVEN REFACTORING

Original programmers working in solo programming cannot be as good at code-driven refactoring of their own programs as they are refactoring programs created by others.

In 2005 five programmers from a technology company in Beijing participated in an on-the-job study of refactoring. Three of them had around 3 years' experience. The other two were randomly assigned to grade the source code on a scale of 1–5 in four areas: readability, style consistency, maintainability, and class relationships.

To support multilanguage programming and communications of terminologies requires professionals in the field to do the translation. As strings appeared on GUI and message box are stored in *.properties file (for JAVA application), we sent these files to translators for language conversion, say, from Chinese to Korean. The return of these files needs examination to ensure the correctness of the file format, for example:

1. Deleting line breaks by mistake
2. Confusion with some symbol such as "or "
3. Forgetting to add \ for \\.

A Java program was written to check the files returned from translators. One of three programmers, Zhao, wrote that program. None of participants were informed that this was part of an experiment; they thought it was just an ad hoc programming task. We asked Zhao to review his program to make it more readable and maintainable and we distributed the source to another program-mer, Qian, for refactoring. In week 3, we asked Zhao to make a final check and again to attend to readability and maintainability. We forwarded Qian's refactored program to Lin for refactoring. The following flowchart shows the proceedings of our study.

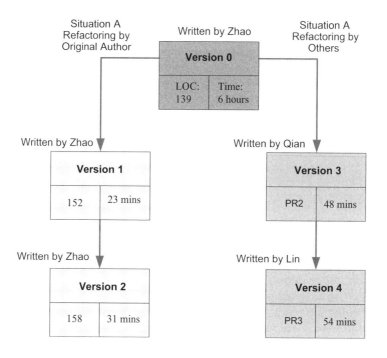

Two programmers graded each version. Their results are shown in the bar charts below. It was concluded that refactoring by multiple developers would achieve much higher software quality in terms of readability and maintainabil-ity than if it were done by the original developer. The limitation of this initial study was its small sample size. This short experiment infers achieving synergies between refactoring and pair programming.

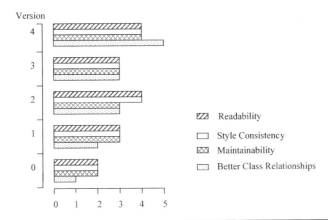

with code-driven refactoring is that the original authors may be blind to any inefficiency in their design solutions. Nevertheless, the original authors can judge readability and maintainability on their own. We are just not as good at debugging our own models as we are at debugging models created by others (Panko 1996).

Original developers will be biased toward the structures of their programs. Methods may have been grouped in an inappropriate class; however, this would hardly be known until the methods would be moved in right object classes. Other people may see better places to put the method. The original authors are so familiar with their code that they take its readability for granted. One person's readability is another person's cryptic text. The naming of variables and methods should be explainable.

Effective refactoring should not be a self-review but an exercise of accumulating design experience from each programmer. The insights we have gleaned from our experience, as well as the experience of others, in developing software provide better refactoring. In this case, it makes sense that pair programming is adopted to maximize the team throughput to achieve code that is more readable and maintainable.

If your teams simply do not like pair programming, try to get them to do refactoring for each other. Two-developer refactoring would still give better quality of code than would refactoring repeatedly done by the same individuals.

8.5.3 Refactoring for Design Patterns

Many "bad smells" apply only for generally accepted programming principles. Therefore, we have valuable and applicable C language techniques such

as "Do not use terse C expression forms even when they sacrifice no readability at all and write 'flat' rather than 'deep' programs, for example, if if if if . . .
then then then then . . ." (Perry 1998).

Here are some more examples of bad-smell advice. We should use a class
method or procedure call to group duplicated code. Anything long is difficult
to maintain and should be divided into smaller units, and this will also
increase reusability. Comments should be concise. The names of the right
variables and methods are self-explanatory. Message chains in which a client
asks to exchange one object for another object should be decoupled as a long
deep chain is not good for maintainability.

However, computer languages such as C do not clearly state the knowledge of purpose (i.e., what this class is supposed to do and why these methods
belong to this class) and knowledge of structure (i.e., class structure, relationships, subclass, inheritance) needed to model real-world systems. Thus,
refactoring C programming to model things that we perceive in the real
world is not very easy. This results in writing in-line comments to achieve
readability and maintainability for other programmers. Sometimes, we rewrite those in-line comments to explain C code rather than refactoring the
C code.

Refactoring is non-zero-point collaboration. Two programmers may start
with the program code; however, they may do refactoring in different ways
even though they perceive the same bad smell. Therefore, we want to know
what good design is so that we can refactor according to that pattern. In a
word, we need design patterns as standards to complement individual design
experience.

Design patterns inspired by Alexander's pattern languages[6] (Alexander et al. 1977) tell us that there are patterns between problems and
designsolutions based on past experience so that programmers can learn
what good object-oriented design is all about (Gamma et al. 1995). Often,
when we are baffled with what we should do to refactor the code, it is time to
brush up Gammea's *Design Patterns*. Almost all design patterns concern
class relationships, which is to say that we have to refactor at levels 2
and 3.

---

[6]Patterns in architecture have a long history in China. It is called *fengshui*, which
addresses what patterns of location and direction of the hill, the bush, the pond, the sun
(rising and setting), the landscape, and the house could make people live more
comfortably and thereby more fortunately. Fengshui was developed 1000 years ago
and did not evolve over a long time. It is less appropriate for modern architecture.

8.5.4 Making Deliberate Mistakes

"Making deliberate mistakes! Are you telling me to write lousy code?" asked an experienced programmer. Hold on; this does not mean that we write programs with bugs. We don't want to make mistakes. In fact, we want to avoid mistakes (Schoemaker and Gunther 2006). However, we can use wrong solutions to confirm that our test cases are right!

Suppose that we write a test case before code. This has two benefits. Like specifications, it helps us clarify our understanding of user requirements, but we can also use the test case for testing. However, we should not be overconfident about the correctness of the test case, which, just like our program, may have defects. Therefore, we either write a quick solution or do hardcoding to see if our test case is right. Then we may work back and revise our solution from bad to good. This development is referred to as "test-driven refactoring development" and this method of refactoring, in contrast with "code-driven refactoring," is called "test-first refactoring" (Mens and Tourwé 2004). Write a quick solution to ensure that a test case works and refactor the solution.

REFERENCES

Alexander C, Ishikawa S, Silverstein M, Jacobson M, Fiksdahl-King I, and Angel S. *A Pattern Language: Towns, Buildings, Construction*. New York: Oxford University Press; 1977.

Beck K. *eXtreme Programming Explained: Embrace Change*. Boston: Addison-Wesley; 2000.

Black JT. *The Design of the Factory with a Future*. New York: McGraw-Hill; 1991.

Black JT and Hunter SL. *Lean Manufacturing Systems and Cell Design*. Dearborn, MI: Society of Manufacturing Engineers; 2003.

Blackburn JD, Hoedemaker G, and Van Wassenhove LN. Concurrent software engineering: Prospects and pitfalls. *IEEE Transactions on Engineering Management* 1996; **43** (2):179–188.

Fowler M. *Refactoring: Improving the Design of Existing Code*. Reading, MA: Addison-Wesley; 1999.

Friedman TL. *The World is Flat: A Brief History of the Twenty-First Century*. New York: Farrar, Straus and Giroux; 2006.

Gamma E, Helm R, Johnson R, and Vlissides J. *Design Patterns: Elements of Reusable Object-Oriented Software*. Reading, MA: Addison-Wesley; 1995.

Harrison DK and Petty DJ. *Systems for Planning and Control in Manufacturing*. Oxford: Newnes; 2002.

Harrison W. Do you learn just in time or just in case? *IEEE Software* 2005; **22** (1): 5–7.

HBR. Don't delight your customer away. *Harvard Business Review* March 2002; 64–65.

Lowell J. *Rapid Evolutionary Development: Requirements, Prototyping and Software Creation.* New York: Wiley; 1992.

Mens T and Tourwé T. A survey of software refactoring. *IEEE Transactions on Software Engineering* 2004; **30** (2):126–139.

Middleton P and Sutton J. *Lean Software Strategies: Proven Techniques for Managers and Developers.* New York: Productivity Press; 2005.

Opdyke WF. *Refactoring Object-Oriented Frameworks.* PhD thesis. Chicago: University of Illinois; 1992.

Panko RR. Hitting the wall: Errors in developing and debugging a simple spreadsheet model. *Proceedings of the 29th Hawaii International Conference on System Sciences.* Jan. 1996; pp. 356–363.

Paulk M, et al. *The Capability Maturity Model: Guidelines for Improving the Software Process.* Reading, MA: Addison-Wesley; 1995.

Perry JW. *Advanced C Programming by Example.* Boston: PWS Publishing Company; 1998.

Pugh K. *Prefactoring: Extreme Abstraction, Extreme Separation, Extreme Readability.* Sebastopol, CA: O'Reilly; 2005.

Schoemaker PJH and Gunther RE. The wisdom of deliberate mistakes. *Harvard Business Review* 2006; **84** (6):108–115.

Schonberger R. *Japanese Manufacturing Techniques: Nine Hidden Lessons in Simplicity.* New York: Free Press; 1982.

Wiegers KE. *More about Software Requirements: Thorny Issues and Practical Advice.* Redmond, WA: Microsoft Press; 2006.

Womack JP, Jones DT, and Roos D. *The Machine that Changed the World: The Story of Lean Production.* London: Harper Perennial; 1991.

9

TEST-DRIVEN DEVELOPMENT

> One death is a tragedy; a million is a statistic.
>
> —JOSEPH STALIN

A desperate-looking guy is sitting in front of a poker machine, shaking his head. Clearly, he has lost lots of money. He slowly stands up and walks away from the machine. Immediately another man rushes over to sit in this place and starts feeding coins into the machine. He looks like someone who has just found a treasure. He thinks that because the machine has not paid out in a long time, it must pay out soon. This is a common belief among gamblers. But it's wrong.

Amateur gamblers—and in life all of us are gamblers in one area or another—are often unconsciously governed by one of four beliefs: (1) an event is likely to happen because it has not happened for a long time, (2) an event is likely to happen because it has just happened, (3) an event is unlikely to happen because it has not happened for a long time, or (4) an event is unlikely to happen again for some time because it just happened. All of these beliefs fail to account for the fact that every toss of a coin has the same odds of producing heads or tails. Even if you toss heads 10 times in a row, on the 11th throw the odds of heads or tails is just the same as at the first throw, 50–50. But this simple fact is not apparent to the amateur gambler. They have their own beliefs and their own view of the world and how it works. And the more they lose, the more they depend on those beliefs to save them in the end.

In software development projects too, we also make decisions on the basis of false beliefs. Experienced programmers—competent, mathematically

Software Development Rhythms: Harmonizing Agile Practices for Synergy
By Kim Man Lui and Keith C. C. Chan
Copyright © 2008 John Wiley & Sons, Inc.

minded individuals—still declare themselves satisfied that a system that has successfully passed 10 test cases stands a good chance of passing the 11th even though the test cases are independent of each other. The discrete nature of software can make every test independent, although software development has nothing to do with probability.

Psychologically, we are trapped by two beliefs: that new tests are assumed to pass because many others have successfully passed, and that the code we have changed to fix bugs will not introduce new ones! Software feasibility and human factors could cause us to fail to cope with randomization from complexity. The software complexity causes us to intellectually deal with a form of logic of probability with software. For example, if we were to accidentally change one command, it might disable functionality, or it could even crash the entire system!

Therefore, a software application is brought to its knees because we don't have enough time for all tests, because we are not clever enough to identify hidden bugs and write useless test cases, or just because we think we are so smart that we think we know how to selectively test system functionality instead of a whole system.

Testing substantially impacts on financial bottom lines. It may consume as much as 40% or 50% of the cost of software development. And as software becomes pervasive in our society and increasingly indispensable to every part of a business, between home and business, between business and business, it becomes both more complex and more critical. This, in turn, means that more testing is needed and testing is even more important than ever. Unless we are able to find more efficient ways to effectively test software, the percentage of development costs devoted to testing will only increase, And there is no way to avoid this. We can't, for example, simply design and code programs better so that they will need fewer tests.

When users tell us that their business cannot afford to have an application down, we become more serious about software quality. Our team extensively devises user test cases and testing data. When the team has accumulated lots of test cases, we have another problem. It is difficult to judge which cases are redundant. Doing exhaustive, overlapping testing consumes project resources. In terms of development times and project running costs, it would be valuable for a project manager to know what the economical (minimum) number of test cases should be run.

Suppose that an application has 10 features. We should at least write 20 user test cases, with each pair of testing true and testing false mapped to one feature (or a story card). The idea of the economical number of test cases contradicts the common wisdom that critical systems demand more test cases for each single feature. However, the economical number of test cases is still practical, and for project managers it serves as the bottom line.

Another way to make testing economical is to prioritize what major features of the software should be tested in order to balance testing with the project resources. This is common in the workplace. In particular, when there is a need to trade off against a project schedule, putting testing effort only into those features that may pose higher risks for the customer becomes critical.

So often, our customers add or modify their requirements without changing the project completion date. They use all kinds of means to get us to accept this, such as project incentives. Uncertain about our estimates, we lack the courage to defend our position against customer pressure (Brooks 1995). To survive in a *death march*, the software team desperately attempts to get the software done by either fair or foul means. The team tries to right the course of the project by throwing out any activity that can be discarded as they hurry to code for the extra requirements without considering the best design solutions. They write fewer documents than necessary. As a last resort, they test only some major functions even though the software now has additional features.

This happens in so many software development projects because software requirements are coupled with coding but both are decoupled from testing (see Figure 9.1), which illustrates the fact that no matter how much one adds or changes, testing efforts remain constant. If, however, we move testing ahead of coding, we ensure that software requirements are coupled with test cases, guaranteeing software quality. This is test-first programming (Beck 2000). And an iterative process that reinforces the practice of test-first programming is test-driven development (TDD) (Beck 2003).

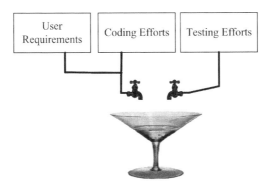

FIGURE 9.1 Testing decoupled requirements from other activities.

9.1 REVERSE WATERFALL

Programmers are aware that the classic waterfall model is not responsive enough to customers' dynamic demands and have adopted more iterative development paradigms and models. These models all variously build software in terms of the four Ps (process, people, paper, and product), but they also apply a repeated *design–code–test* rhythm. Whether a cycle of the design, code, and test processes is carried out in small steps or bigger ones, programmers are still thinking design–code–test, and that also applies to experienced programmers who may adopt "design by code" to write less complicated applications but whose reflexive approach remains design–code–test. Although there are no physical laws governing how to build software, programmers can test programs they have not yet coded or work out test cases for a system that hasn't yet been designed. Also we can reverse the rhythm design–code–test to test–code–design, and then testing and coding become much more interdependent.

9.1.1 Design–Code–Test

The order of software development activities is not accidental: requirements, design, coding, and testing. The order has been established for decades. We collect requirements from users. Then we formulate specifications to confirm our understanding and distribute them to a development team. Or, for less complicated requirements, we go directly to software design. Next, we build the software. Finally we test it before releasing it to our customers. As for incremental design, we may either continually, or regularly collect user requirements and feedback. However, what we do in our minds is design–code–test. It seems so completely natural that we never even try to imagine an alternative.

Design involves planning what a software team is going to do. For any project including software development, there can be several ways to reach the same goals. Some ways are uneconomical and some are risky. Therefore, the more we design, the more likely we are to see faster and better ways to develop a good design blueprint for execution and to ensure that team members can discuss the blueprint at an early stage. Fixing errors early avoids rework.

Coding is the execution of software design. We can use a design to devise test cases and data to examine external behavior of modules or pieces of code even before coding. At this point, we have to write test cases in a programming language, because there may not be user interfaces ready for testing. However, there is a problem with this approach. We see the test code failing only because the implementation has not yet been done. In other words, we can determine the correctness of our test cases only after the program has been written. We do not have to wait for the whole program to be done before we test. As long as we have a piece of code that is complete enough to be executable, we can go ahead and test it. As each test case itself is a tiny program, the real problem here is that there could be defects. We can be misled by the system passing the wrong test case. Worse yet, we may assume the test case works because its logic is so small.

9.1.2 Test–Code–Design

The test–code–design rhythm means putting design after coding. It also implies that something was not right and that some sort of redesign is needed. Clearly, this kind of redesign is avoidable as long as we think over what to do before execution. Then why should we go for test–code–design?

Some experienced programmers can do "design by code" well. On the basis of their experience in knowing how the code will be tested, they write test cases in advance. But it is not that beneficial. In this case, testing first or testing later does not appear to be significant. Then when does test–code–design work better?

As for the test–code–design rhythm, test cases are written beforehand to confirm the existence of features. It helps couple test cases with user requirements so that no single requirement goes untested. To make test before code work, we have to write a quick solution to ensure the correctness of our understanding and the tiny program (i.e., test case). The solution can be a dummy one just to check whether the test case really works. But it must be quick enough to be productive. This critical step gives us early feedback on both requirements and programming.

As the solution can be just temporary, incomplete, or hardcoded, we have to redesign a better one or just rewrite it for maintainability. Obviously, test–code–design does not straightforwardly reverse design–code–test. The tasks at each phase are different. Our thinking is now driven by test-first, which aligns the programming mind with customers, and we are centered on seeing what a system does before seeing how it works.

9.2 TEST-FIRST PROGRAMMING

Psychologically, those people who make things that did not exist before should be optimistic; otherwise, nothing would have been created. Programmers should also be optimistic. They might not fully test each feature or programming logic that they think is too simple to be wrong. They might ignore and deemphasize the impact of defects. This approach can be characterized by what we often say to our colleagues and customers: "We can fix it in 15 minutes!"

As for test-last programming, because of the constraints of software contracts, time, and budgets, a common strategy is to reduce the number of test cases so as to shorten testing time and deliver the product on schedule. We "assume" that the software has passed. If need be, we can release a patch later on. Another strategy used in some small software houses is called "paid by bug." Ask a number of freelance programmers to find 50 bugs within 3 days. Have your team fix them all in 3 days and release the program to customers on day 7. But why identify just 50 bugs? There may be thousands! Well, it has been estimated that the team could have only 3 days to fix that number of bugs.

This section will take a deeper look at what test-first programming really is.

9.2.1 Testing and Verification

Testing is a means of improving our understanding of the software we are building, not just a way of assessing its quality. Testing requires the execution of the software, often referred to as *dynamic analysis*. It often involves three steps: testing cases with data, program execution, and generation of results. The opposite form of testing, a form of verification that does not require execution of the software, such as mathematically proving properties about a given source, is referred to as *static analysis*. A flowchart for obtaining yes/no-type results through the testing–verification procedure is shown in 9.2

Testing has several advantages over static analysis techniques, which often makes testing necessary and verification sufficient. The developed software should be executed in a target environment including hardware

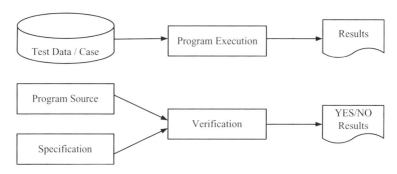

FIGURE 9.2 Testing and verification.

requirements and the version of the operating system specified. The success of these executions with the test cases provides a software configuration baseline on which the software will perform as intended. For example, if the application has been tested only on Windows 98, it would not be expected to also run on another operating system.

Output from execution and the comparison of expected results can be used to identify the test cases on which the software did not pass. We can therefore assess the software functionality and code quality (such as performance and runtime errors) by the test case requirements. The same test case with different testing data can often be regarded as different cases. Therefore, ideally, testing should be automated. In this case, test cases can be regressively used for future testing as the software evolves.

Testing, however, has some limitations, and hence we have to rely on software verification to complement testing for critical applications or zero-defect software. Test cases are quite independent and cannot be easily generalized to other cases. Therefore, we might think that we have developed lots of test cases to measure software quality but in fact many of them can be totally redundant. In addition, when we change the requirements, we have to rework the test cases involved. Furthermore, testing cannot determine, for instance, whether faults are absent. It can only show that they are present.

Unfortunately, many application programmers find software verification complex. Testing has often been used to provide the level of confidence in the quality of software. Since there is no formal notation required to conduct testing activities, test case requirements can be prepared by programmers or users. Testing has become generally accepted as a way of assessing software quality in the software industry.

9.2.2 Breakpoint Testing

A key element of testing is unit tests. Unit tests differ from user acceptance tests (UATs) in that they do not involve programming. Crispin (2003) explains that unit tests are written in the same language as is used to directly interact with programming modules. Thus, *unit testing*, as the name implies, examines a piece of code or a unit of functionality. User acceptance tests are often prepared by customers to ensure the completeness of functionality rather than software quality. Naturally, the user acceptance test cannot be conducted until all required modules including external user interfaces are ready.

A unit test has a structure of input parameters, expected return output values, and exception handling (see Figure 9.3). We may write unit tests covering (1) valid parameter values that return correctly, for example $(-5/2) = -2.50$ and $(10/3)! = 3.34$ and (2) invalid that which cause appropriate

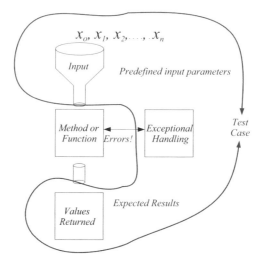

FIGURE 9.3   Unit tests.

exception such as 5/0. Boundary values, rounding numbers, negative values, null, and February 29 are often selected as test data. In addition, throwing an exception may also be done by testing records not yet set up in master tables such as nonexistent customer code.

Writing exhaustive unit tests for each user function is costly. We should try to write test cases that probably break the system (called breakpoint testing) rather than typical expected behavior with valid parameters and a few negative paths. There are two reasons for this: (1) these test cases make us think about exceptional application behavior, and (2) they are often the cases that will fail once we change the code in the future.

For this reason, when a software team has incrementally built or refactored a program for some time and never sees any of its old test cases failing, this could be an indication that the team has not understood that they should write unit tests that will probably break the function. For example, an application is designed to allow six characters in a password field. We should at a minimum examine two passwords of six and seven characters long.

9.2.3 Supporting Practices

Let us just look at test–code; more precisely, write test case before coding. The test cases serve both for quality assurance (QA), avoiding the introduction of defects, and quality checking (QC), detecting for any defects that may have been introduced. When we automate our testing so that test cases are reusable, testing before coding implements both QA and QC. Test-first programming is a software practice in which unit tests are written down before coding and then these test are regressively executed.

Writing unit tests before coding helps us understand user requirements from a programming perspective. Requirements may not be the same as application functionality. Even though well-written story cards can make good documents, descriptive stories in plain human language aren't the same as exact blueprints. Instead of developing program specifications for a software team to collaborate on and share, writing unit tests before coding can achieve more or less the same objectives as do technical specifications. Moreover, when unit tests are repetitively used throughout development and maintenance, it is much more economical and productive than having extensive non-machine-executable program specifications.

Moving unit tests development closer to requirements activities binds each story card with unit tests. This ensures the overall quality of software because it covers every function of an application. However, writing unit tests without making sure that they are correct is just talk without action. We need to quickly write a solution to confirm the validity of each case. To make the unit tests reusable, they must be free of error.

Solutions aren't always easy to find or write, especially when the requirements for a unit test are very complicated. But in these cases it is still better to quickly develop a "dummy" solution, that is, one where the programmers know that the solutions are dummy (hypothetical), partial, incomplete, or even hard to code, but where the solutions can at least be used to study testing inputs and expected outputs. At the minimum, applying dummy solutions knowingly allows us to test our assumptions inside unit test cases (Schoemaker and Gunther 2006) and is a way of alerting us to any accidental code changes in the future. Dummy solutions that pass these test cases help us explore better design solutions. This is the spirit of test first programming, which not only introduces a new way to program but also helps us think about programming in a new way.

Practices that support test first programming include

- Coupling requirements and test cases
- Using test cases for specifications
- Executing a quick solution for test cases as quick feedback
- Writing unit tests in computer code. (So that they can be used to test pieces of code rather than any sort of submodule)
- Taking an iterative approach
- Accumulating unit tests
- Automating test cases for reusability

- Making simple designs
- Having breakingpoint testing
- Making deliberate mistakes

An iterative software process from these principles and practices of writing software is called *test-driven development* (Beck 2003).

9.3   RHYTHM: TEST—CODE—REFACTOR

Beck (2003) suggests two rules be adopted for test-first programming.

1. Don't write even a single line of code if an automated test has failed. This rule can be regarded as an essential precondition. It can also be applied when working with a third-party package. A test for all third-party library functionality should be done before it is used.
2. Have all tests run at 100% all the time. This rule is a criterion for the beginning of coding and the completion of refactoring.

Now that we have described the key principles and practices of test–code–design, we can formulate them as 11 essential steps called test–driven development:

1. Pick a user story (i.e., a user requirement log) that may have a number of pieces of functionality.
2. Add a unit test that can specify each piece of functionality and think about how that test "may" break the system.
3. Run all tests including the one that has been added in step 2.
4. See that the new test is failed as that code has not yet been implemented.
5. Write the code to pass the new test or fake it if the code cannot be implemented quickly.
6. Run all tests and see them all succeed.
7. Refactor the code.
8. Run all tests and see them all succeed.
9. Decide whether to do more refactoring. If yes, go back to step 7.
10. At any time, if a bug is detected, write a unit test to detect that bug and fix it.
11. Go back to step 1 until finished.

Principles and practices summarized in Section 9.2.3 are embedded in test-driven development. Depending on how the tests were done in steps 5 and 7, we could either just improve the design or rewrite the solution; however, we should conserve the external behavior of the program to pass all accumulated written test cases as in step 5.

In particular, we should pay attention to simple design, breakpoint testing, and deliberate mistakes for dummy solutions in test-driven development because some programmers are not used to thinking in this way. Some programmers read the user stories and often associate some other features that they think the application is likely to have. They then proceed to code solutions for the present but also for the unforeseeable future, but this is contrary to the principle of "simple design." Worse still, since unit tests are coupled with requirements (i.e., story cards), they may break the first rule; that is, they may write system features without writing corresponding test cases.

Simple design, breakpoint testing, and deliberate mistakes distinguish test-driven development from other methodologies. Just reversing the order from design–code–test to test–code–refactor (where design becomes refactoring) does not improve our thinking— and good programming is all about better thinking. The good news is that, from our experience, once we elaborate these points to programmers in the workplace, they soon begin to develop test-driven minds.

Test-driven development is fractal-like iterative. Each loop not only comes from the previous one but also results from work in step 5, which has a corresponding refactoring in step 7 that fulfills the same set of test cases. Still, we regard the development rhythm as test–code–refactor. As shown in Figure 9.4, the curved line indicates that two activities are connected in such a way that both the inside of a previous activity and its results contribute to the next activity. In addition, coding a quick solution as suggested in step 5 makes our development rhythm fast and vivid. The rhythm is "vivace!"

9.3.1 Simple Example

The following brief example illustrates the operation of test-driven development. More examples showing the detailed use can be found in Beck's book

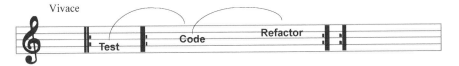

FIGURE 9.4 Test, Code, and Refactoring are all done in the same programming language.

(2003). This example is given in Python code as it is self-explanatory. In Python, a function block begins with the keyword `def` followed by the function name and parentheses, and the pound # sign is used for comments.

Our team wants to develop a payroll submodule for an ERP system. Monthly income for sales and managerial staff often includes a basic salary and a performance bonus. In the calculation for a regular employee, there will be no bonus. Our customer writes down on a story card that staff income before tax is the sum of the basic salary and bonus.

Straightforwardly, we immediately think of a method for adding both salary and bonus as `calcMthIncome(salary, bonus)`. Before doing anything else, we have to add a unit test case for `calcMthIncome()`, which can be `assert(calcMthIncome(1, 2) is 3)`. The test does not seem quite right. No staff has ever earned less than $100 per month in the company. Similarly, `assert(calcMthIncome(987654321.123, 9876543) is 997530864.123` does not make any sense either. We cross both out and ask what the maximum wage is that staff could get from the company for just one month. We have to talk to our customer, who then agrees that the system should not be able to mistakenly process an unreasonable amount. The highest basic salary is less than 99999.99 and the bonus less than 9999.99. The unit test becomes `assert(calcMthIncome(99999.99, 9999.99)= 109999.98)`. In the same fashion, more unit test cases are written.

Assume that we have no idea how to write a quick solution. We just fake it by returning a value irrespective of the right calculation:

```
def calcMthIncome(salary, bonus):
    return 109999.98
```

This does not implement any logic for `calcMthIncome()` at all. The value of "fake it" is that programmers can anticipate the expected result and roll back to the last point at which all tests ran with a 100% pass rate. Starting from this point as a baseline, we proceed to implement `calcMthIncome()`. Human programmers sometimes make mistakes even though they know better. So let's absentmindedly do some stupid coding as follows:

```
def calcIncome(salary, bonus):
#    return 109999.98
    return salary × bonus
```

A typo like "+" never causes backsliding as it will not pass our test case and we can go back to the previous point for correction. Of course, we do not always begin by faking everything. When a solution is known and simple, we should try to quickly complete it. Notice that these testing tasks are regressive.

If they are not automated, testing will become more tedious and time-consuming than before.

9.3.2 Automation

A tool to automate the execution of accumulated unit tests is indispensable in test-driven development. It integrates unit test cases with the tested program. The tool displays which tests fail and measures the overall percentage. Erich Gamma and Kent Beck developed an open-source tool to automate unit testing called "JUnit". As discussed, unit test cases are written in the same language that we use to program. JUnit is used only for Java programming. However, testing frameworks for other languages have been developed, and this kind of code-driven testing tool is known as "xUnit"

JUnit is also helpful for refactoring alone. As the tool is designed to automate unit testing, programmers will develop a number of automated test cases to make assertions about external behavior reserved after refactoring. By continuously running these automated test cases, JUnit will identify where refactoring breaks anything in the existing program.

JUnit creates a thorough regression testbed, which allows smooth integration of new features into and refactoring for the code base. The two rules for test-driven development are framed by JUnit. In Figure 9.5, the purpose of "see it fail" is to have a failing automated test before coding. All tests running at 100% all the time are objectively controlled by JUnit. Since software development can never be fully automated, it is best to use an automation tool on a regular basis. It helps to control and monitor the whole cycle.

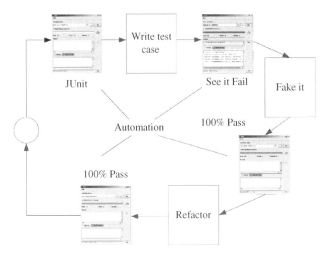

FIGURE 9.5 JUnit for automation.

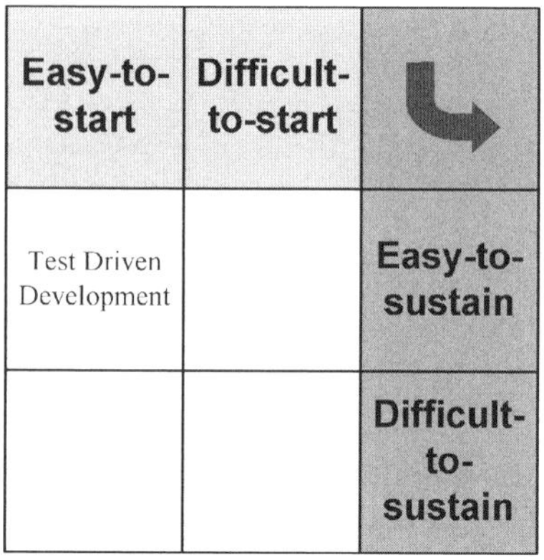

Easy-to-start	Difficult-to-start	↳
Test Driven Development		**Easy-to-sustain**
		Difficult-to-sustain

FIGURE 9.6 In–out diagram for test-driven development.

There are three major benefits to automated testing: (1) productivity, (2) reusability, and (3) quality improvement. Using the automated tool, it is easier to adopt and sustain test-driven development, as shown in Figure 9.6. In a real environment, one of the authors I has seen programmers fail to write meaningful unit tests, and some may even test after code occasionally. In general, however, test-driven development is easy to sustain. There is no need to be strict. As long as straying programmers can get back on track, the test–code–refactor rhythm can be sustained.

9.3.3   Revolution in Consciousness!

Superficially, test-driven development gets programmers to write testing code that is automatically testable and that can be checked against expected results. The obvious benefit of this is improved task understanding and focus. Yet these benefits can be realized in essentially any development method simply by moving test cases before implementation. Test-driven development is not significantly related to productivity. As long as unit test cases are written in an automated way, it is possible to reduce the burden of rework. It does not matter whether it is done before or after. In addition, the amount of automated unit tests does not truly represent quality because software testing can show the presence, but not the absence, of defects. It simply ensures that system features are well covered by unit tests and that programmers have not abandoned testing just to meet a deadline.

Test-driven development is more than writing automated test cases first. It must come with test-first thinking, which is not merely a step-by-step set of actions but a problem-solving method (see Section 9.2.3). (For instance, as depicted in figure 9.7, the path followed to go forward might not be the same as the path used to come back; in other words, order reversal necessitates new

FIGURE 9.7 Order reversal necessitates rethinking.

thinking). This is similar to what Ohno in the Toyota production system talks about, a revolution in consciousness, a change in people's attitudes and viewpoints (Ohno 1988).

What will happen if our team just mechanically exercises test-first but their minds fail to think test-first? From our experience, the team will not see any significant improvement out of test-first programming. Quality may tend to improve owing to the coupling of requirements and test cases. This is the worst that can happen, as test-first programming without test-first thinking does not appear to be worse than test-last programming (see a short summary of test-driven development in Table 9.1).

We were once learned that a smart software team in Japan was doing both test-first programming and test-last programming (Figure 9.8). The key to getting the best of both worlds is to do both test-first programming and test-last programming, switching as needed with a suitable rhythm. Before coding, write unit tests that probably break and, after coding, write essential unit tests. This won't improve productivity but it will help the team pay attention to breakpoint testing for software quality while they

TABLE 9.1   Research Findings on Test-First Programming and Test-Driven Development (TDD)

Subjects			Experiment Focus								
				Test Cases							
Type	#	Write Test Case Before	Solo–Pair Programming	that Probably Break	Deliberate Mistake	Refactoring Emphasized	Code Quality	Productivity	Conclusion		Reference
Students	19	Yes	Solo	No	No	No	N/D[a]	N/D	Conservative, need more study		Muller and Hagner (2002)
Programmers	24	Yes	Pair	No	No	No	TDD is better	TDD takes 16% more time	Constructive		Maximilien and Williams (2003)
Students	35	Yes	Solo	No	No	No	N/D	N/A[b]	Better task focus, faster learning		Erdogmus et al. (2005)
Students	10	Yes	Solo	No	No	No	N/D	TDD is better	Constructive		Janzen and Saiedian (2005)

[a]No difference.
[b]Not applicable.

FIGURE 9.8 A rhythm for test-first and test-last.

are writing code. The team composes a very strong rhythm. The flexibility to change is a central part of applying effective software development rhythms.

9.3.4 Test Case for Collaboration

We had all seen nervous team leaders. They want to be kept in the loop, so they tend to hover around a project, asking questions but not ones that seem to matter much to the programmers. Their main issue is usually deadlines, so they want to know about the latest project progress but they really already know about the *overall* progress, so they ask about details so that they can solve small problems before they snowball into big ones.

So, what do programmers tell the team leaders about when asked about their progress? Telling them which part of a program they are working on does not provide any new information. Telling them exactly what they are doing right now might just be about DO-loop or IF-THEN logic. Perhaps it would be more informative to talk about the unit tests they have just developed. Since each unit test is a solid example for the system, they are easy to understand and even comment on, perhaps helpfully!

Our ability to communicate with others what we are doing and thinking in the workplace is very important. But, personal bonding aside, the talk-to-information ratio has to be worthwhile. We all know that effective communications save time and resources, but how do we improve a programmer's ability to communicate well with his or her peers? Unit test cases are one way to do this.

In test-driven development, we write unit tests at the beginning. Each unit test is a tiny example with data and expected outcomes. We can make mistakes there, but there is no gray area for communications. For example, a unit test like `assert(add(1,1) is 3)` is just wrong but it causes no confusion for team communications.

Given a piece of a requirement, there can be many programming solutions. And even if you explain until your head falls off, your partner may still misunderstand one or two points. So why not start by talking about unit tests? Test cases are unambiguous, objective, and concrete. They have inputs and expected results. Once we have a unit test on hand, collaborating on its solution and pair communications are greatly simplified. In particular, when developers will be collaborating closely with other, team members on the

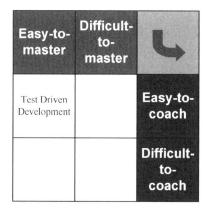

FIGURE 9.9   Master–coach diagram for test-driven development.

same task, as in pair programming or side-by-side programming, starting by communicating unit tests quickly builds some ground-up understanding. Then they can get down to the business of writing code.

Even where software teams do not adopt pair programming, test-driven development is still practical. Their experience in writing good unit test cases that are embedded with domain-specific knowledge and testing skills can be shared with other team members. Depending on programming experience, it normally does not take long to absorb the principles we discussed in Section 9.2.3. In addition, mastering JUnit is not that difficult, and so a software team can easily get test-driven development right. As for new joint programmers, the best way to learn test-driven development is through on-the-job training, which is a kind of all-around learning activity including practice, skills, thinking, and attitude. New joint programmers can learn how test-driven development works by seeing for themselves how each unit test case should be designed and how making deliberate mistakes can help developers explore solutions. Figure 9.9 shows a master–coach diagram for test-driven development.

Although we have discussed many principles, practices, and rules for test-driven development, the important element is to develop test-first thinking. We see nothing wrong with test-driven programmers sometimes adding more unit tests after implementation or occasionally coding before testing. This doesn't matter as long as programmers have internalized test-first thinking and the rhythm for test-driven development.

9.4   RAPID SOFTWARE PROCESS IMPROVEMENT

Capabilities of programmers in developing countries are likely to be diverse. In particular, programmers who have less than 3 years' experience are coders more than developers. To manage a team composed of many of these programmers is very challenging. In this case, project managers may prefer a process-oriented approach, like CMM (or CMMI).

Capability maturity modeling is a regular choice for software managers who are not sure which software practices will be most important to project success in their unique environments and teams. CMM addresses so many practices that it is hard to miss anything (Zahran 1998). It's like the slogan: "Just do it!" CMM is a scattergun approach where managers do little follow-up on when each practice is used or how it works. Maybe this is okay, if you've got the budget.

In contrast, agile team leaders have to catch and/or explore rhythms among people and practices. This is a very hands-on and human-centered and not at all robotic approach. Agile practices should be adopted according to the values that they deliver to the team and the software. Among many agile practices, test-driven development is a process that includes a number of practices organized in a strong rhythm. Yet there are also tools available to support test-driven development so test-driven development is not hard or costly to adopt and can be quickly learned, applied and adopted in all kinds of environments, including developing countries, to improve team capabilities in a very short time.

9.4.1 Training Program

Programmers in developing countries work in an ad hoc environment and consequently do not perceive in any significant way a correlation between software and software methodologies. Yet while they are not so interested in software methodologies such as CMMI or eXtreme programming, these developers do have a strong interest in programming techniques such as thread programming and computer languages such as C#.

Many programmers in developing countries are code gurus or enthusiasts. They may take time to appreciate the importance of a software methodology in team collaboration and a longer time to discover their rhythms with their development methodology. They may not be able to give up old ways and adopt new software practices as quickly as they can learn a new testing tool. The way to go with these guys is to view test-driven development as a tool (e.g., JUnit) rather than as a method. Mastering a development tool will definitely interest many programmers more than understanding how to use templates for quick documentation or learning software paradigms. Progressively implement a software paradigm through a testing tool. It may be that in this way JUnit has contributed to the wide popularity of the software methodologies, XP and TDD (Janzen and Saiedian 2005).

9.4.2 Project Planning

One of the major problems with project planning in developing countries is that programmers find it harder to estimate how long it will take to code a piece of a program. They tend to underestimate the time required for their planned tasks. They even try to correct their errors in estimating by cutting down testing efforts. In addition, too little time is devoted to testing relative to programming, with ratios as great as 4 days of code to 2 hours of testing. This has a substantial impact on project planning.

Here is a daily scenario we often see in the workplace. A project manager asks two colleagues how much time they need to write a program for a problem. On the basis of their replies and the manager's own assessment, the manager will work out the time estimation for the task. The estimate is subjective and can deviate unpredictably from the actual outcome (see Figure 9.10).

We may adopt agile planning to manage rapid iterative development cycles as discussed in Section 8.1.1. However, most software teams in developing countries are conservative and actually greatly prefer step-by-step change. A conventional project plan should be done at the beginning of the project.

Here is our advice for developing that plan. Let the team members spend a little time on getting a number of unit tests randomly selected from user requirements and getting their quick solutions done. Having the unit test establishes a specific goal; the programmers are more confident about their estimates of the amount of effort required after they write unit tests. This is not a perfect approach, but many programmers have told us that it is better than what they are used to.

9.4.3 Project Tracking

Programming progress should be tracked in terms of completeness. When a programmer reports 40% of coding done, it is by no means clear what this means in terms of progress. The work isn't 40% functionally complete since it can't be executed—and 40% complete in terms of time? If she did that 40% in 4 days, does this mean that she will do the rest in 6 days? And if she hasn't yet finished it, how can she know the length of her complete program? If she doesn't know how many lines of code the program will have, how can she report 40% done?

When requirements are decomposed into story cards and each story card is examined by unit tests, we may determine our current progress against the outstanding user stories, completed stories, and, most importantly, the velocity (see Section 8.1.1). Even using test-driven development with traditional project management, we can use velocity to track our progress.

FIGURE 9.10 Planning dilemma.

Another metric is the number of times that the project team is working on something current but previous unit tests fail (see Table 9.2). This is an interesting metric. When it is low, this probably means either that the team has written many typical unit tests or that the team rarely makes mistakes so that old unit tests are always passed. A higher value indicates either that the team has worked out a number of amazing unit tests that have broken the system many times while the development is ongoing or that the team has

TABLE 9.2   Unit Test Cases that Probably Break

Metric		n	Iteration $N+1$	$N+2$	
Number of unit test cases written at the current iteration	...	3	4	4	...
Total number of accumulated unit test cases from previous iterations	...	100	103	107	...
Number of accumulated unit test cases failed at the current iteration	...	0	2	8	...
Old unit tests failed in percentage (%)	...	0	0.19	7.4	...

made lots of mistakes. Get to learn more about this metric. While this does not tell us how long the developers will require to complete the program, it does provide reliable information that assists us in overseeing the process, especially in relation to team performance.

9.4.4   Software Quality

As for programmers in developing countries, software quality is unpredictable. For instance, developers can repeat the same kind of mistake and deliver work products to other team members without testing them thoroughly. The most noticeable benefit of test-driven development in such an environment is to have software quality improved as test-first thinking and making deliberate mistakes becomes the development strategy. With test-driven development, many defects are systematically identified through the accumulated reusable test cases after we refactor the program or add new features.

How much has software quality improved after software teams have adopted test-driven development to build software? In 2004 we collected some industrial data. Because different teams wrote different commercial systems, it is not possible to analyze the defects on the same baseline, so we compared how much time programmers needed to fix defects reported by users during user acceptance testing and production operations. We collected 643 and 212 bug fixes from non-TDD teams and TDD teams in China, respectively. With automated unit tests, 97% of defects can be fixed by TDD teams in one day (see Figure 9.11). TDD helps to fix defects faster.

9.4.5   Software Configuration

One of the biggest but most neglected problems for many inexperienced programmers is software configuration management. We have all heard

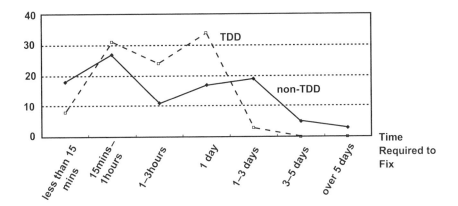

FIGURE 9.11   Shortening time to fix reported bugs.

stories like this. At the beginning of the day, we each get the same copy of the program and make separate changes. At the end of the day, we upload our program back onto the server, and so do you. The next morning, we download the program and code the other parts. Only after 2 or 3 hours do we realize that this is not the right version. Our program was accidentally overwritten yesterday.

In traditional software development, when tasks are assigned to programmers, they will be busy with their work and may not talk to each other very often. They even take it for granted that what they are working on has no relationship to what others are working on.

In test-driven development, we have to communicate with each other closely because unit tests must pass 100%. Anything wrong will immediately cause our work to be lost! This seems messy, but it is good to know that we will at worst lose only hours rather than days of work.

It is about discipline and team cooperation. Test-driven development does not address software configuration management. However, if the team does not have a mechanism for version control in place, they will more quickly encounter configuration problems than when using other methods.

There are two artifacts that are so closely associated that we have to manage their versions all the time: unit test cases and programs. Unit tests must be shared with others. To avoid mistakes, the team has to integrate the software at least daily. Perhaps the biggest benefit of test-driven development for software configuration is that any version control problem will quickly stop the development rhythm, which avoids any sort of snowball growing big enough to ruin the development efforts of weeks.

9.4.6 People Discipline

Programming activities in test-driven development are easily tracked. If, owing to personal lack of discipline because they misunderstand test-driven development, the developers do not follow the framework, they can be quickly identified. However, this is not why programmers who adopt test-driven development tend to be more disciplined. Writing unit test cases is just the same as writing code. We do not ask programmers to do things like write documents and fill in forms. Testing is an automated process. In addition, coding and refactoring are both about technical programming. This is why so many programmers we met like the methodology and are willing to keep to its practices.

In 2003 a speaker in an international software engineering conference asked the audience what they thought was the best methodology. Among many answers, including XP, CMM, and the waterfall model, the most popular answer seemed to be "ad hoc." Programmers do not follow software models in a disciplined way. As no programmer hurts or dies during software development, we don't take our practices seriously.

It would be hard to believe that the ad hoc method, which is regarded as an undisciplined way to build software, could be acceptable to so many people. Why? Some programmers may understand that their methods are ad hoc because they cannot be clearly classified by one of the models or paradigms suggested by CMM, CMMI, Lean Software Development, Scrum, eXtreme Programming, and so on. However, if you look deeply at when their practices work and when the practices are used, you may notice that the success is due to their own ways of playing software development rhythms well.

REFERENCES

Beck K. *Extreme Programming Explained: Embrace Change*. Boston: Addison-Wesley; 2000.

Beck K. *Test-Driven Development: By Example*. Boston: Addison-Wesley; 2003.

Brooks FP. *The Mythical Man-Month: Essays on Software Engineering*. Reading, MA: Addison-Wesley; 1995.

Crispin L. *Testing Extreme Programming*. Boston: Addison-Wesley; 2003.

Erdogmus H, Morisio M, and Torchiano M. On the effectiveness of the test-first approach to programming. *IEEE Transactions on Software Engineering* 2005; **31** (3):226–237.

Janzen D and Saiedian H. Test-driven development: Concepts, taxonomy, and future direction. *IEEE Computer* 2005; **38** (9):43–50.

Maximilien EM and Williams L. Assessing test-driven development at IBM. *Proceedings of the 25th International Conference on Software Engineering*. 2003; p. 564–569.

Muller MM and Hagner O. Experiment about test-first programming. *IEE Proceedings Software* 2002; **149** (5):131–136.

Ohno T. *Toyota Production System: Beyond Large-Scale Production.* Cambridge, MA: Productivity Press; 1988.

Schoemaker P and Gunther R. The wisdom of deliberate mistakes. *Harvard Business Review* 2006; **8** (6):108–115.

Stephens M and Rosenberg D. *Extreme Programming Refactored: The Case Against XP.* Berlin: Springer; 2003.

Zahran S. *Software Process Improvement: Practical Guidelines for Business Success.* Reading, MA: Addison-Wesley; 1998.

EPILOGUE: MEDLEY

If music be the food of love, play on!
—SHAKESPEARE

A first piano lesson starts with learning to sit upright with the chest forward and shoulders pulled back and the arms and hands relaxed. We then practice playing C, D, E, F, and G with our right hand. By the end of the first lesson many of us can play a simple tune. On the surface, playing the piano is easy! But when we start to learn to play with two hands, we have two rhythms to play, and then it's not that easy at all.

Unlike many other musical instruments like the violin or the saxophone, we often play the piano melody with the right hand and chords with the left. Software development rhythms are like this. One rhythm is for the theme, and the other is for the chords that support the theme.

Software development rhythms are embedded in any executing paradigm. There are two areas: a theme that guides or moves us forward and chords that support our theme practices. However, in many cases, we may have to alter the rhythms to match changes in the project environment. We could start to play another rhythm and thereby alter our accompaniment or our theme. This is the reason why we prefer development rhythms that are easy to start and easy to sustain in a rapidly changing environment or in an uncertain commercial world.

No musician in an orchestra will hand in a resignation letter to the conductor and then leave during the performance. However, in the presence of relatively high personnel turnover in the software team, we have to

Software Development Rhythms: Harmonizing Agile Practices for Synergy
By Kim Man Lui and Keith C. C. Chan
Copyright © 2008 John Wiley & Sons, Inc.

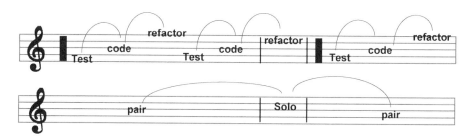

FIGURE E.1   TDD as theme + pair programming as chord.

consider the master–coach diagram, which helps us understand the impact on the development rhythms we are playing.

All these considerations will help you discover the right rhythms for your team in the workplace.

Rhythms and You

In this final section we hope to stimulate the reader's thinking. The two rhythms that you see in Figures E.1 and E.2 worked well with small teams we coached in agile software development in China. We suggest that you read the stave chart and think about

- When these rhythms would work for your team and when they most definitely would not
- When these rhythms have been used in a project in your workplace

Then you might like to consider the kinds of rhythms that you might employ with your team or your staff in a particular project in your workplace.

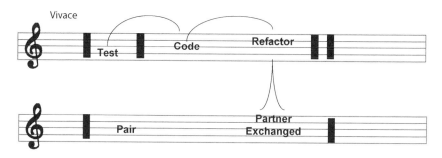

FIGURE E.2   TDD as theme + pair programming as chord.

Rhythms for More Repetitious Programming Tasks

All test cases and their code source have been written in pairs. When the same code patterns have previously been done in pairs, they can be refactored by individuals (see Figure E.1).

Rhythms for Challenging Tasks

All test cases and their code source have been written in pairs. The pair is ready to change partners when both know what and how to refactor a piece of code. Change partners so that new partners bring a fresh view to the pairing (see Figure E.2).

INDEX